# Downtown Los Angeles
## In Photographs
# 2013

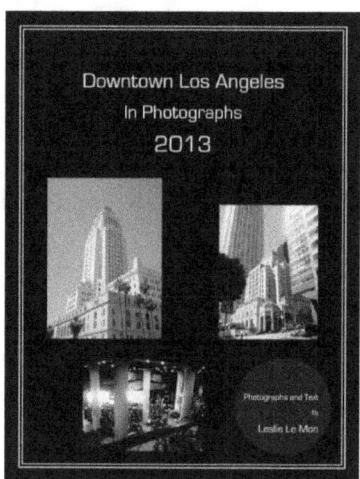

Photographs and Text

By

## Leslie Le Mon

# TABLE OF CONTENTS

## Contents

4

# DEDICATION

For my father, Warren James Le Mon (1929 – 2011), a New Yorker, born in the Bronx, a man who loved the lights and shadows and music and poetry of great cities, particularly New York City, Paris, and Los Angeles.

6

# INTRODUCTION

Photograph books, by their very nature, should be visually rich, with a few historical comments to give each photo a context. This book is intended to be a leisurely photographic "stroll" through some of downtown L.A.'s notable landscapes. There are many wonderful photo books of *historic* Los Angeles on the market. This is a book that shows how the city looks *today*.

Downtown Los Angeles is a big place. The photos within this book include some of L.A.'s most interesting and iconic features. However, the subject selection was, well, subjective. And selective. The pictures within focus on contrasts between historic corridors like Spring Street and Broadway, and newer districts on Grand Avenue and Figueroa Street. There is a lot more to photograph in downtown Los Angeles. Wilshire. Hill Street. Chinatown. So anticipate future collections.

All photographs in this book were snapped in 2013, except a handful taken in 2012. All of the photos were snapped in downtown L.A., in color, and then rendered in black-and-white.

Los Angeles – the city of film, the city of noir – is a black-and-white sort of place. Dazzling lights. Deep shadows. Stark contrasts. Los Angeles is gritty even in its beauty, and lovely even in its ugliness. With color washed away, the city's patterns and lines, its darks and lights, the grit and beauty of Los Angeles emerge in their purity.

Enjoy.


*Leslie Le Mon*, Los Angeles, May 2013

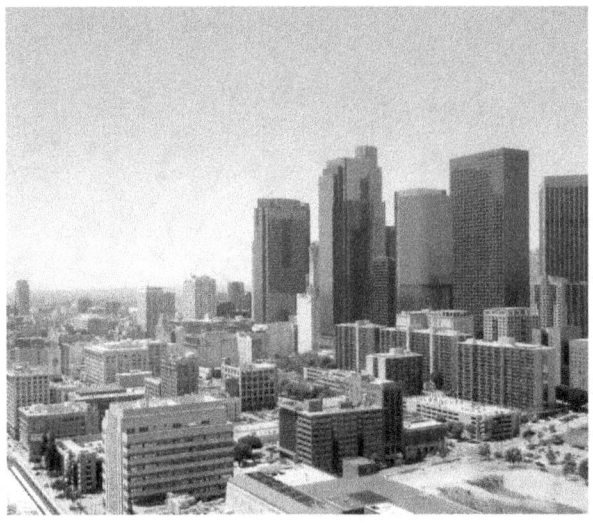

# THE PHOTOGRAPHS

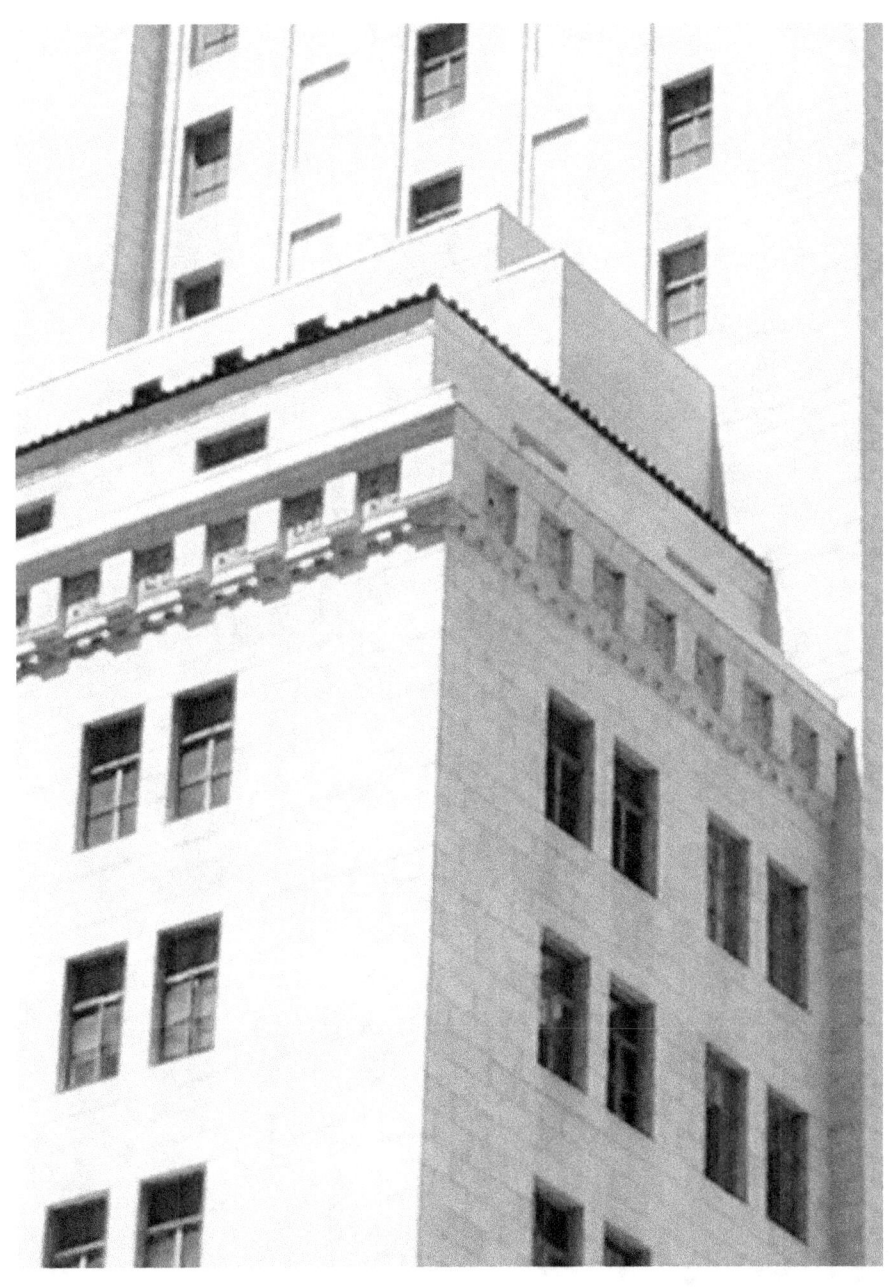

## UNITED STATES POST OFFICE – LOS ANGELES TERMINAL ANNEX

900 N. Alameda Street

*L.A.'s downtown mail processing center, the Terminal Annex, opened in L.A.'s northeast quadrant in 1940, when L.A. handled 2 million pieces of mail per day. The facility closed in 1989; a flow of 14 million pieces of mail per day – an astonishing figure – necessitated a move to larger premises in South L.A. Elements of the Terminal Annex were crafted in a style meant to complement neighbor Union Station, which was completed one year earlier, in 1939. Today the interior has an eerie, abandoned atmosphere, although the customer service counter is still staffed.*

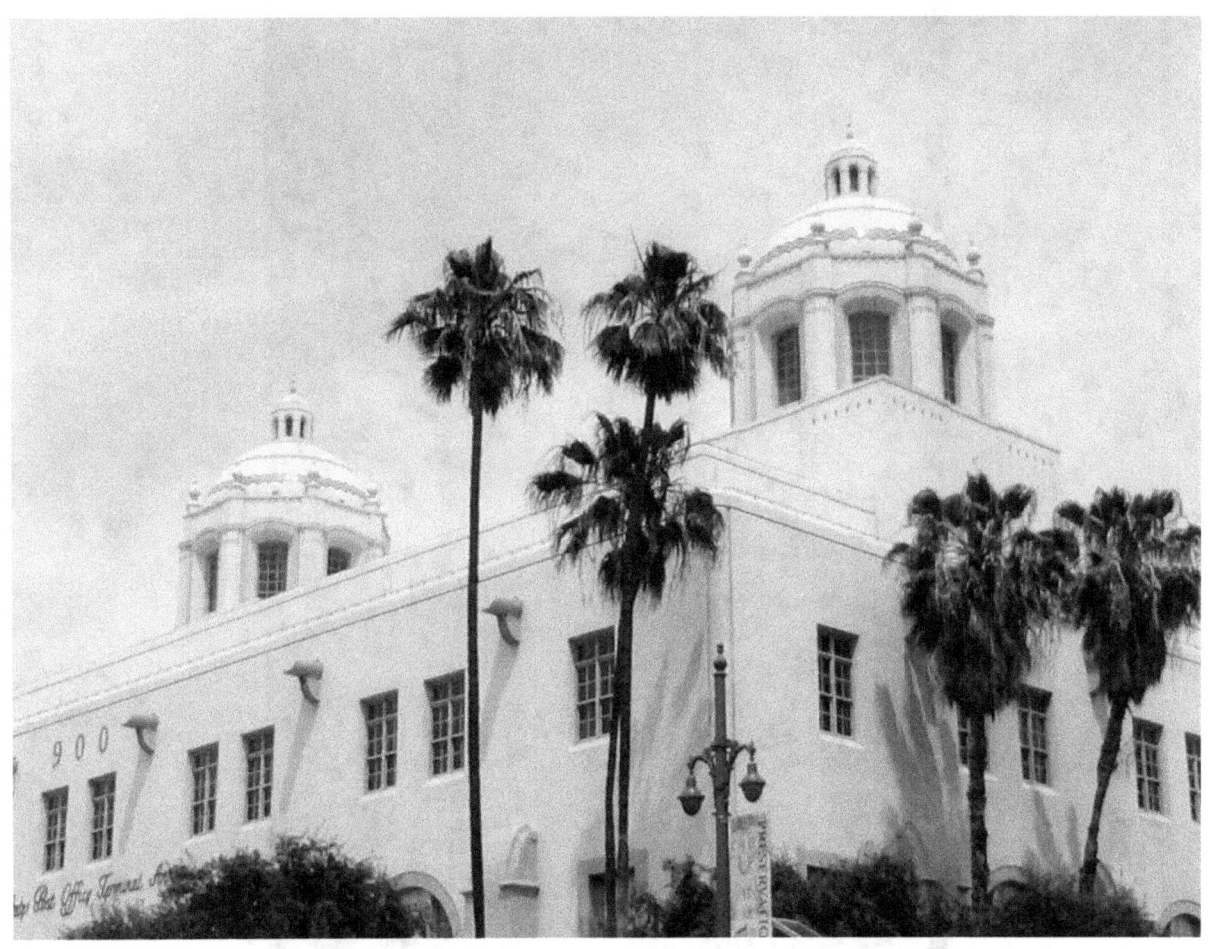

# UNION STATION

800 N. Alameda Street

*Union Station in Los Angeles is often described as the last of the great train stations. It opened in 1939, just before World War II, and not long before the great age of rail gave way to the age of airplanes and automobiles. Surrounded by palm trees, Union Station's Mission Revival-style exterior has a distinctly Californian flavor. Union Station was designed by multiple architects, including British-born John Parkinson, his son Donald B. Parkinson, and Jan von der Linden, who was born in Holland.*

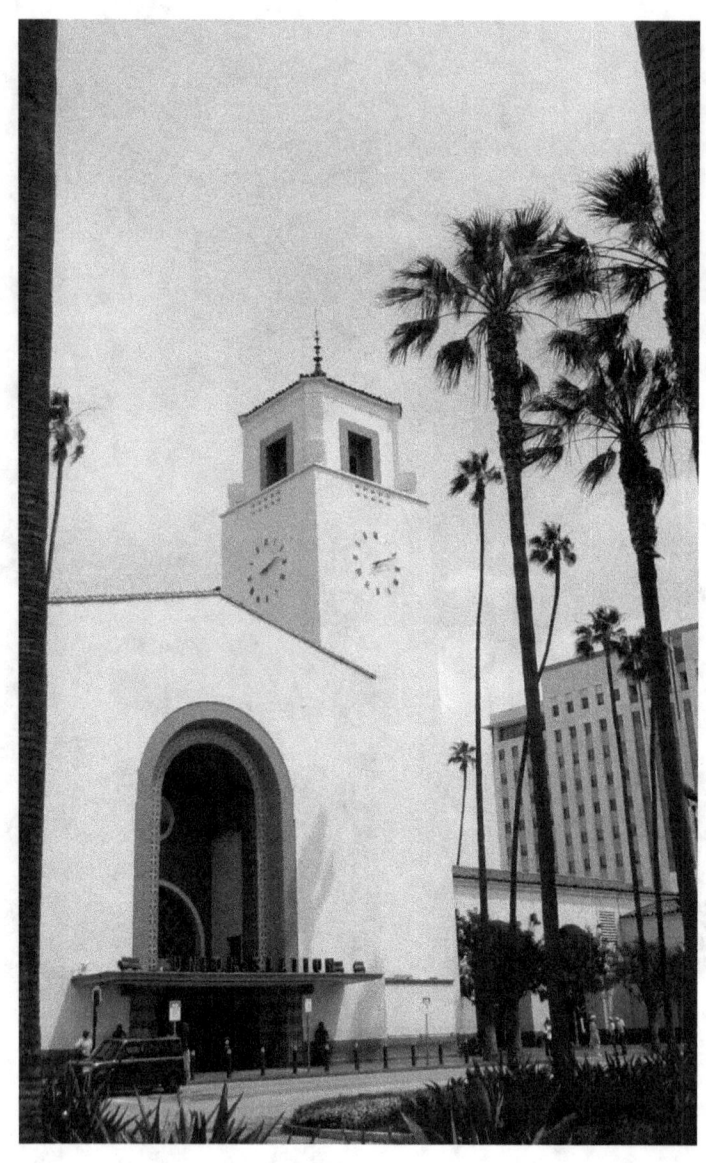

# UNION STATION

800 N. Alameda Street

*Amtrak and Metrolink passenger trains share 14 train tracks. (Two additional underground tracks accommodate the Metro subway lines.) This is a view looking northwest from Platform No. 2, toward Chinatown and the northern industrial district that surrounds the tracks.*

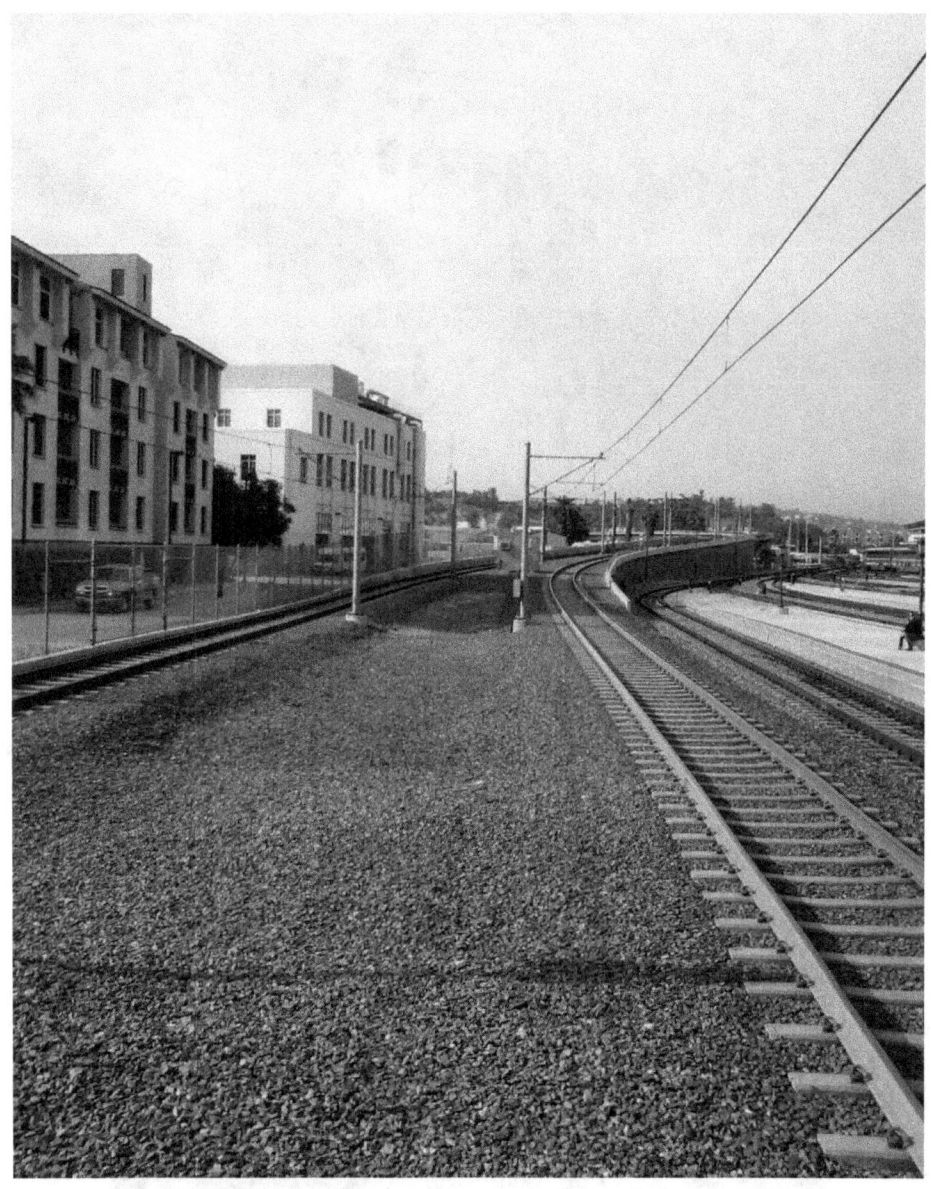

## UNION STATION

800 N. Alameda Street

*Metro headquarters stands just east of the train tracks and Patsaouras Transit Plaza (named for transit advocate Nick Patsaouras). Metro headquarters (located at One Gateway Plaza) opened in 1995 and contains a multi-level lobby with striking transportation murals.*

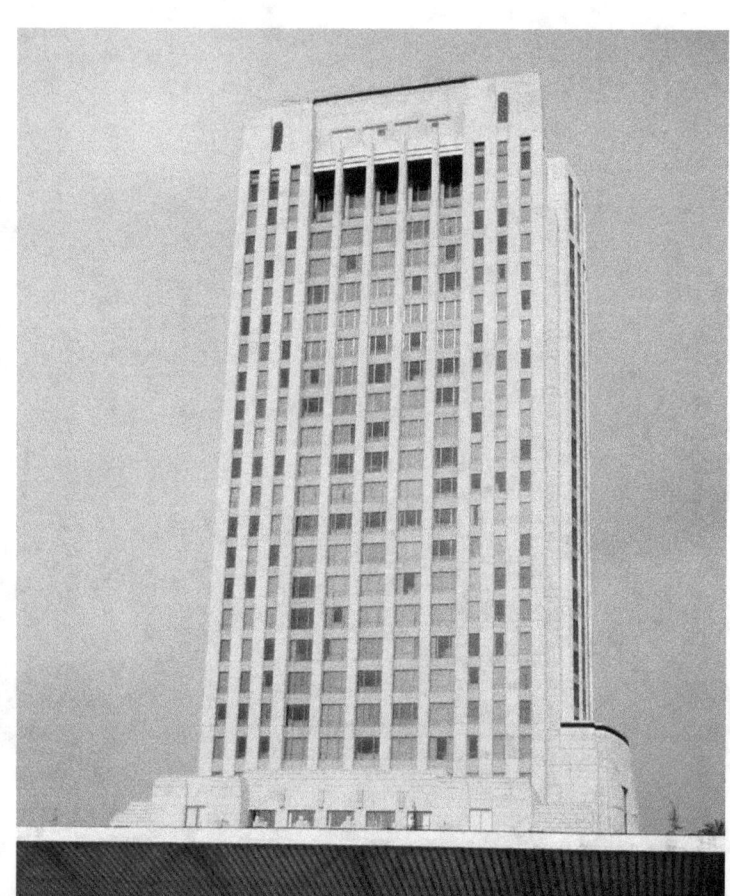

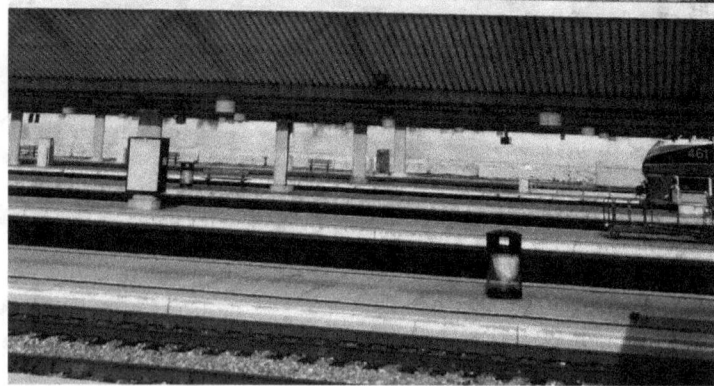

## UNION STATION

*Union Station's elegant interior is known for its fine carved and painted woods, terra cotta tiles, marble, and recurring motifs (like stars). This photo provides a glimpse of the painted wood ceiling (top). The information booth is usually staffed during the day. Union Station was constructed on the site of L.A.'s original Chinatown, as noted by a marker in the south garden off the main waiting room. Old Chinatown flourished until around 1910. After decades of decline, it was razed. The present Chinatown northwest of Union Station is a fascinating blend of the old and new, the authentic and the Hollywoodized. Union Station's Gold Line train connects travelers to the new Chinatown.*

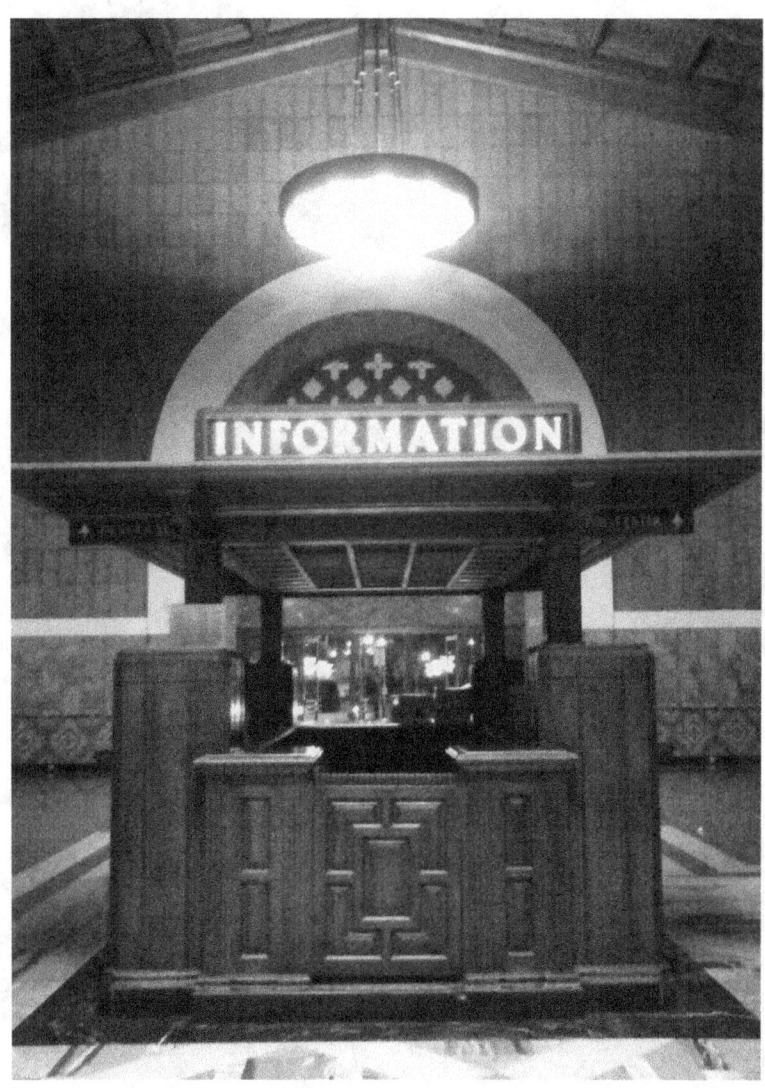

## UNION STATION

800 N. Alameda Street

*Cavalcades of films and TV shows have shot scenes at Union Station since it opened, including "Blade Runner," "To Live and Die in L.A.," and "Gangster Squad". A recent McDonald's commercial featured young people tossing beach balls in the grand waiting room. Pictured below: The cathedral-like windows of the old Ticket Seller area, which is off-limits to the public but available for filming.*

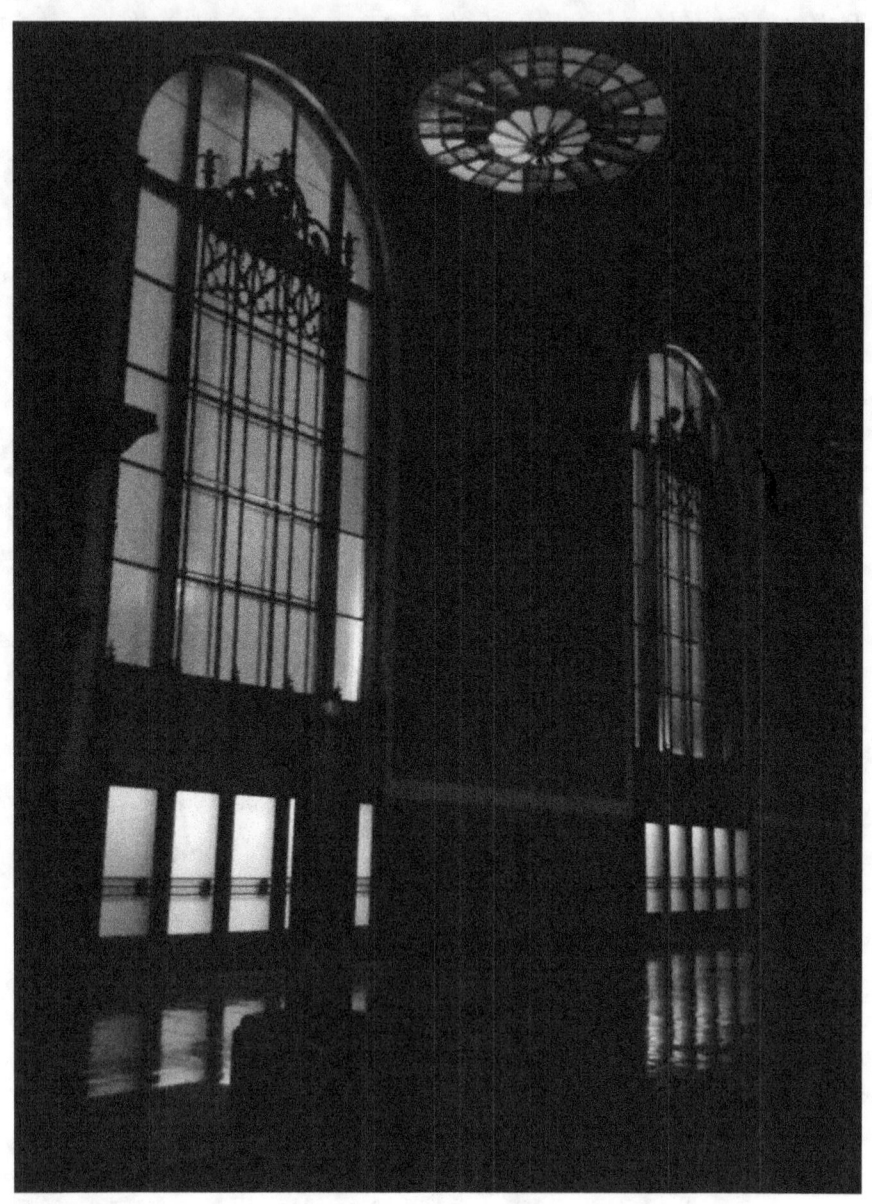

# UNION STATION

800 N. Alameda Street

*Deep below Union Station, Red Line and Purple Line subway trains carry tourists and Angelenos to destinations in Hollywood and along Wilshire Boulevard. Connections at the 7th & Metro station transport riders to destinations like Long Beach, USC, and Culver City.*

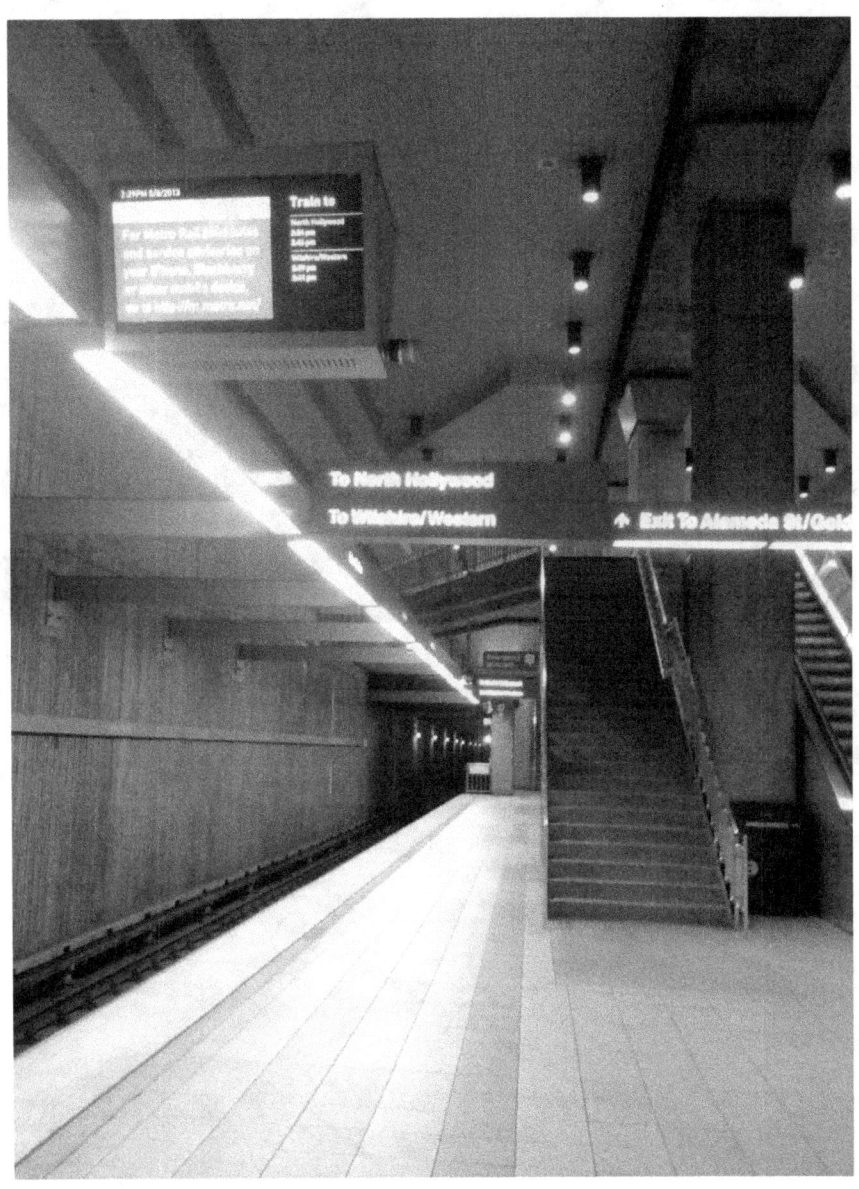

## UNION STATION

800 N. Alameda Street

*A train rumbles into Metro's subway terminal below Union Station.*

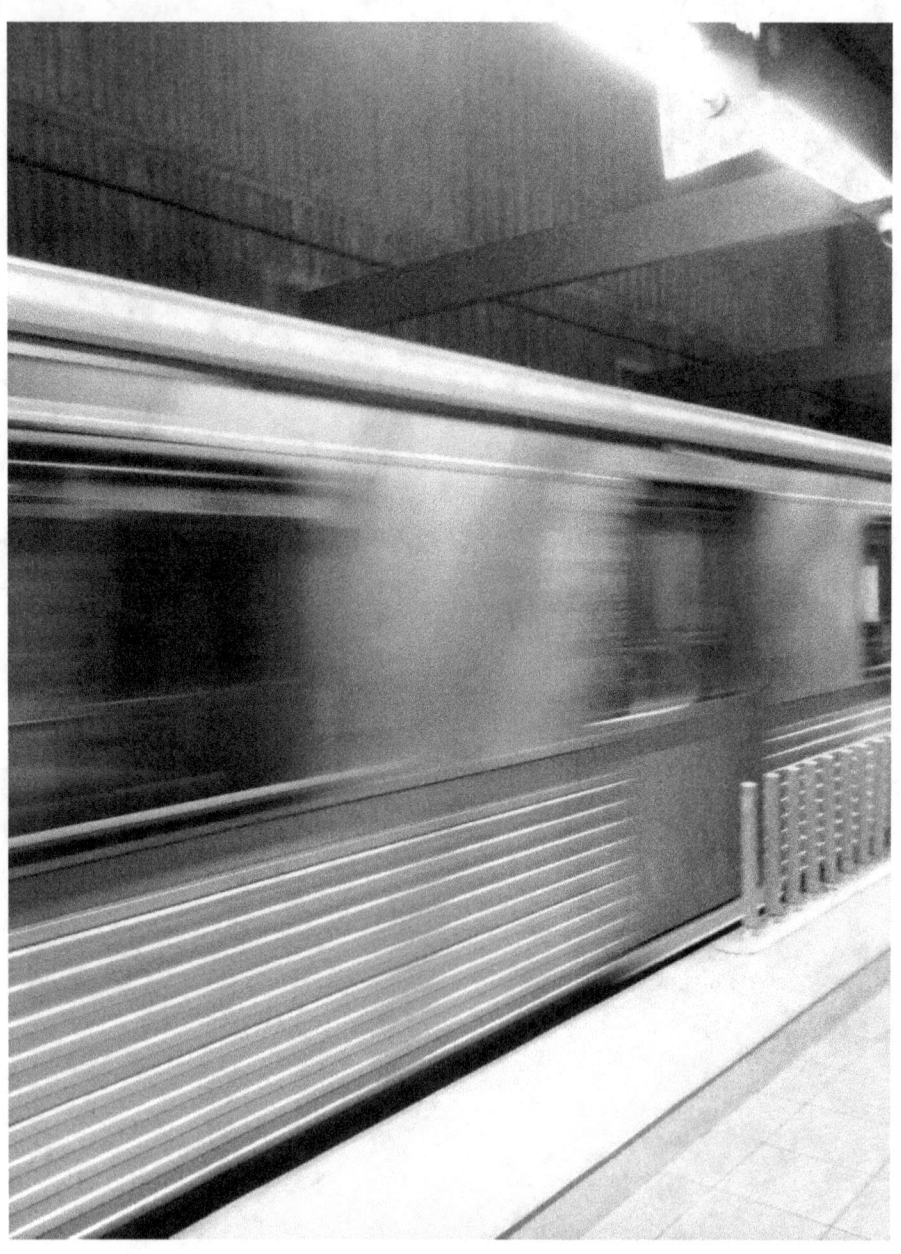

## SUBWAY – PERSHING SQUARE STATION

Pershing Square

*The underground station at Pershing Square (near Bunker Hill, the old bank district, and the new arts district) features one of L.A.'s distinctive art forms: glowing neon.*

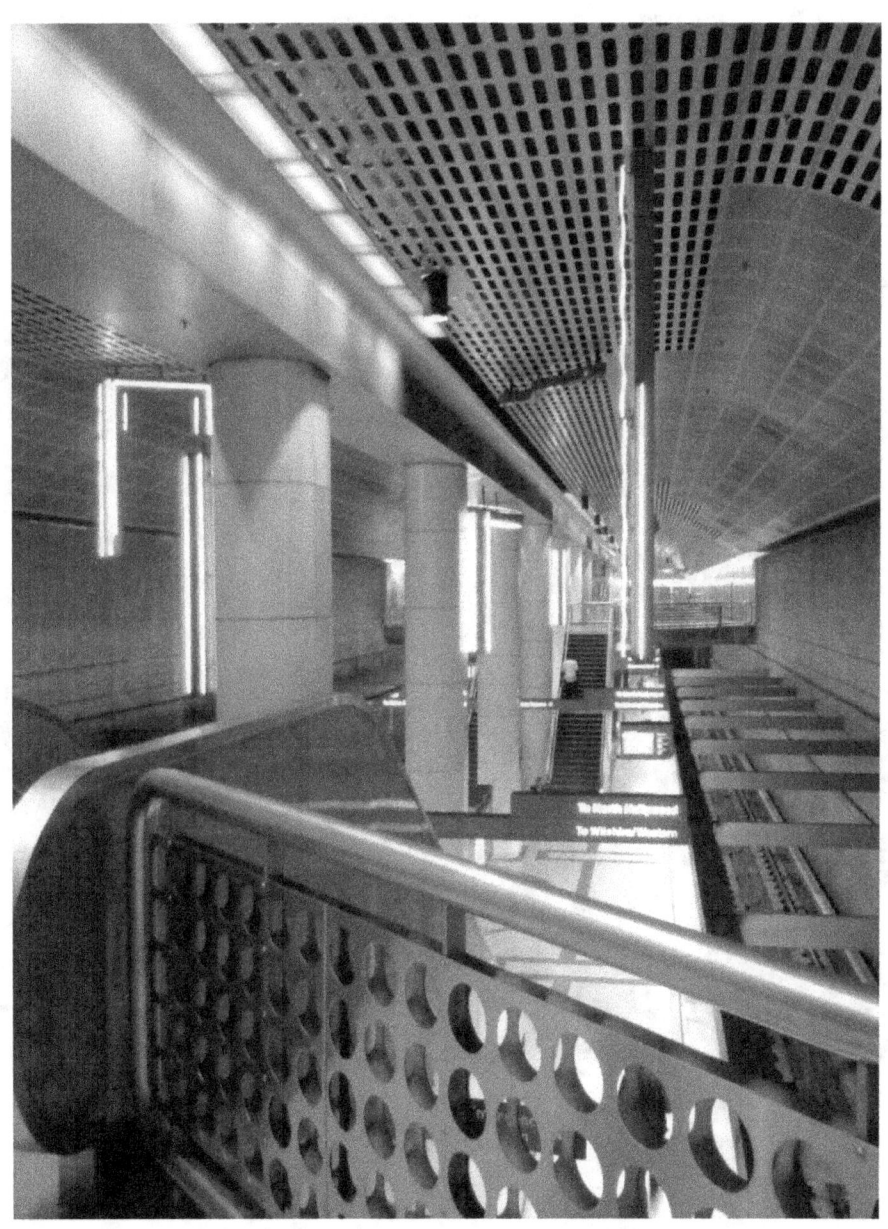

## PICO HOUSE

430 N. Main Street

*Built by Pio Pico, Alta California's last Mexican governor, Casa de Pico was L.A.'s first luxury hotel. Opened in 1870, its fortunes rapidly declined – fortunes shift very quickly in Los Angeles. The hotel witnessed everything from an 1871 riot to elegant events. By the mid-20th century, Pico House had fallen into decay, but was rescued due to its historical importance. Pico House has been designated a state and national landmark, and still hosts events. As recently as May 2013 it hosted an art exhibit.*

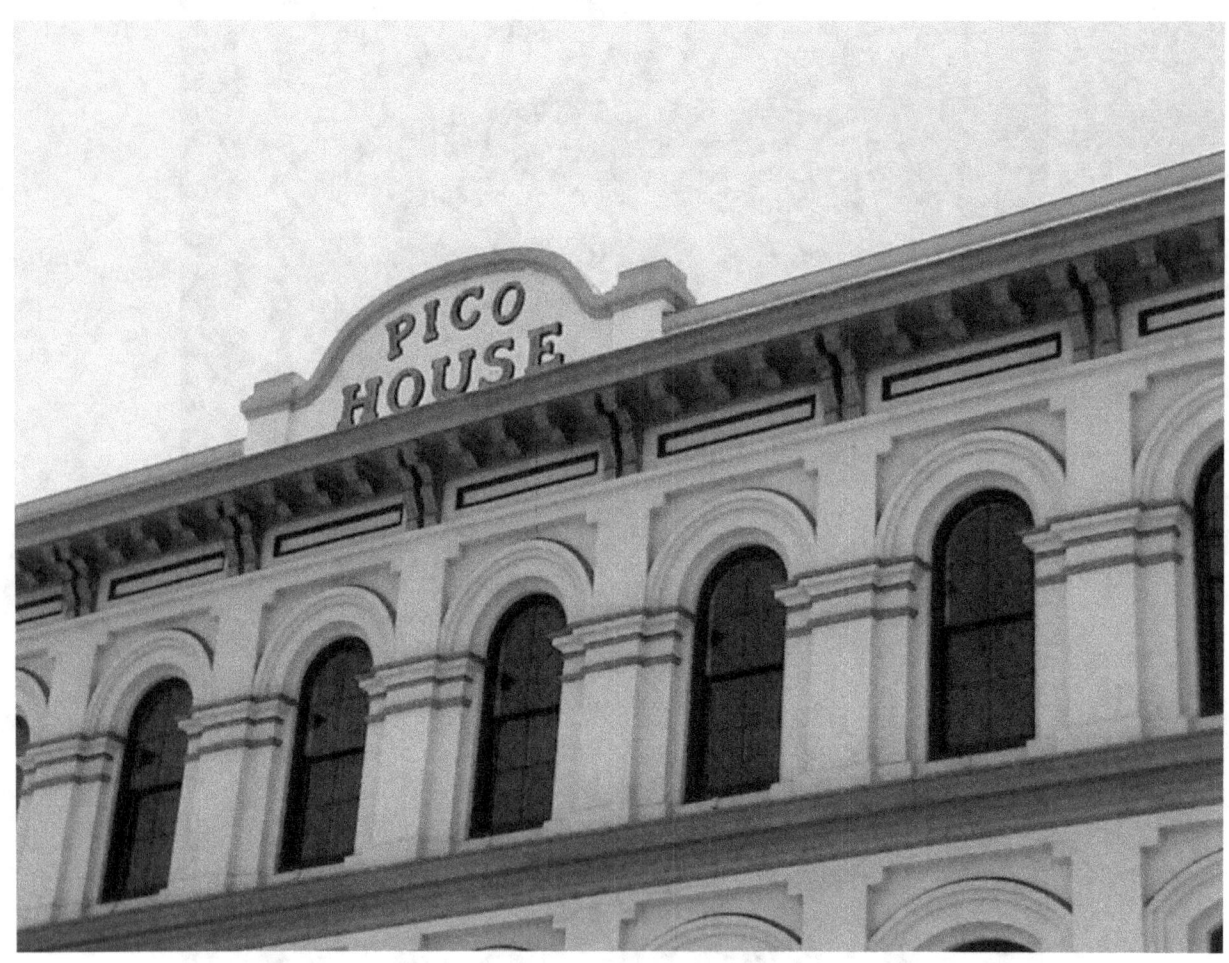

## PICO HOUSE

430 N. Main Street

*A full view of Pico House's north entrance. L.A.'s new federal building is visible in the distance, on the left side of the photo; L.A. City Hall and the United States Courthouse are visible on the right.*

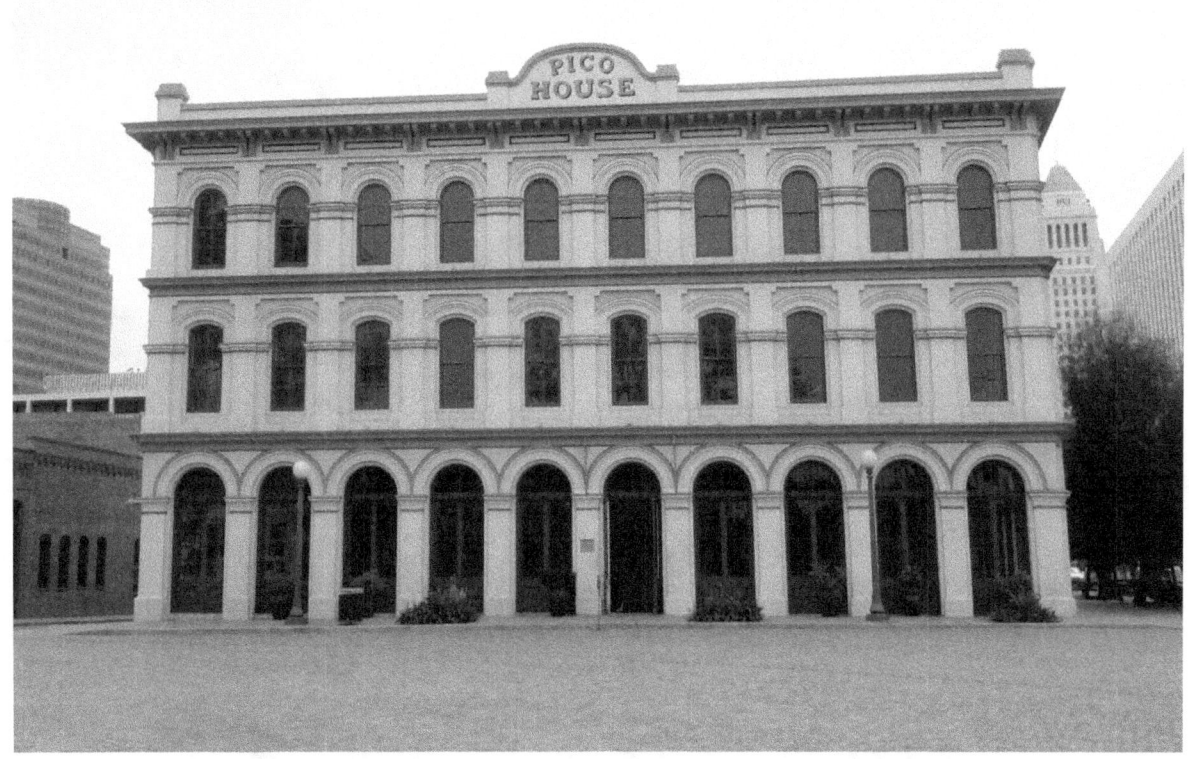

## OLVERA STREET

125 Paseo De La Plaza

*Olvera Street runs parallel to Alameda Street to the east and Los Angeles Street to the west, and for decades was a simple dirt lane. In 1930 it was transformed into a picturesque collection of restaurants, shops, and museums that honors Mexican culture and history in Los Angeles. Olvera Street as a celebration of Mexican heritage was the brain-child of society luminary Christine Sterling, who was also behind the creation of China City, one of the precursors of today's Chinatown.*

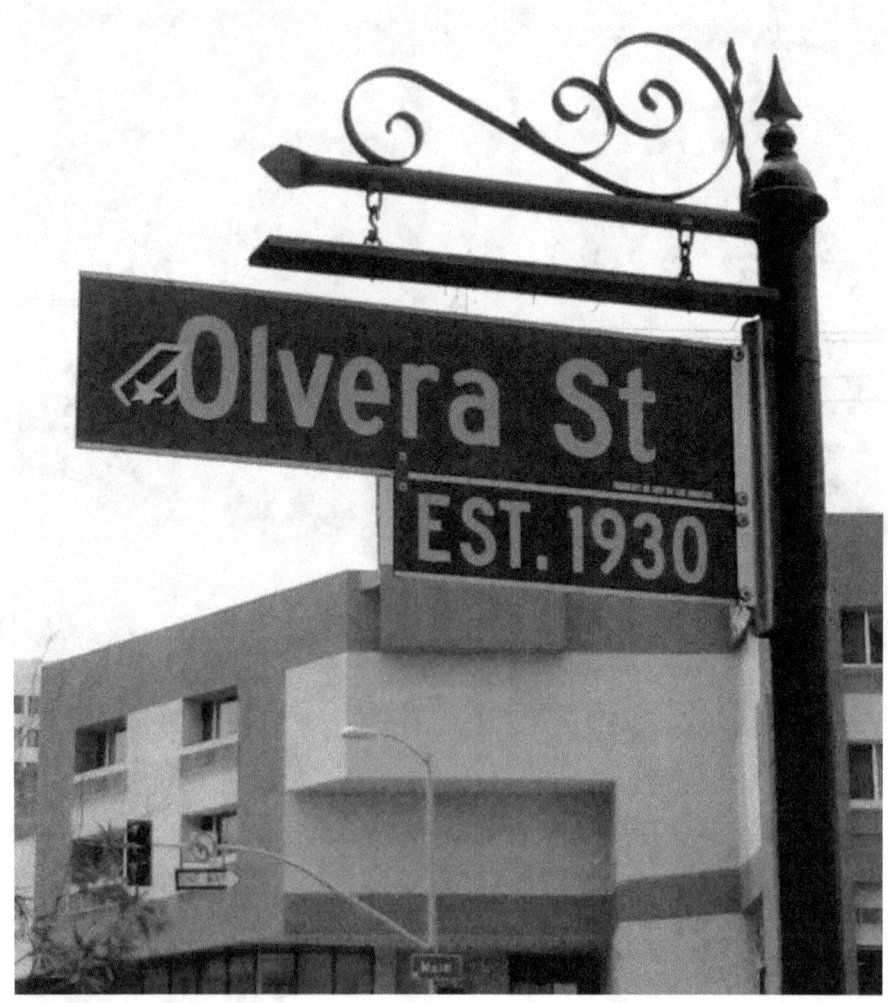

# OLVERA STREET

125 Paseo De La Plaza

*It looks like it's been a part of Olvera Street forever, but the statue of Mexican actor Antonio Aguilar astride a mighty steed is a new addition. Crafted by local sculptor Dan Medina, the sculpture of Aguilar was unveiled on September 16, 2012, and anchors the southern approach to Olvera Street.*

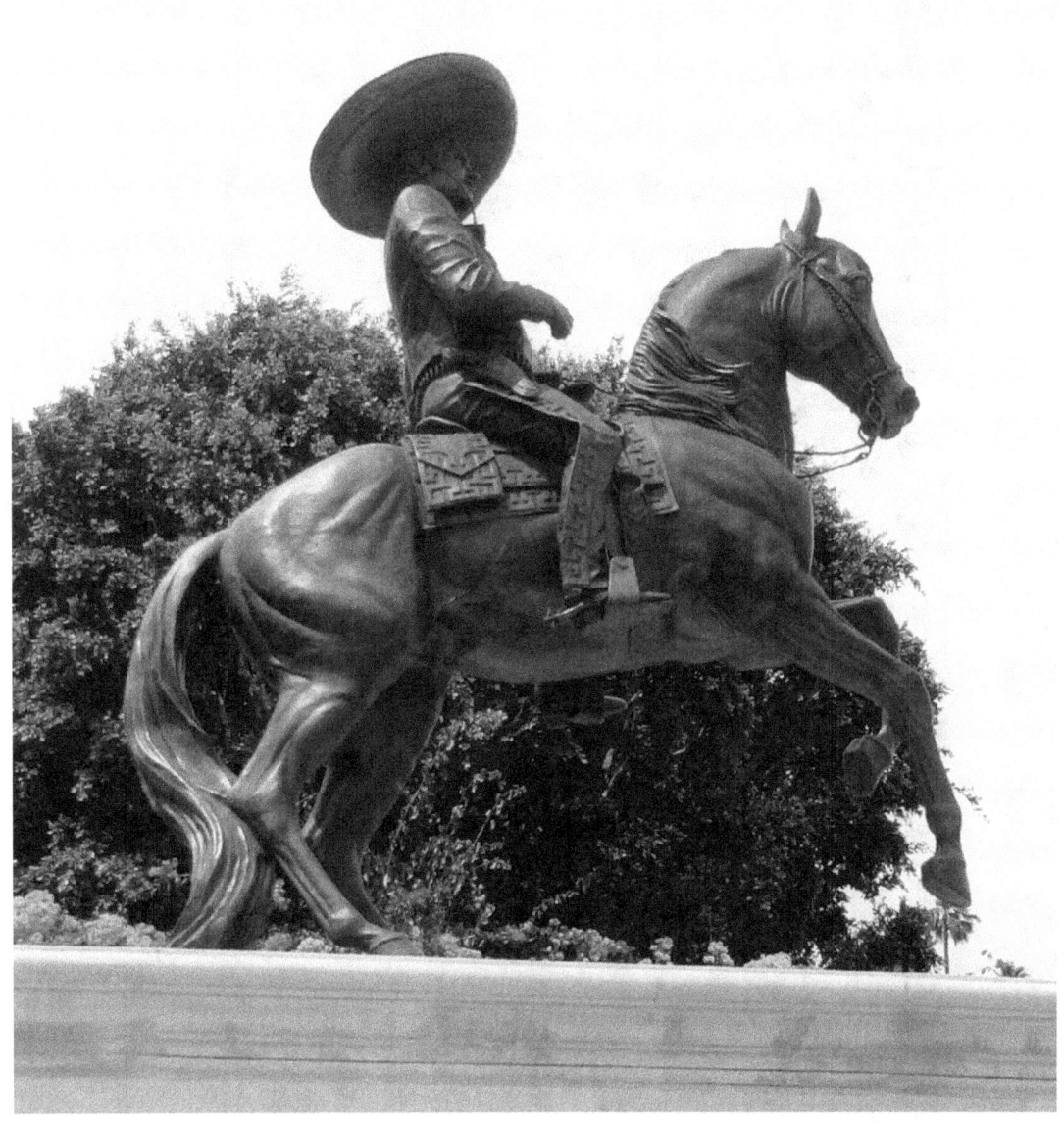

# OLVERA STREET

125 Paseo De La Plaza

*Wares sold at Olvera Street's open-air booths include traditional Mexican leather goods and woven clothing, as well as toys, postcards, and novelty items like these guitars.*

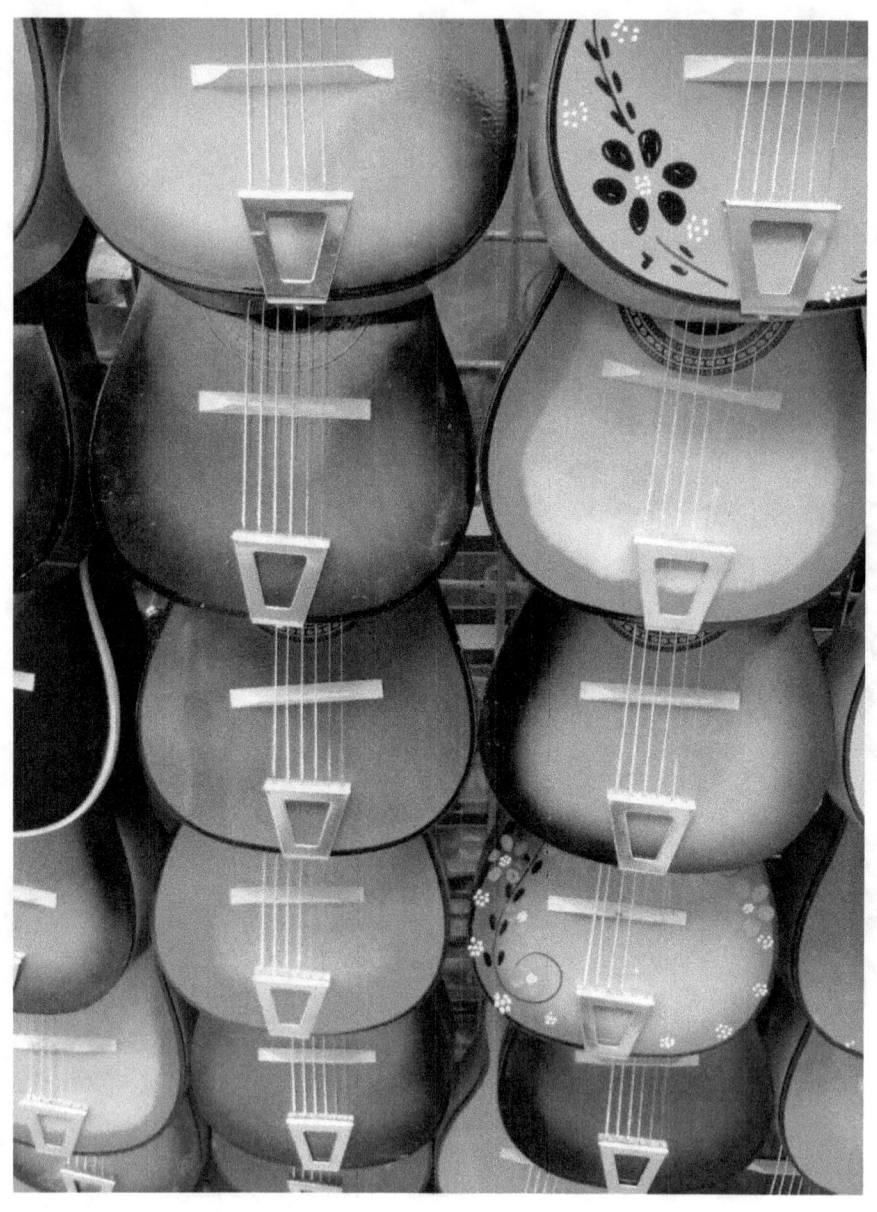

# OLVERA STREET

125 Paseo De La Plaza

*Banks of flowers, bells, and an ancient tree grace the front of Olvera Street's Avila Adobe, built in 1818, the oldest standing house in Los Angeles.  Now a museum, the Avila Adobe offers an authentic view of early life in Los Angeles, and a display about William Mulholland's quest to bring water to L.A.*

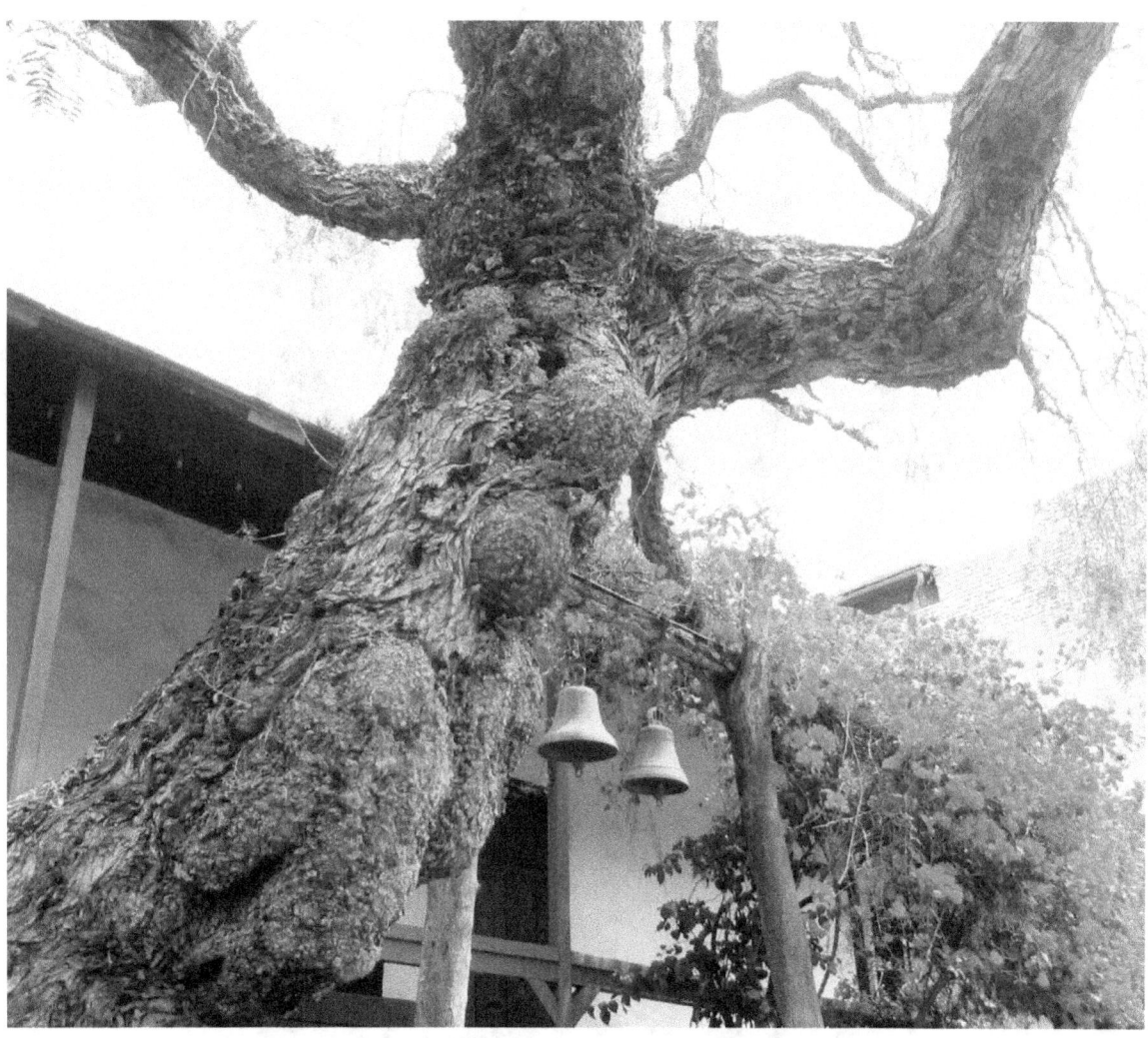

## OLVERA STREET

125 Paseo De La Plaza

*Blink and you'll miss the narrow entrance to the Avila Adobe.  Budget bonus – admission is free.*

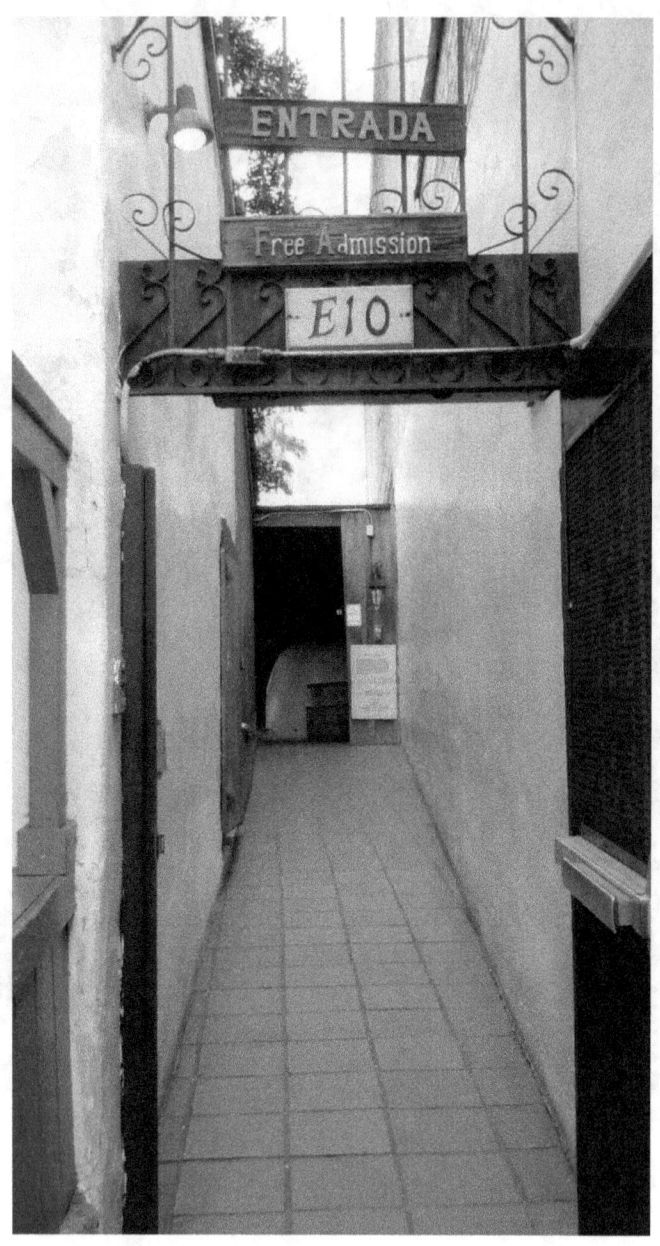

*The Avila Adobe dining room.  Helpful docents are on hand to answer questions about the era.*

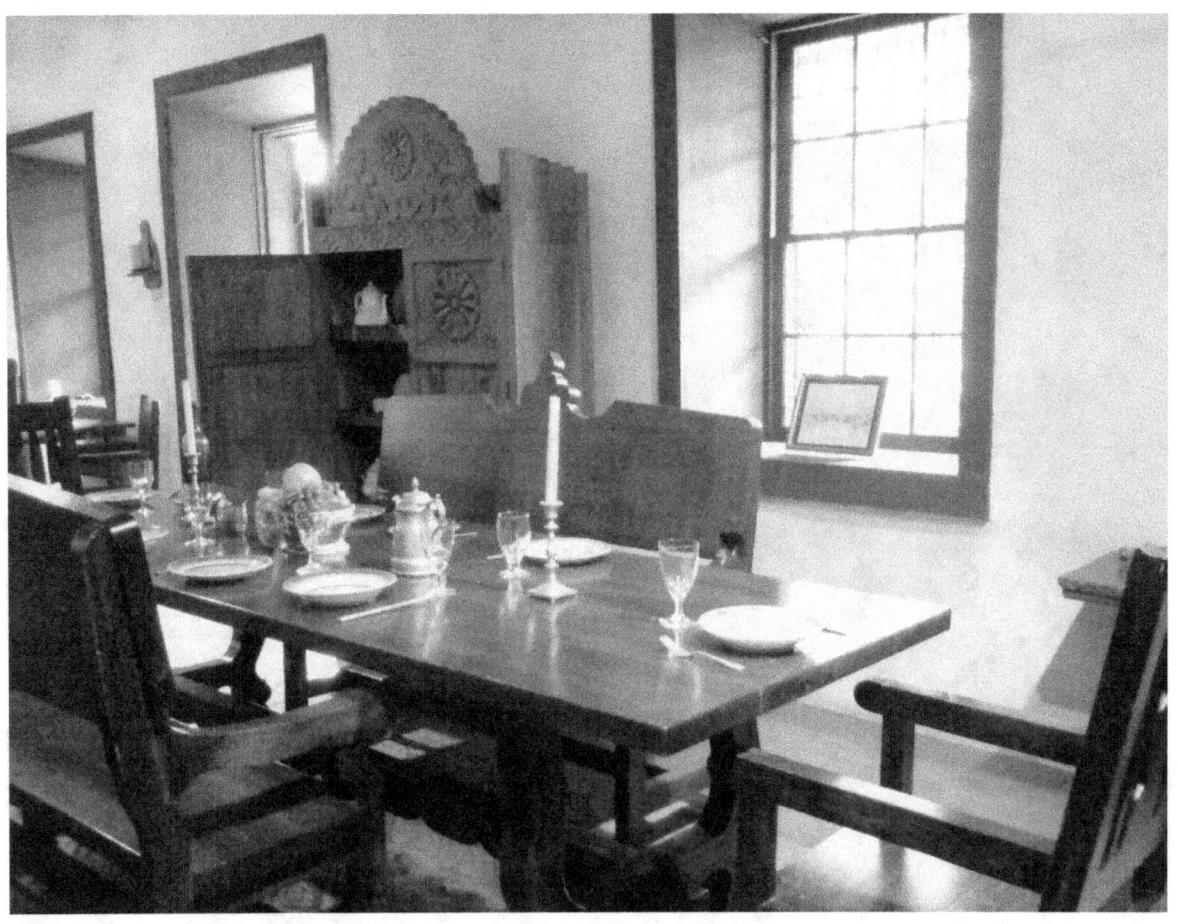

125 Paseo De La Plaza

*The Avila Adobe parlor. Francisco Avila was a wealthy rancher; he attended mass at the nearby church Nuestro Señora Reina de Los Angeles. The Adobe was occupied briefly by American forces in 1847 during the Mexican-American war. By the 1920's the house was in dire need of restoration, which was spearheaded by Christine Sterling.*

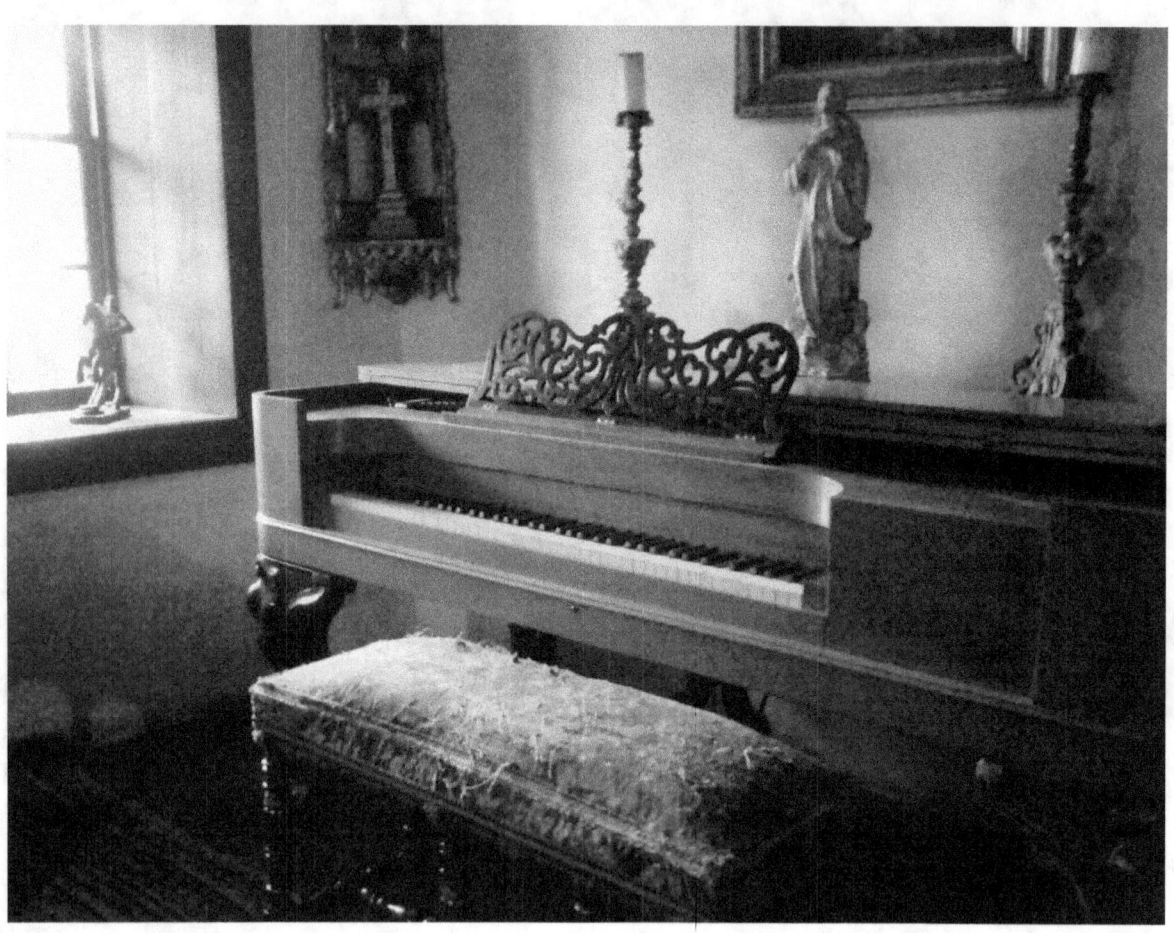

# OLVERA STREET

125 Paseo De La Plaza

*The church where Francisco Avila worshipped, Nuestra Señora Reina de Los Angeles ("Our Lady Queen of the Angels"), was founded in 1781. Just across Los Angeles Street from the plaza and the market, it continues to welcomes locals and tourists alike.*

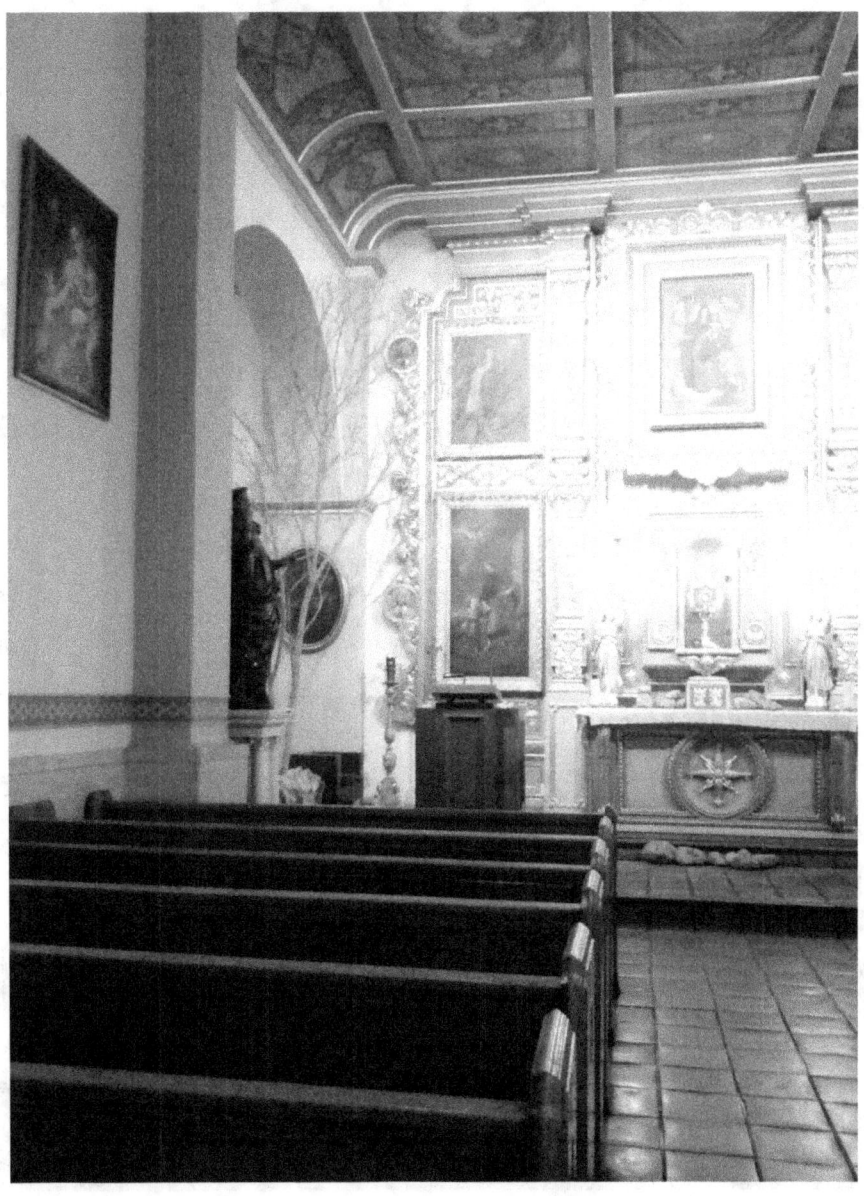

*Pictured below is Nuestra Señora Reina de Los Angeles' stunning reredo.*

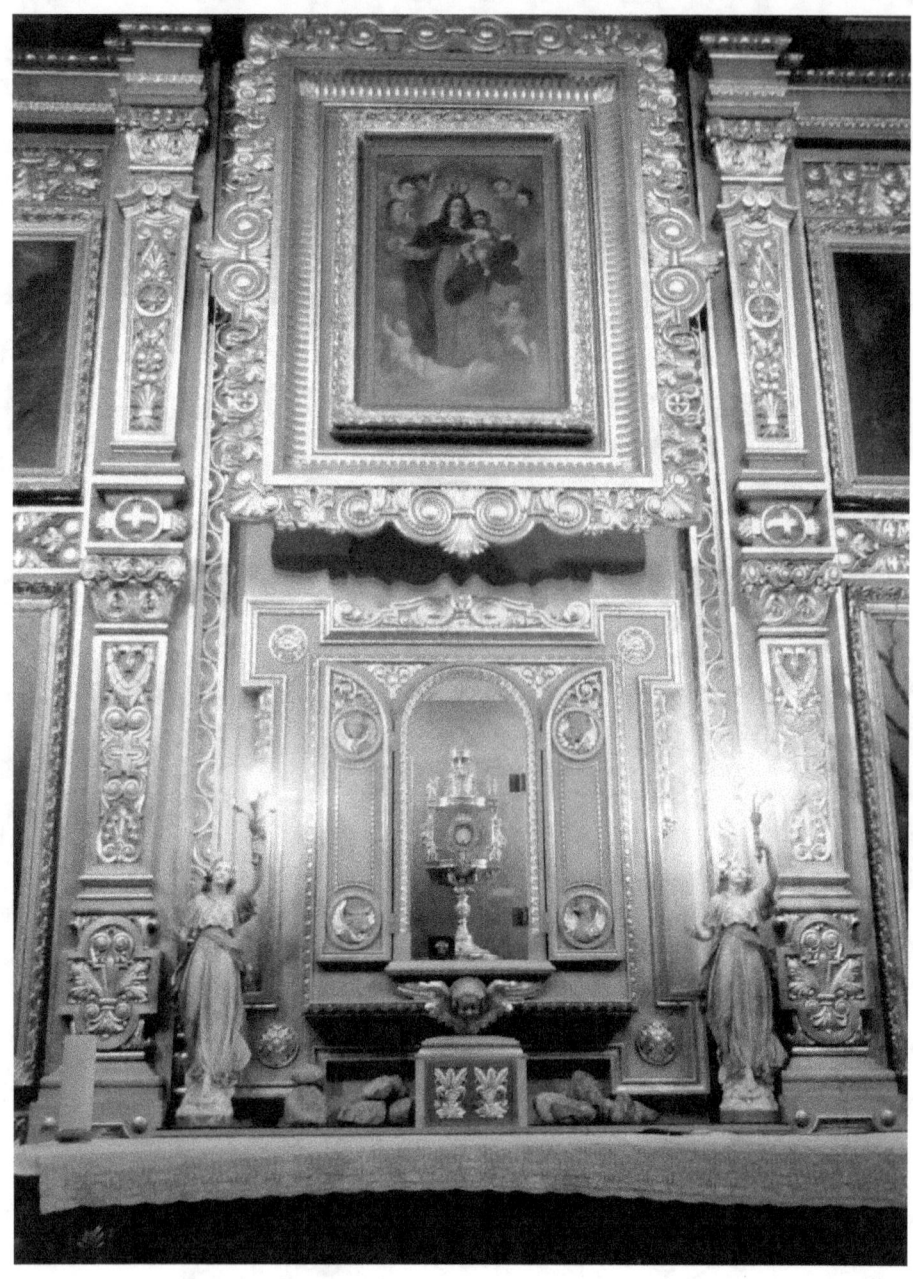

## UNITED STATES COURTHOUSE

312 N. Spring Street

*Opened in 1940, this Art Moderne edifice, designed by Gilbert Stanley Underwood, was built on the site of a previous federal building which had proved too small to accommodate L.A.'s booming population. Cases involving celebrities such as Clark Gable were tried in this national landmark. Although L.A.'s newer federal building, the Roybal Building, also holds a federal courthouse, the U.S. courthouse at this location remains active. The lobbies are notable for their murals and sculptures. The building is seen here from the Los Angeles Street side.*

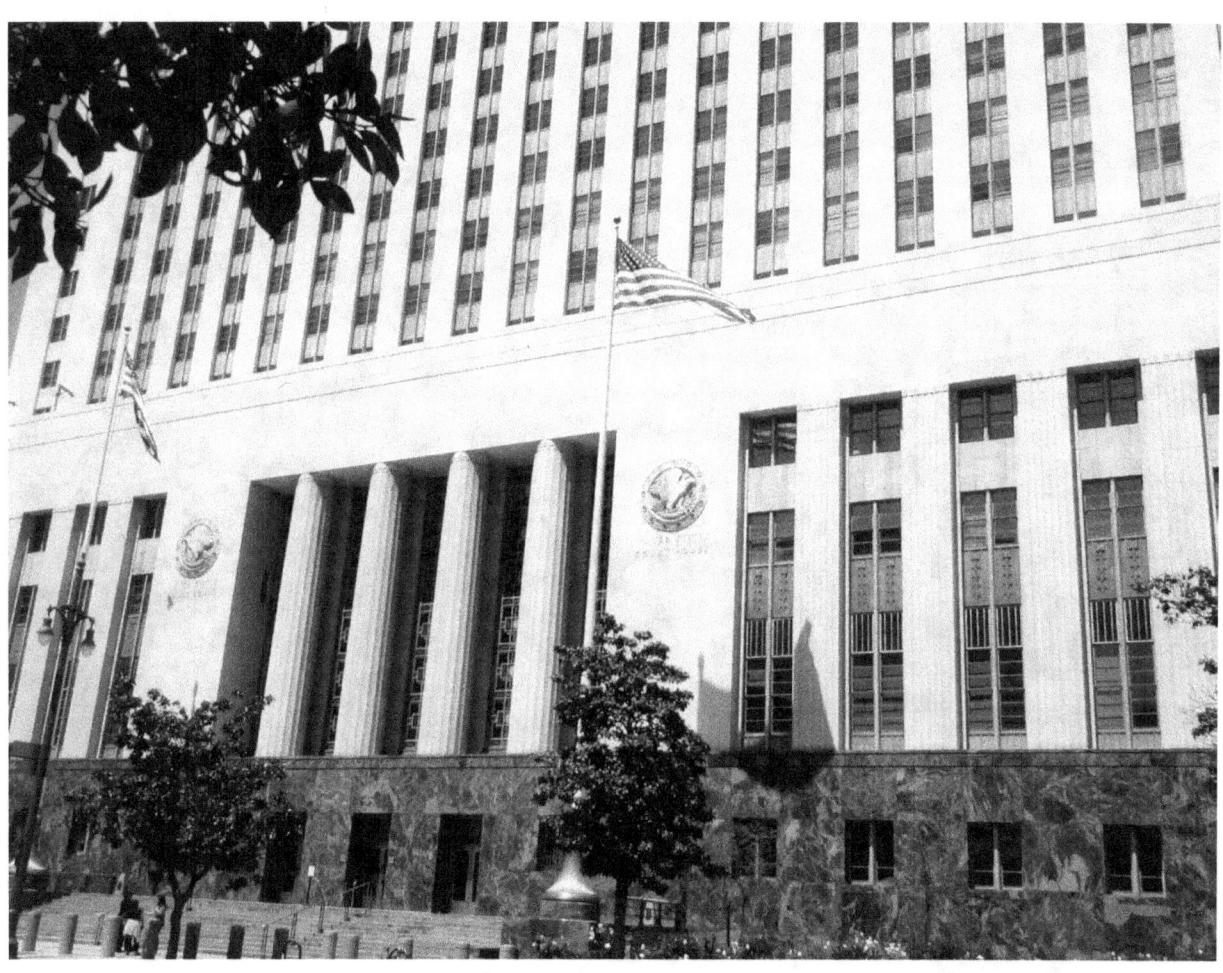

## UNITED STATES COURTHOUSE

312 N. Spring Street

*A view of the United States Courthouse from Temple Street. Note the graceful gravitas of the structure's geometry, and the handsome lawns, shrubs, and flowers that soften it.*

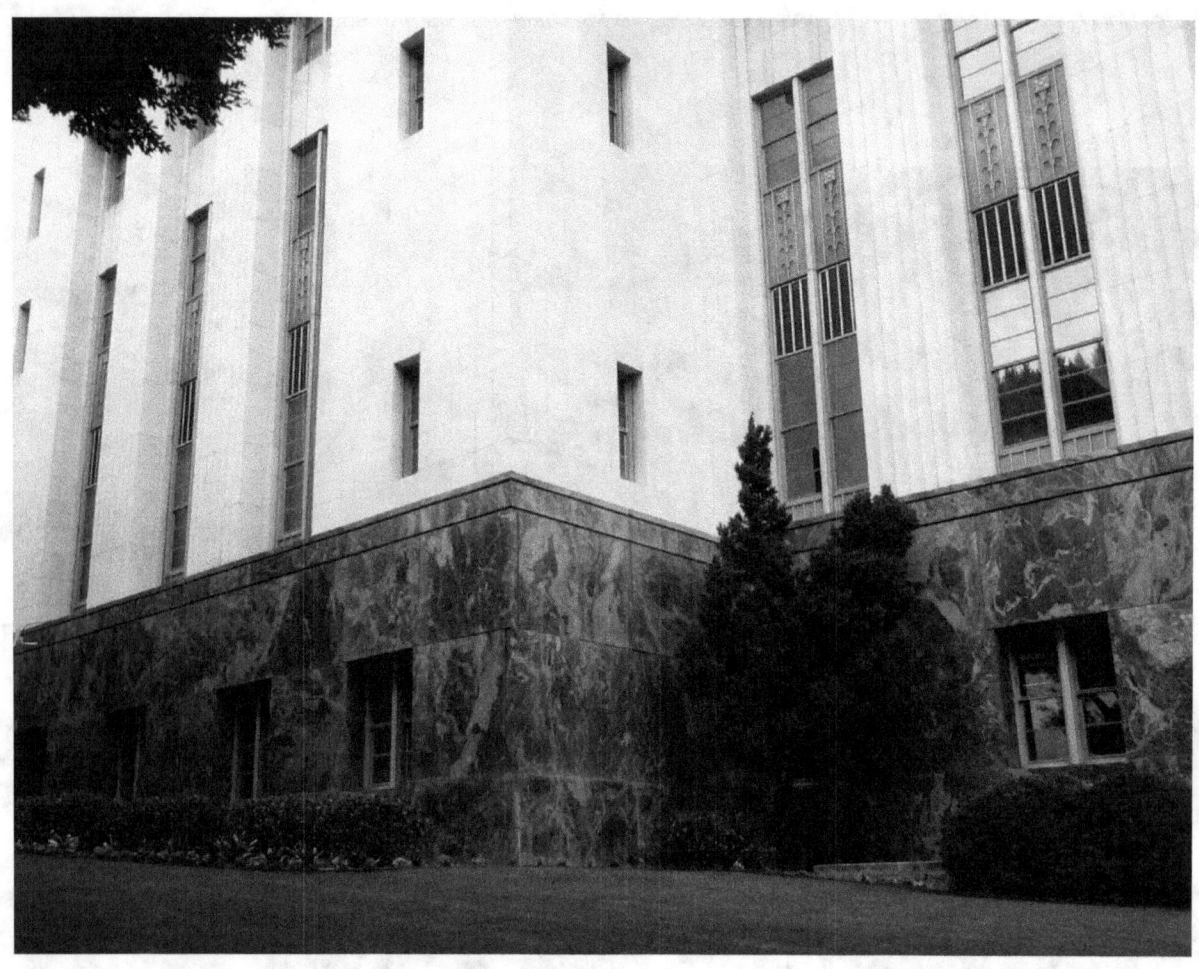

## LOS ANGELES CITY HALL

### 200 N. Spring Street

*An elegant work of architecture that visually communicates L.A.'s broad foundation and towering aspiration. The 32-story civic building opened its doors in 1928. "Dragnet" made city hall's silhouette famous, as the image appears on the badges of L.A. Police officers. The design of the distinctive tower is based on a Turkish mausoleum, and houses a large meeting/event space and observation deck that tourists and citizens can visit (for free) to see staggering views of the city and its environs.*

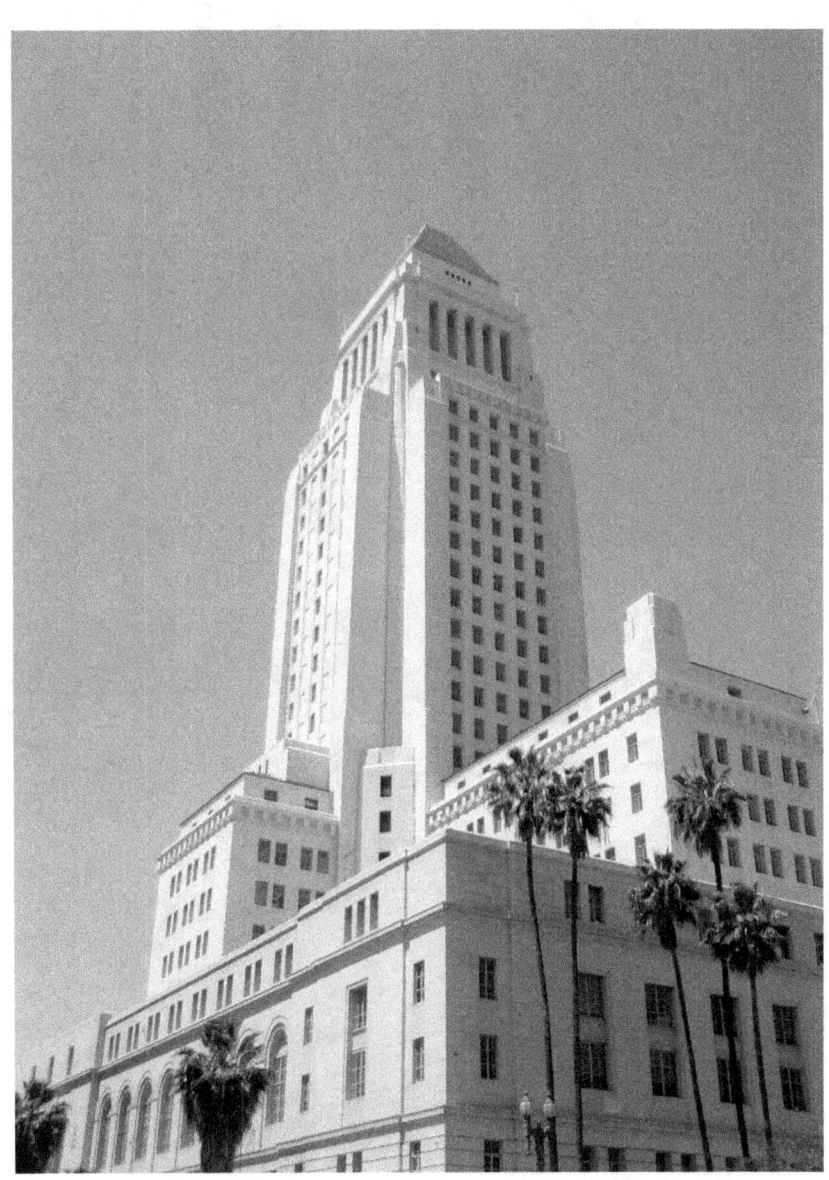

## LOS ANGELES CITY HALL

200 N. Spring Street

*The entrance for visitors who wish to ascend to the observation deck is on Los Angeles Street.*

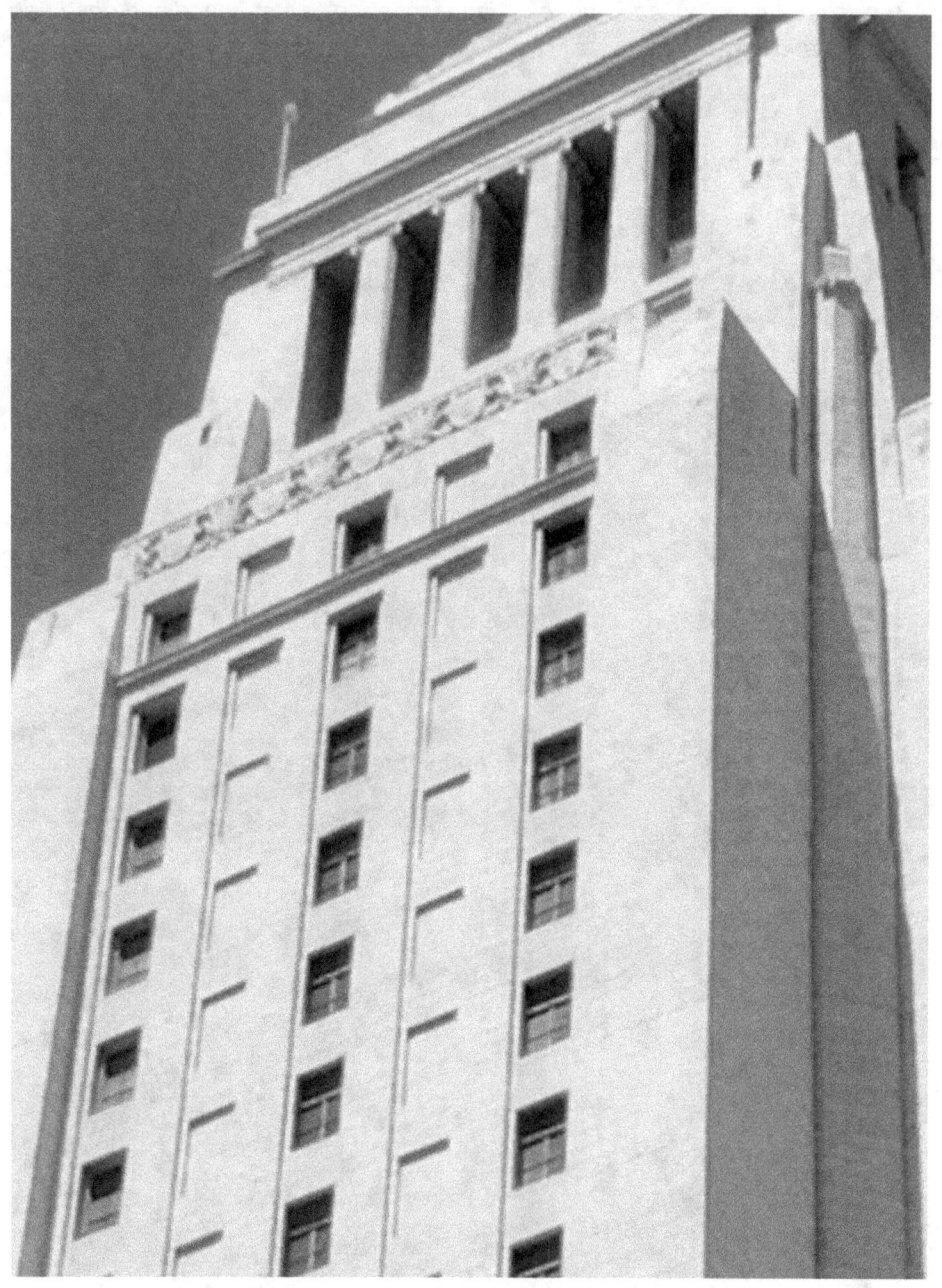

*A striking meeting chamber occupies the 27th floor. Events and press conferences are held here.*

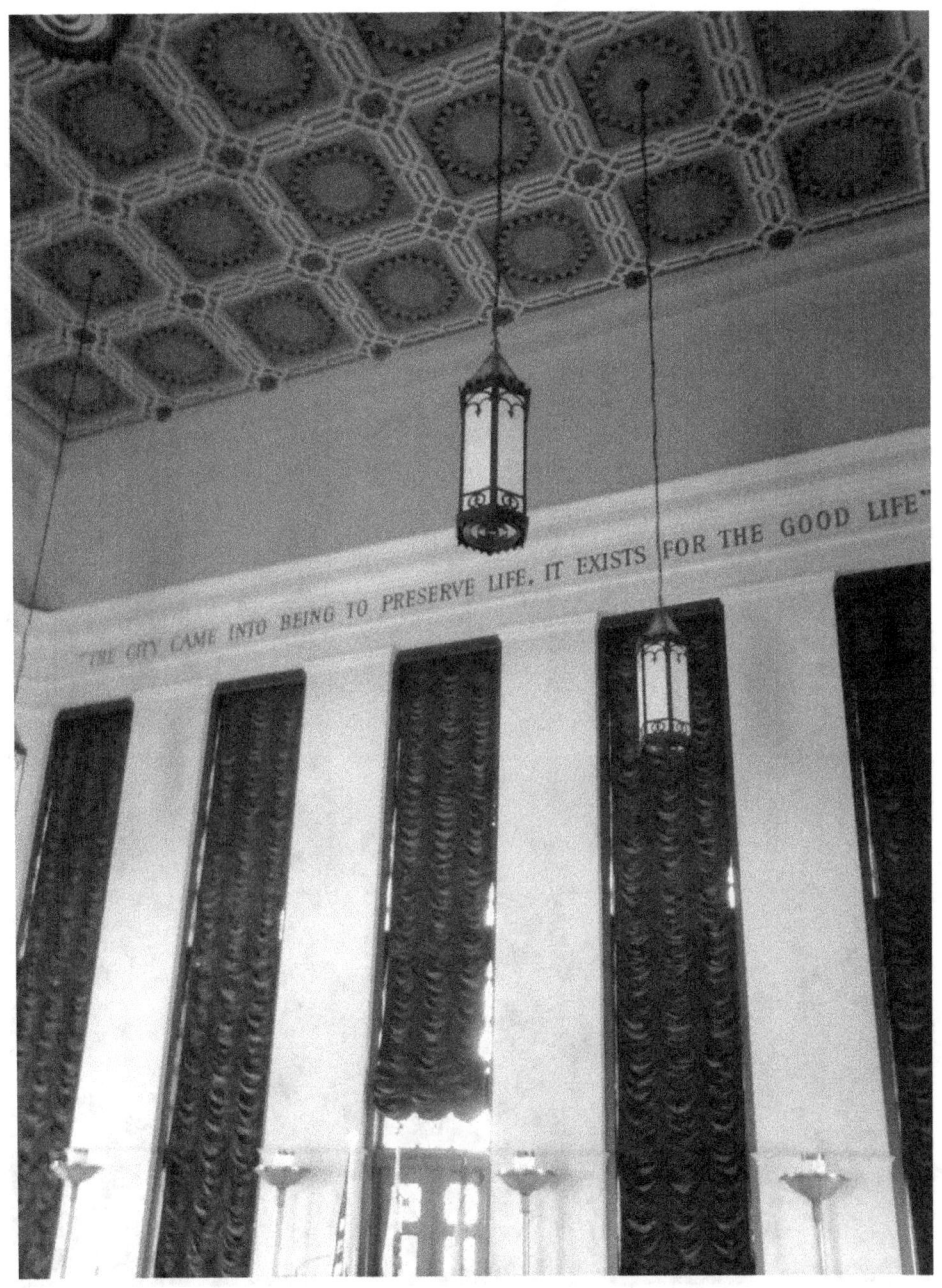

# LOS ANGELES CITY HALL

200 N. Spring Street

*A high view of the U.S. Courthouse, looking north from City Hall's observation deck.*

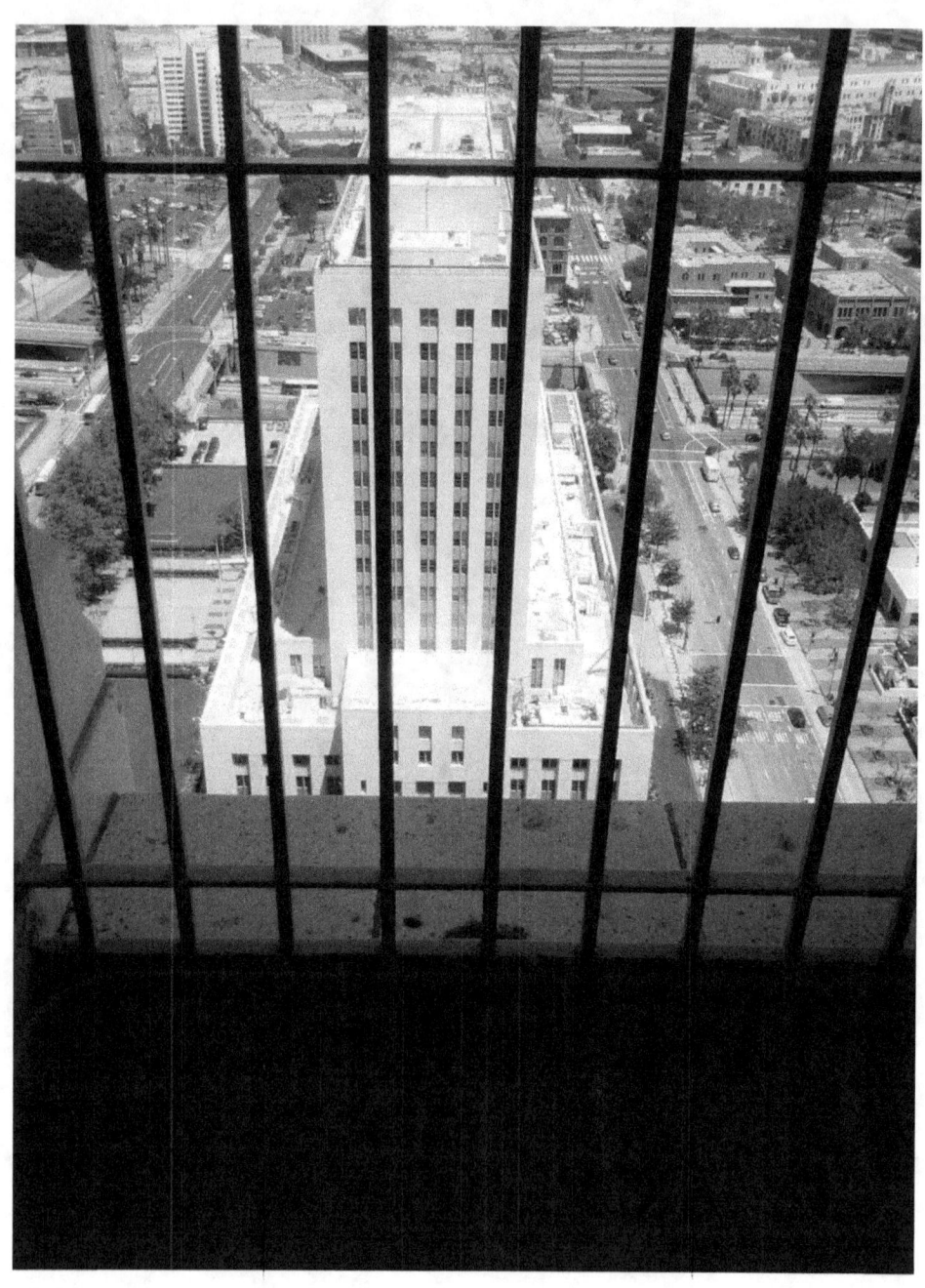

## LOS ANGELES CITY HALL

200 N. Spring Street

*A view of L.A., looking south from the observation deck of City Hall. Note the lower profile of the older buildings on the east (left) side of the downtown, and the Manhattan-like towers of the newer financial district on the southwest (right). Known for its "sprawl" rather than height, Los Angeles has few pockets of soaring skyscrapers; the financial district is one of them.*

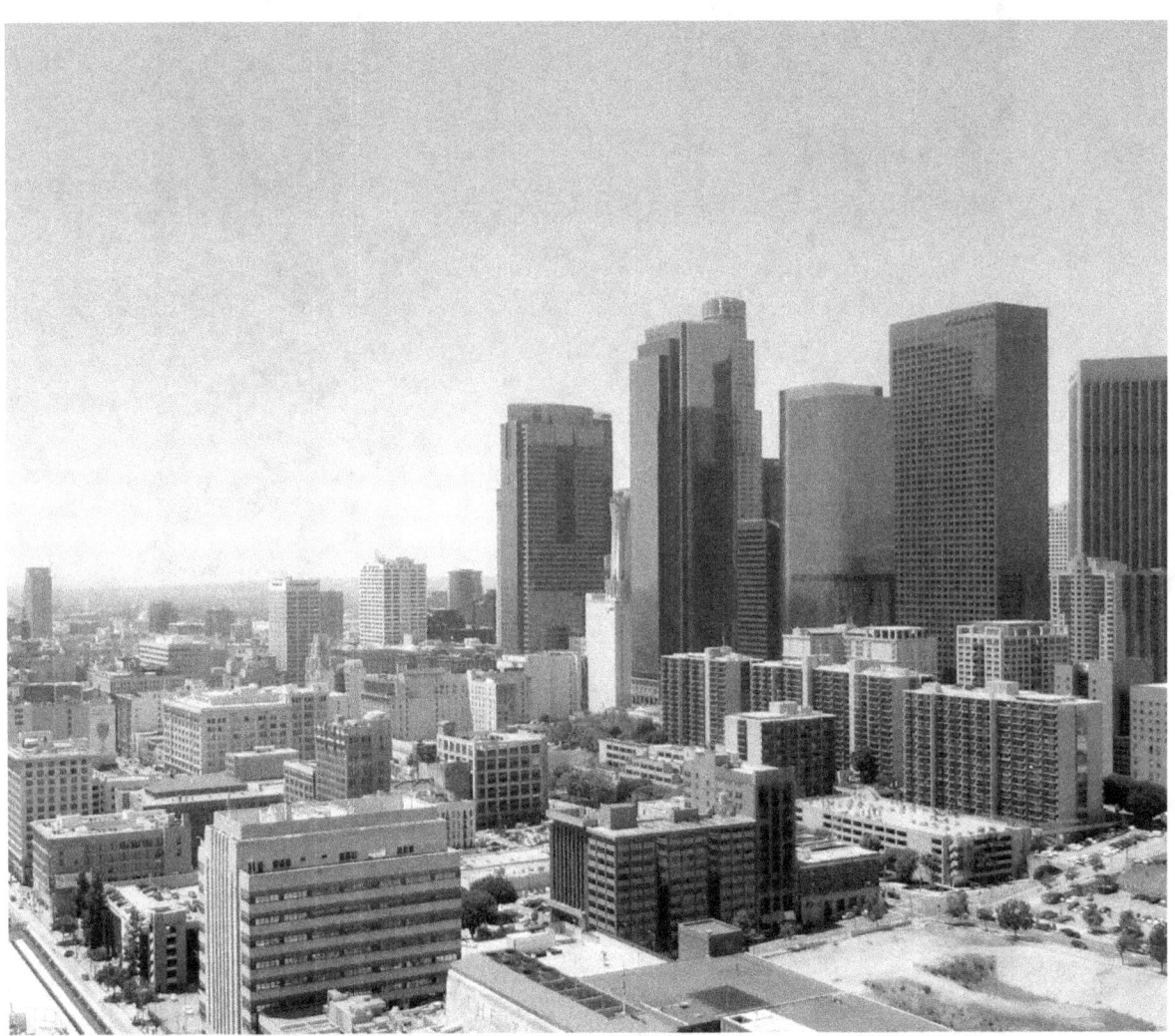

## LOS ANGELES CITY HALL

200 N. Spring Street

*A north corridor on the 3ʳᵈ floor of City Hall.  City workers in this section of the building enjoy marble,
mosaics, sculptures – a feast of lovely, classical, architectural details.*

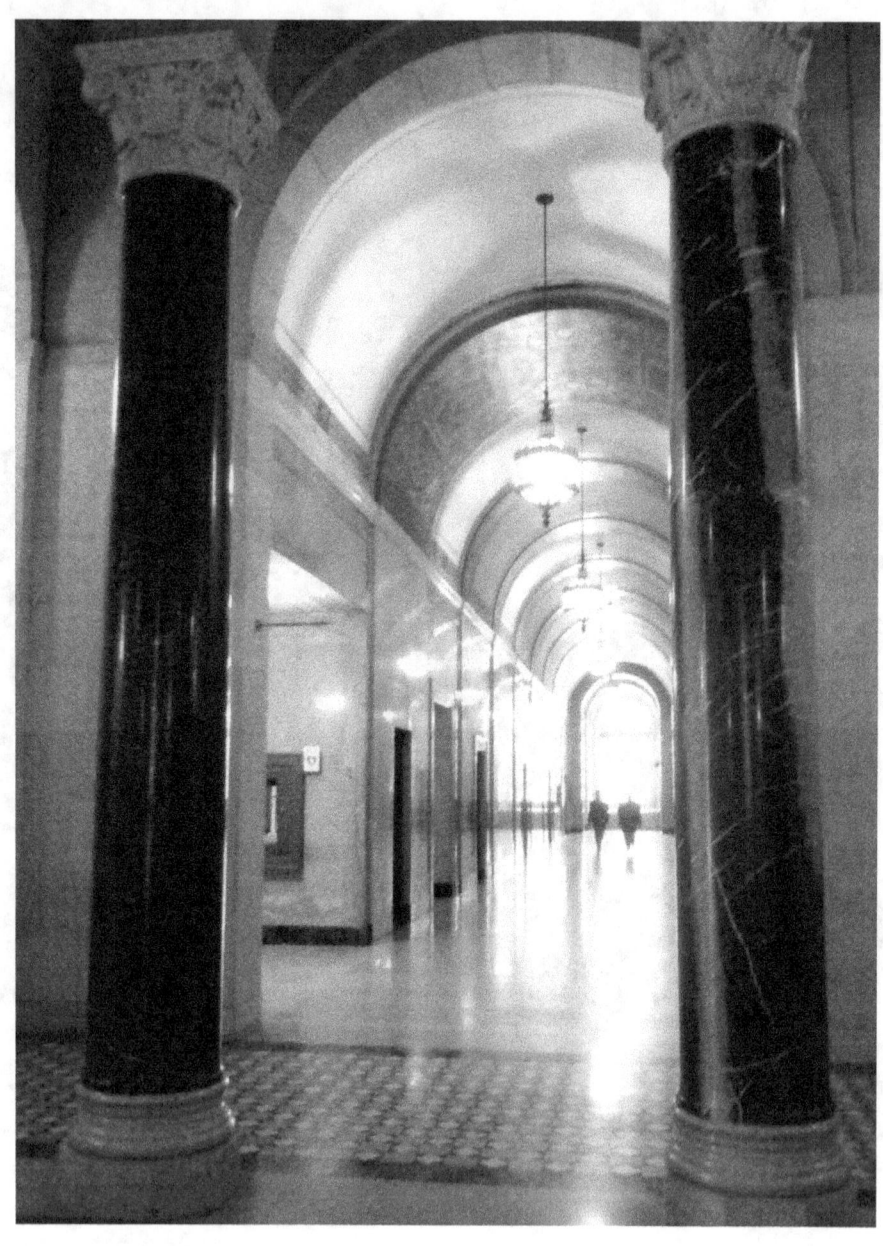

## LOS ANGELES CITY HALL

### 200 N. Spring Street

*Atrium, 3ᵈ floor of City Hall.  Note the symmetry of the classical columns and arches; the lace-like delicacy of the balcony; and the Egyptian influence in the tiled mosaic below the top arch.*

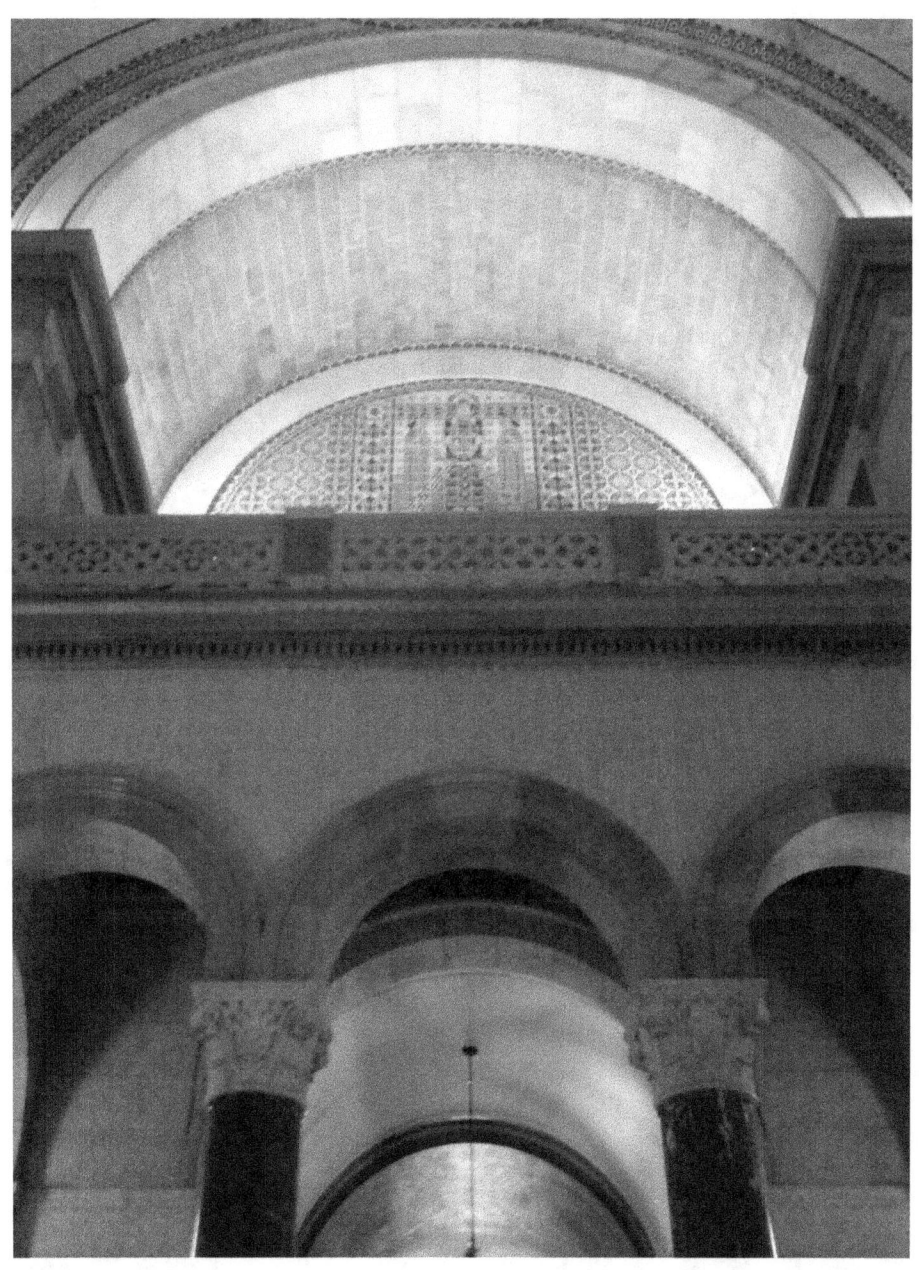

# LOS ANGELES CITY HALL

## 200 N. Spring Street

*The courtyard fronting the Spring Street entrance of City Hall is surrounded by arches featuring these sinuous interlocking patterns. The result is a vision of elegant, perpetual flow.*

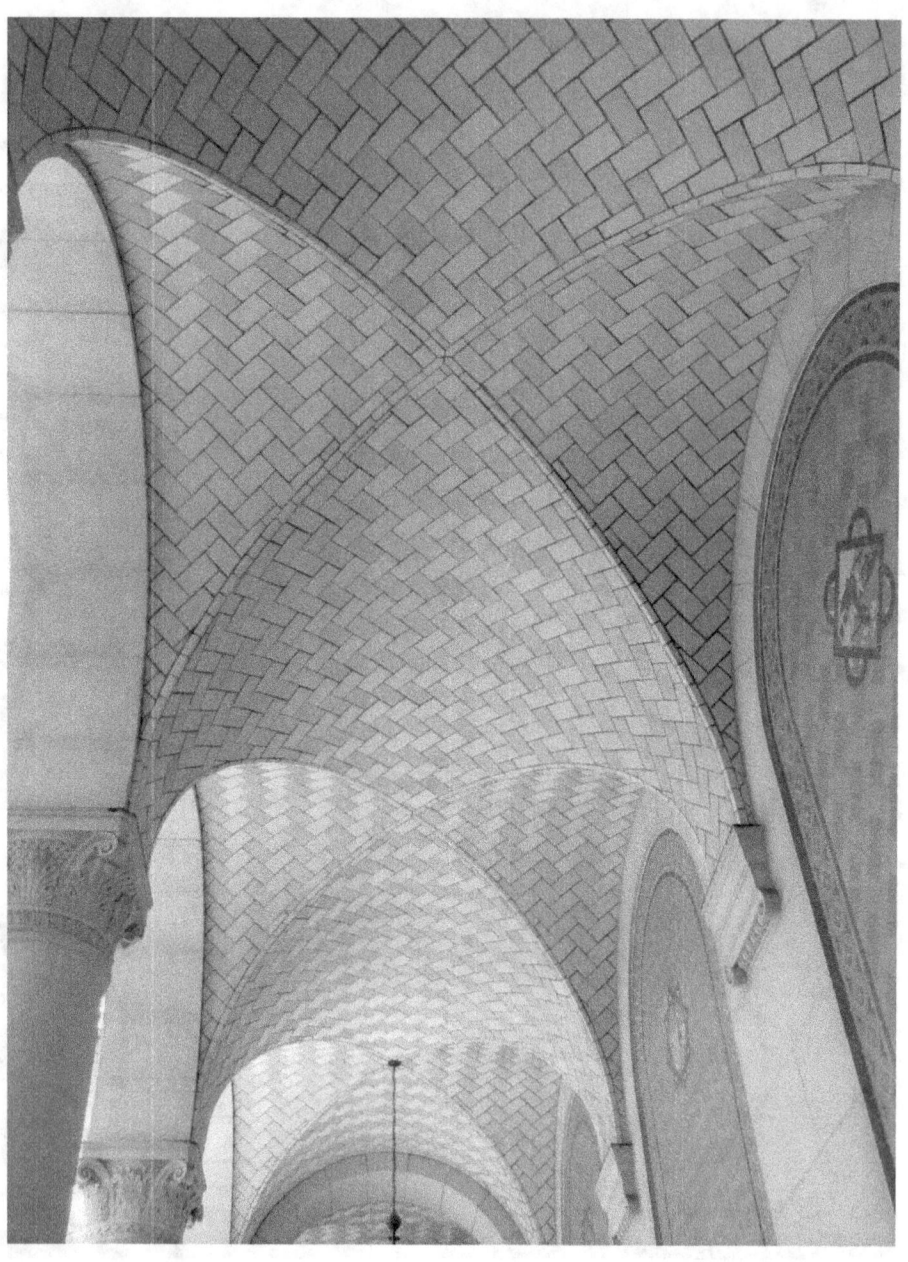

# OLD BANK DISTRICT / ARTS DISTRICT

## Spring Street

*A few blocks south of City Hall, the handsome historic buildings of the Spring Street corridor – many of which were formerly banks and hotels ("the Wall Street of the West") – are being refurbished as art galleries, sidewalk cafés, and trendy lofts. A wave of young people and developers has swept this formerly forlorn corridor. While the revitalization is certainly welcome, it has raised important questions about how to assist the homeless populations displaced by the wealthy young newcomers.*

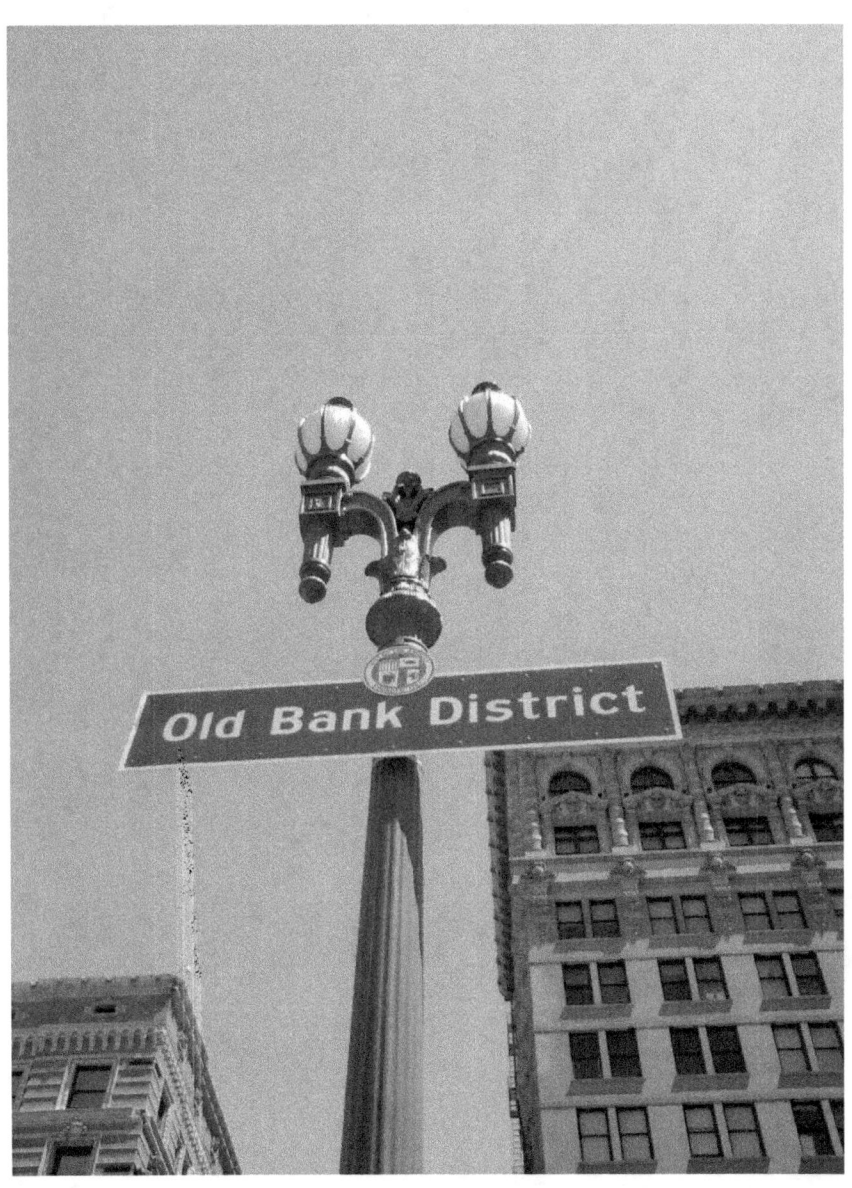

Spring & 4th Streets

*A young man walks his dog at the northeast corner of Spring Street and 4th Street. Many of the artists and students moving into the revitalized neighborhood own dogs; dog-walking hipsters are a new subculture in downtown Los Angeles.*

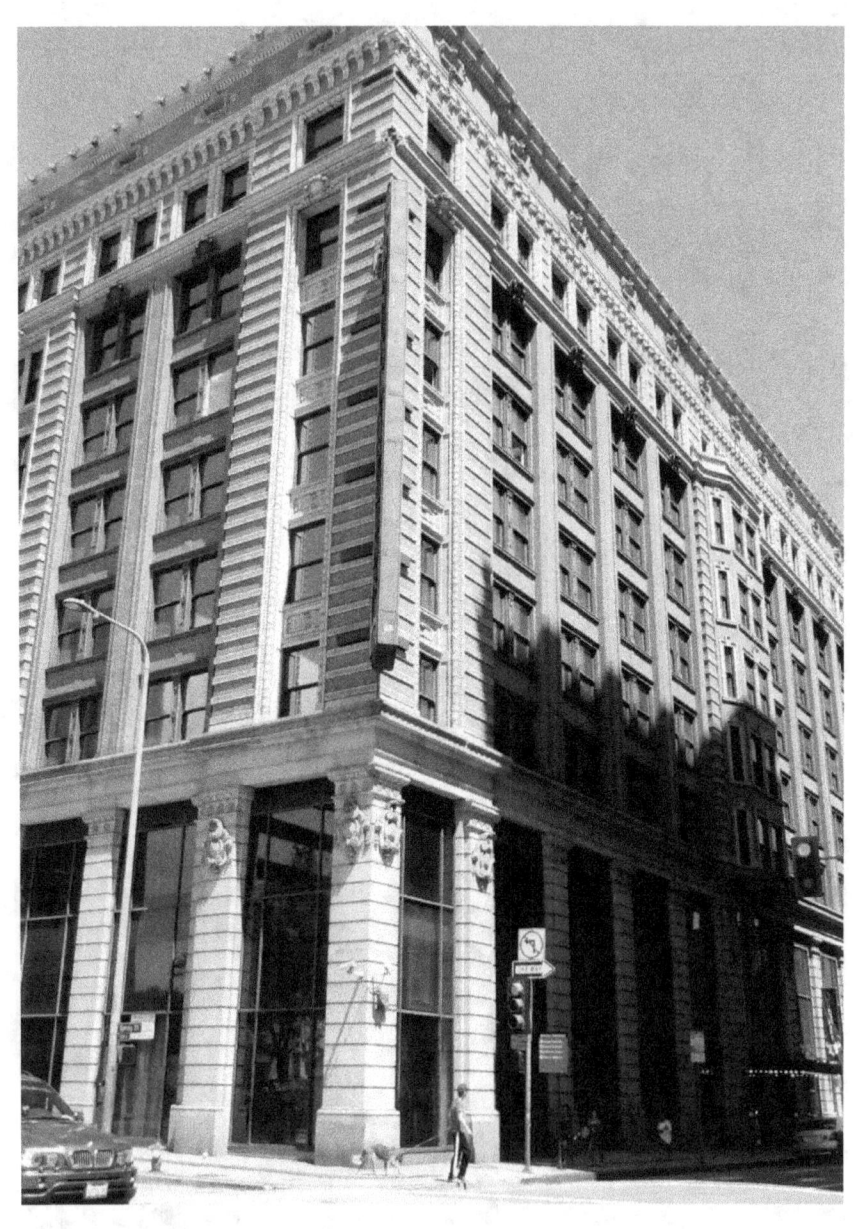

416 S. Spring Street

*The El Dorado (formerly the Hotel Stowell, 1913) is one example of the lovely architecture in this district that has benefited from restoration. Charlie Chaplin once stayed here (when it was the Stowell). Contemporary loft-dwellers enjoy the hotel's restored original tiles and ornamentation.*

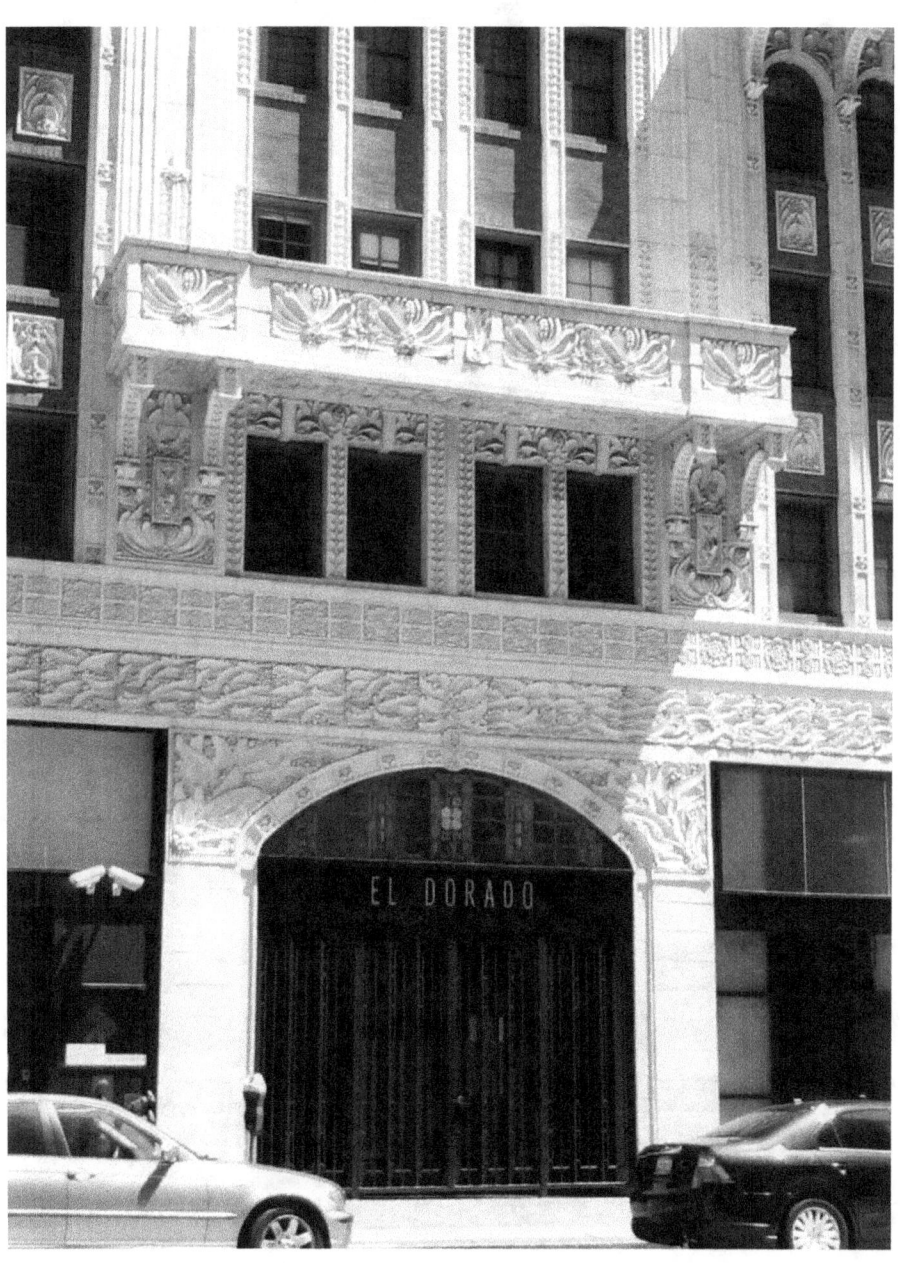

433 S. Spring Street

*A tile mural on the façade of the Title Insurance Building (1928), a Moderne treasure designed by John and Donald Parkinson, the father and son team so instrumental in Union Station's design.*

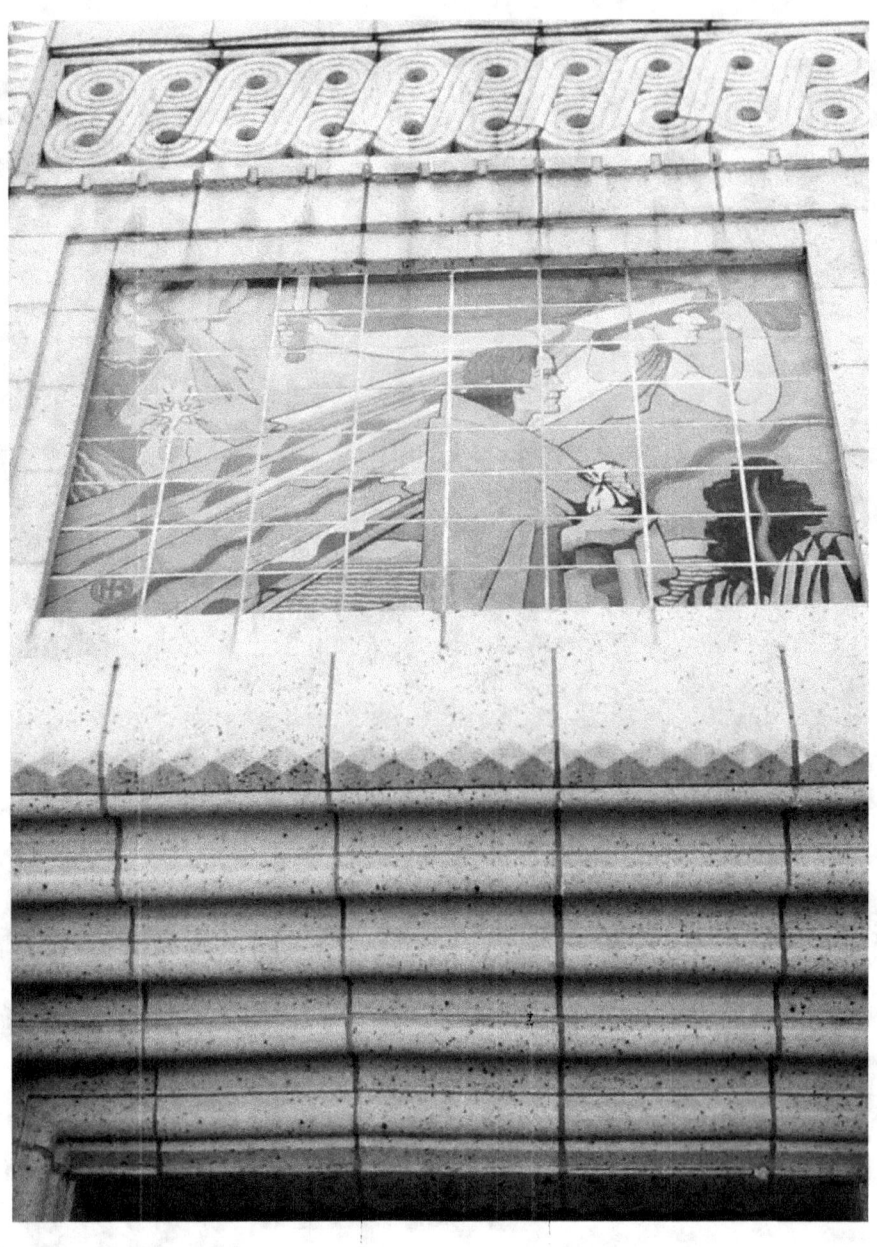

# ARTS DISTRICT

### Spring & 5ᵗʰ Streets

*This tree-shaded view looking south along Spring Street is largely unchanged since the mid 1900's. Note the sign for the venerable Alexandria Hotel hiding behind the tree on the right. An indicator of the changing times: the sign advertising lofts for rent (top left side of the photo).*

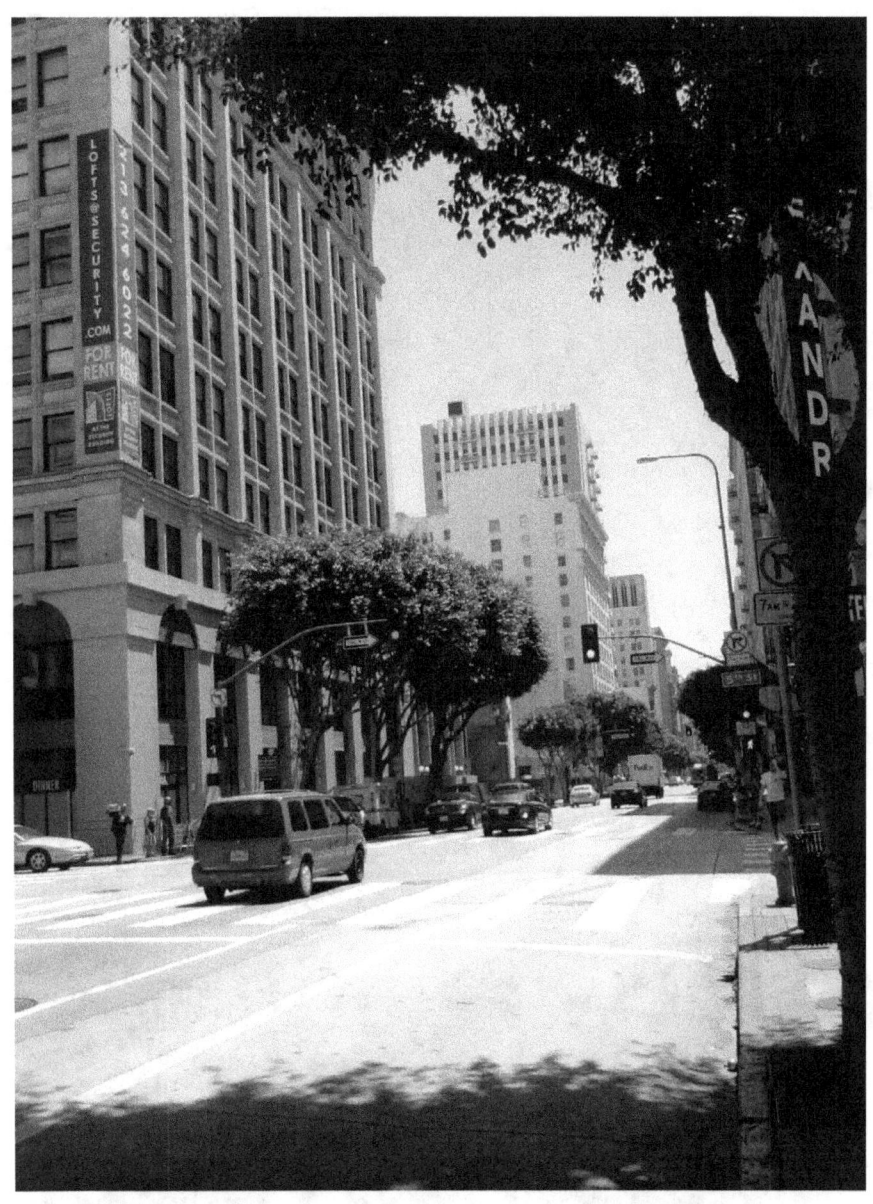

# SPRING ARTS TOWER

453 S. Spring Street

*Originally the Crocker Bank Building, this stunner composed of marble, oak, and brass was completed in 1914 for the Crocker Citizens National Bank. In the new millennium, the restored building hosts artists, filmmakers, and a massive bookstore. This entrance leads to the upscale and quite modern Crocker Club, which, while retaining the 1920's flavor and the bank's infrastructure (like the vault), serves modern appetizers and cocktails while DJs spin contemporary tunes. The Crocker Club features a "Ghost Room" and is reputed to be haunted.*

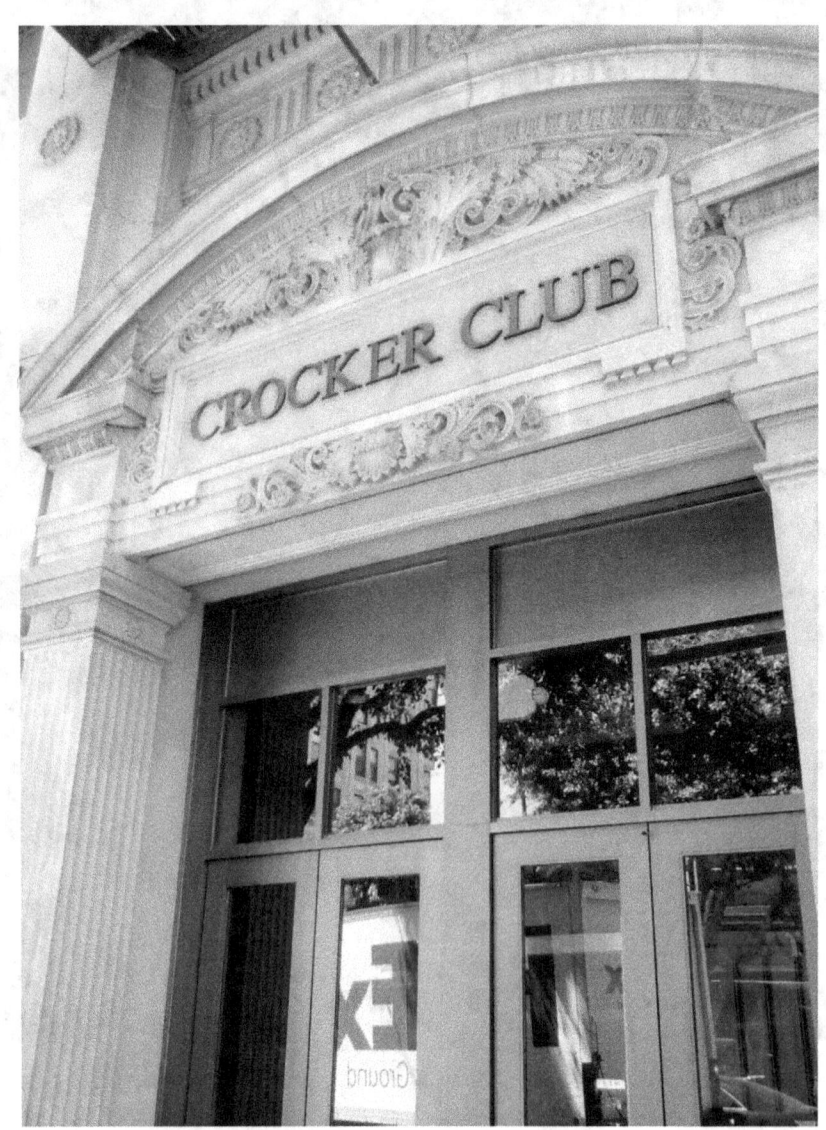

## THE LAST BOOKSTORE

453 S. Spring Street

*Pictured below is the Spring Street window of one of the district's hot spots. The Last Bookstore features funky furniture, paintings, poetry readings, an open mic night, .concerts, art installations, a labyrinth – and, of course, thousands of books. The main entrance is around the corner on 5th Street; this is the book sellers' entrance.*

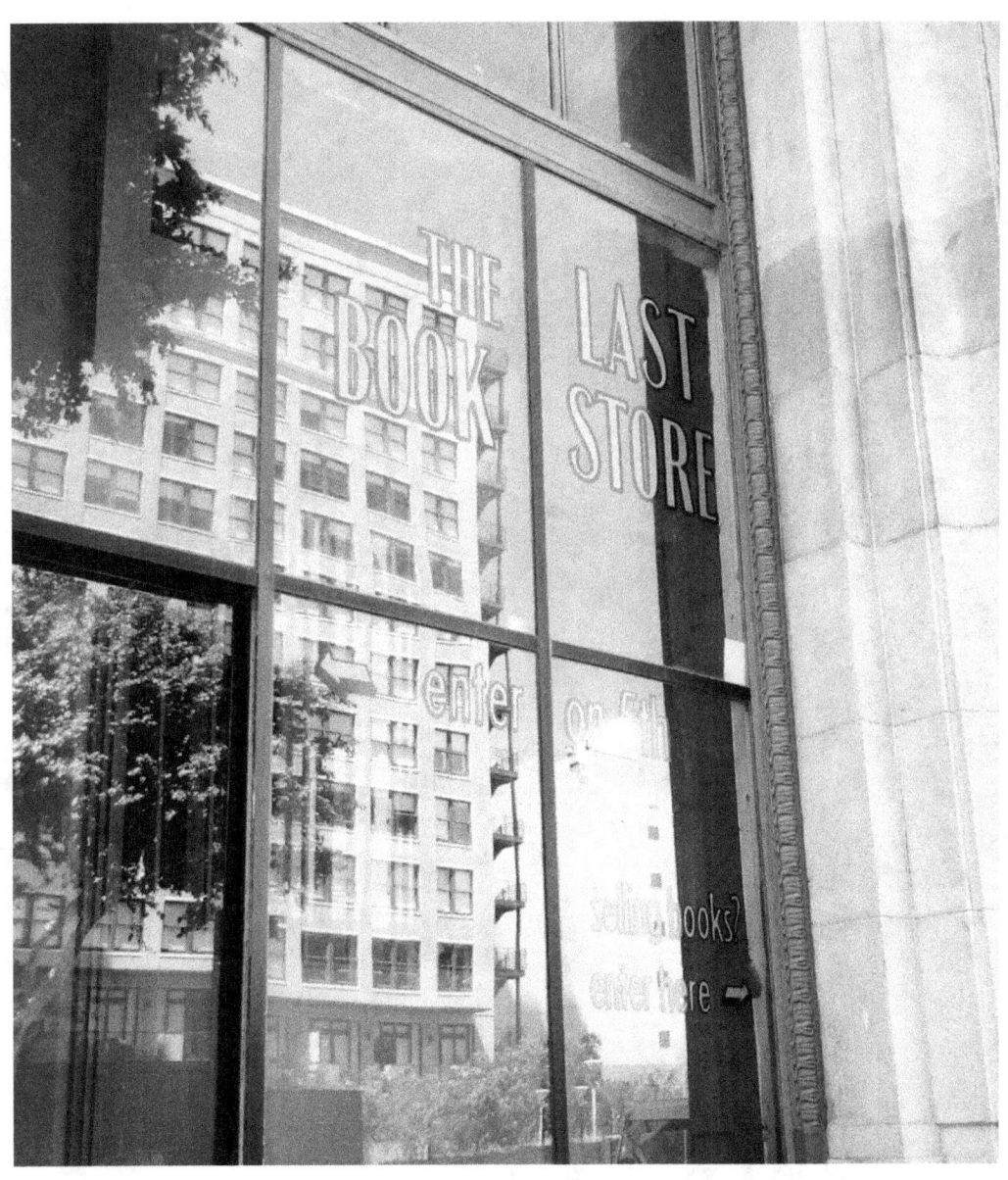

## THE LAST BOOKSTORE

453 S. Spring Street

*A view from the balcony at The Last Bookstore. The store originally opened quite modestly, in a loft, in 2005, then in 2009 moved to a small storefront on Main Street at 4ʰ. The Last Bookstore was such a hit, and became such a central part of the developing downtown arts community, that in summer 2011 it moved to these much larger quarters at 453 S. Spring.*

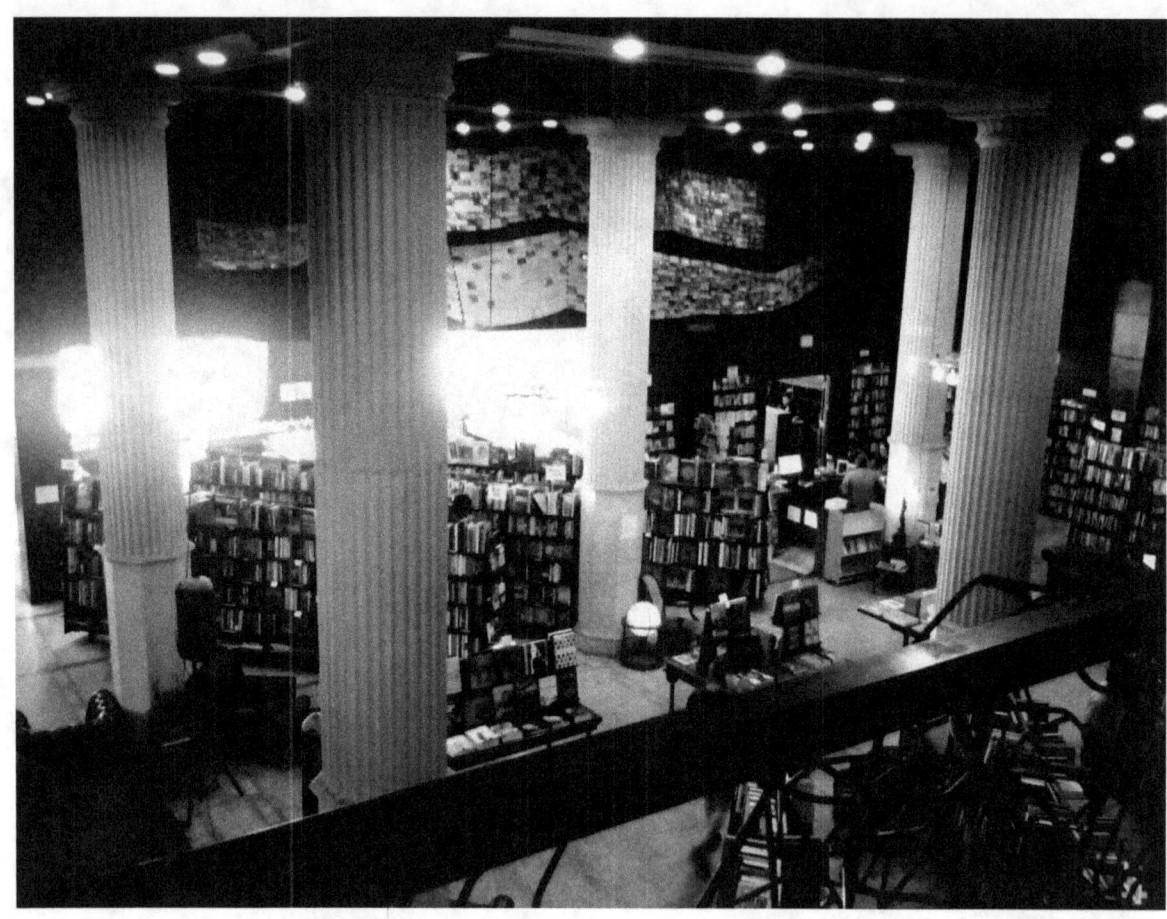

## THE LAST BOOKSTORE

453 S. Spring Street

*The book labyrinth on the second level of The Last Bookstore features 100,000+ bargain books (yes, you read that correctly) and a meandering maze of shelves and artwork and startling little alcoves.*

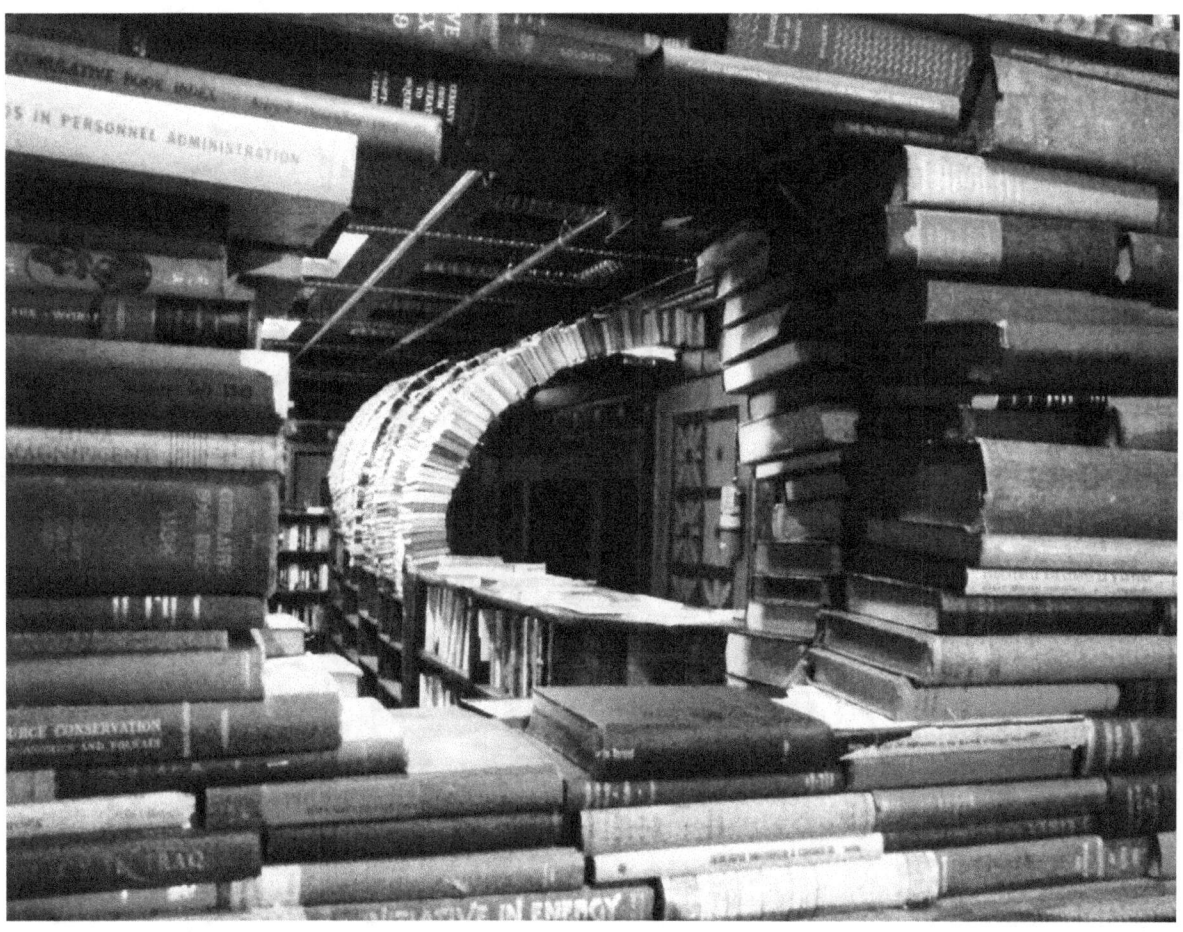

## THE LAST BOOKSTORE

453 S. Spring Street

*Anything seems to be possible at The Last Bookstore. Here, books fly off the shelves, and a typewriter floats, in this creative art installation.*

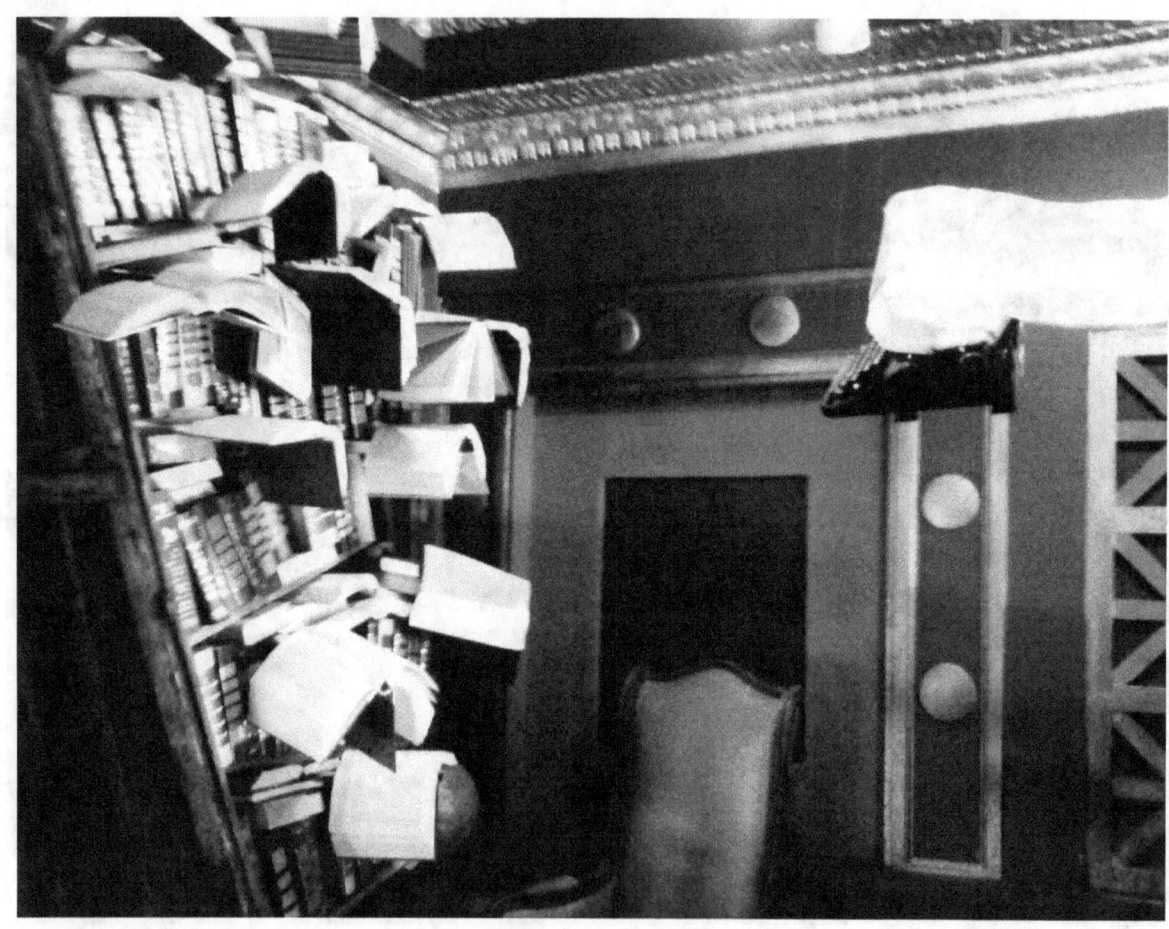

## ALEXANDRIA HOTEL

210 W. 5th Street

*The Alexandria Hotel was completed in 1906. It might be hard to believe now, but this was once the most elegant hotel in downtown L.A. Celebrities of the day stayed here, and the décor and ambiance were top-drawer. By the 1950's and 60's it had deteriorated into a flophouse. In the early 1970's it was converted to an apartment house.*

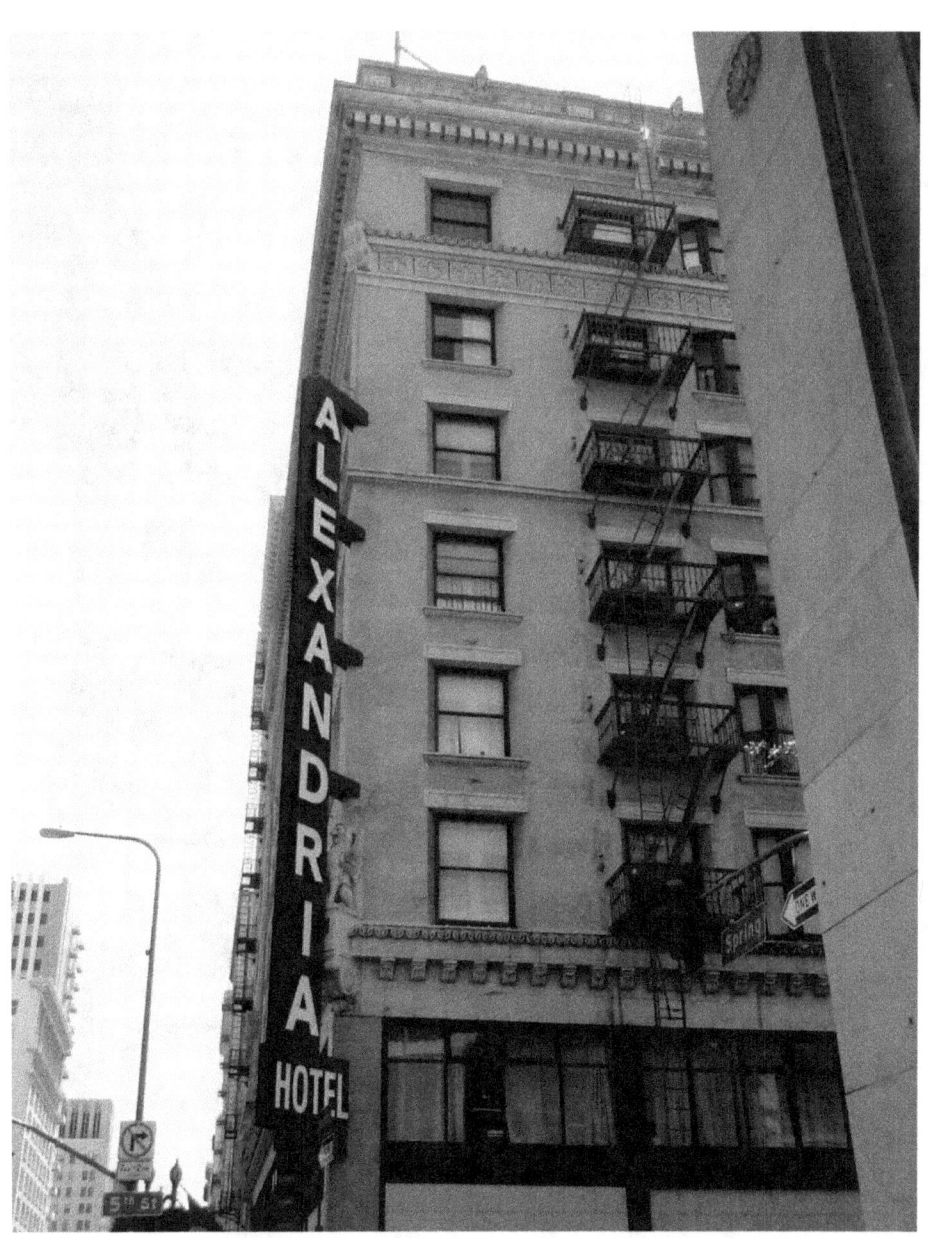

5ᵗʰ & Spring Streets

*This is the view looking west along 5ᵗʰ Street from Spring Street. The peaked tower in the distance (center of the photograph) is the modern portion of L.A.'s famed Biltmore Hotel (now called the Millennium Biltmore) which opened in 1923 and, by wooing glittering guests from the Alexandria Hotel, sparked the Alexandria's tragic decline. The truck in the lower left corner of the photo is carting away rubble from an interior that's being gutted. The building façades and streetlamps shown here are vintage, but note the modern recycling receptacle at the bottom right-center of the photo.*

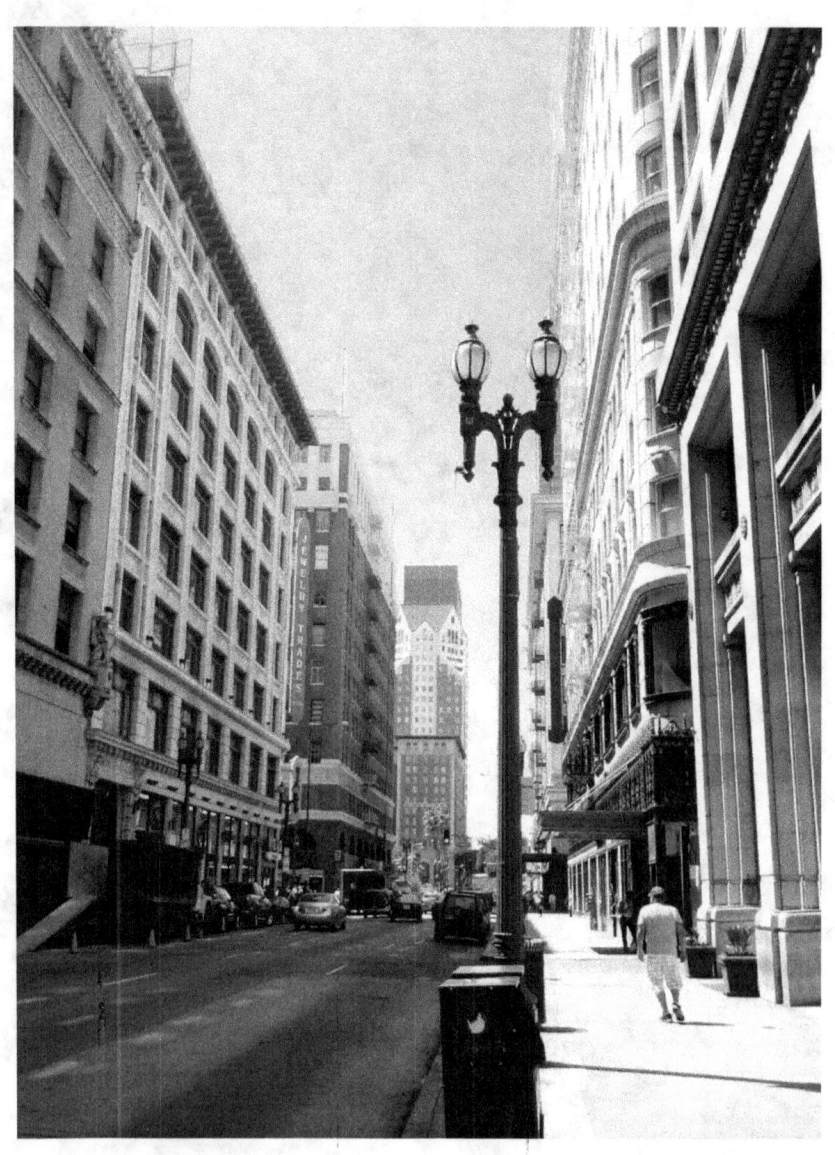

## CLARA SHORTRIDGE FOLTZ CRIMINAL COURTHOUSE

210 W. Temple Street

*We've circled back north, to the southwest block on Temple Street – the block between Spring Street and Broadway. On the site where there once stood an elegant sandstone courthouse, with a graceful clock tower, the Clara Shortridge Foltz Criminal Justice Center, an imposing modern structure now stands. It opened in 1972. Foltz (1849 – 1934) was a descendant of Daniel Boone and the first female lawyer in the western United States. Trials held here have included the O.J. Simpson and Phil Spector murder trials. In the bottom left of this photo, a corner of the Hall of Justice (1922), swathed in a massive dark tarp, is visible; the Hall of Justice underwent major renovations in 2013.*

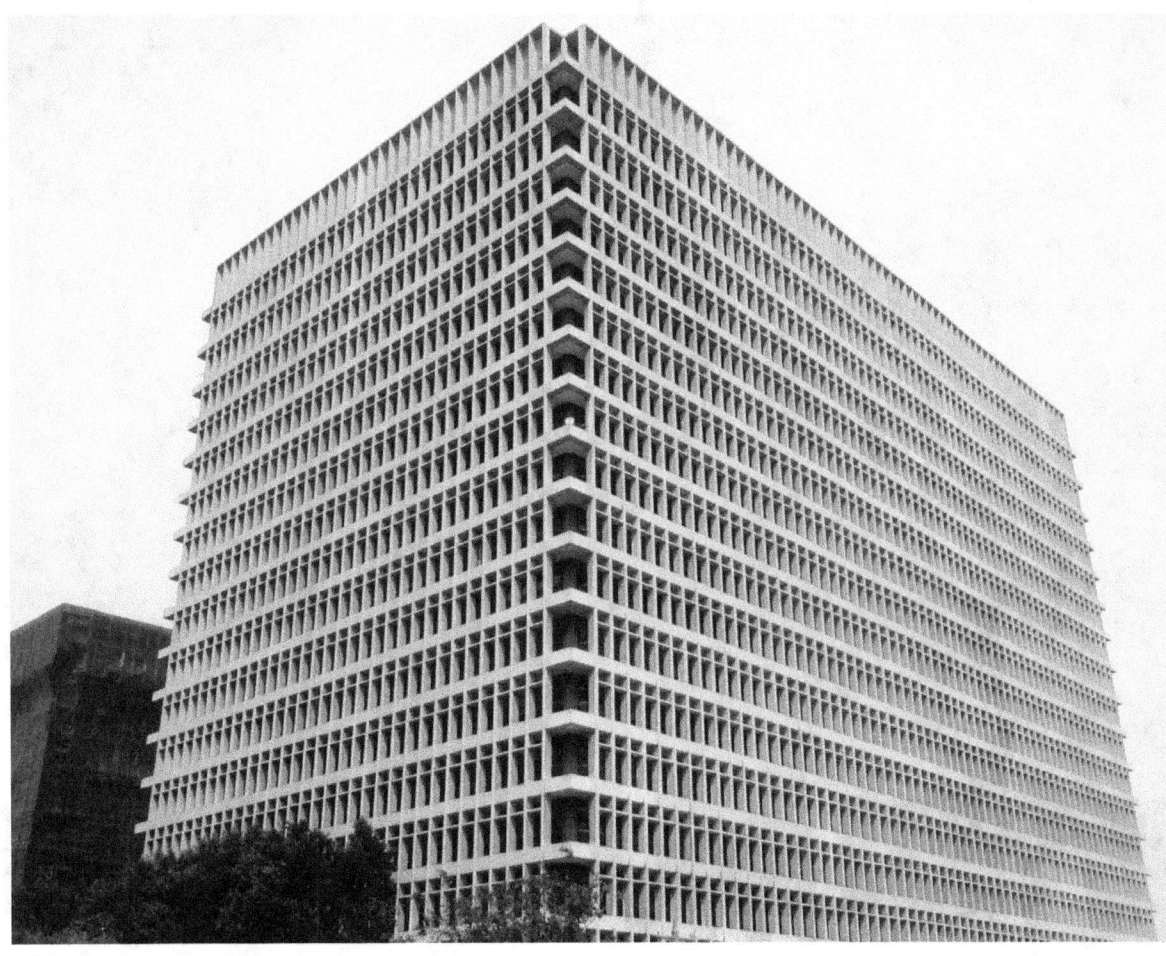

## CATHEDRAL OF OUR LADY OF THE ANGELS

555 W. Temple Street

*The old song says "they pulled down paradise and put up a parking lot" – but in this case, Los Angeles razed a parking lot north of the Criminal Courthouse and Hall of Justice and put up a cathedral. L.A.'s cathedral opened in 2002. It includes worship spaces, gardens, fountains, a grand plaza, a restaurant and gift shop, and an underground mausoleum where regular people – not just clergy – can arrange to be interred. The vista as one approaches the cathedral is engineered to inspire awe.*

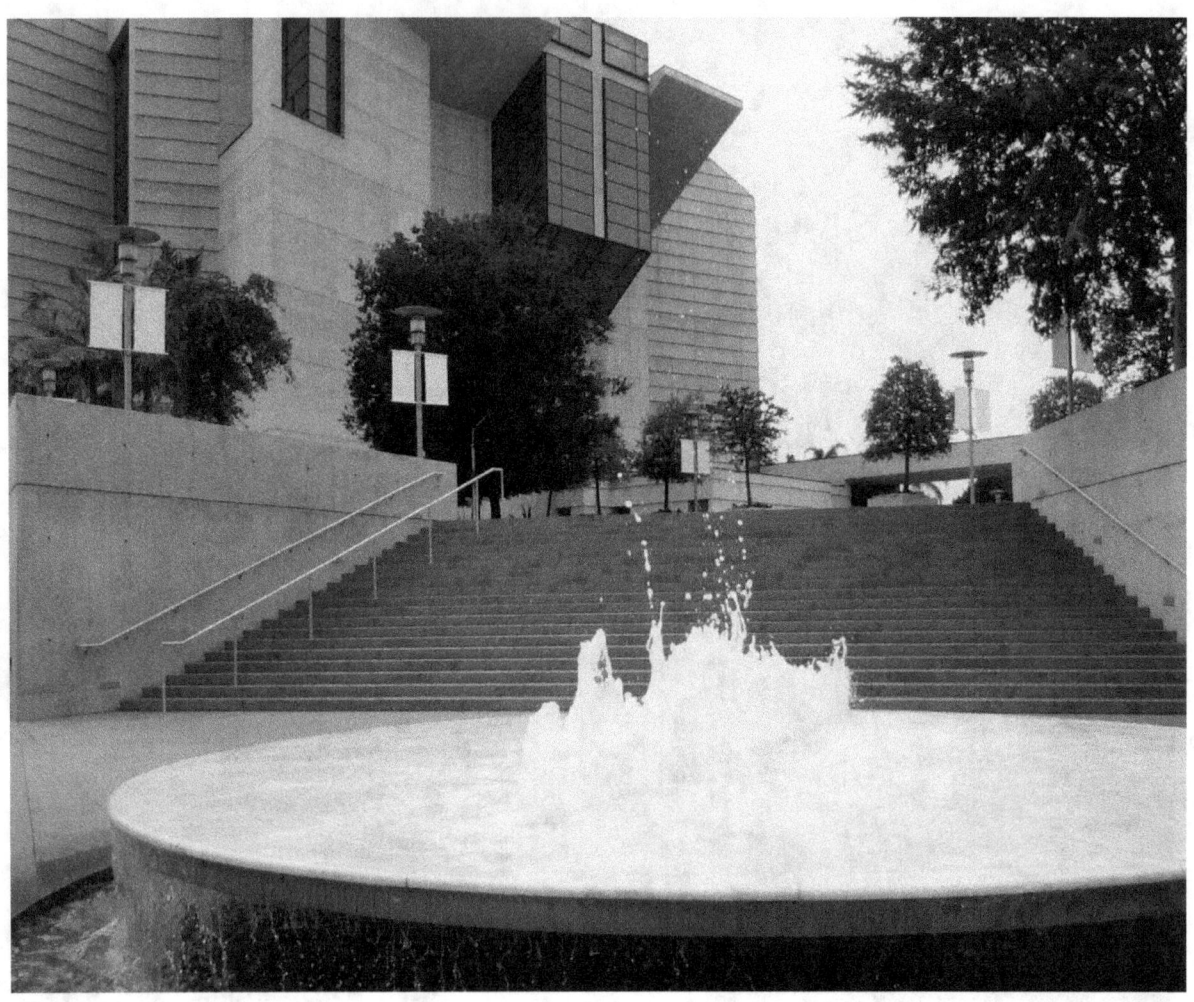

# CATHEDRAL OF OUR LADY OF THE ANGELS

555 W. Temple Street

*In the children's garden, animal statues inspired by the bible and designed by a children's artist are accompanied by tiles explaining each animals' symbolic meaning. Pictured here, the lion, nicknamed "Simba," and symbolic of courage and dignity.*

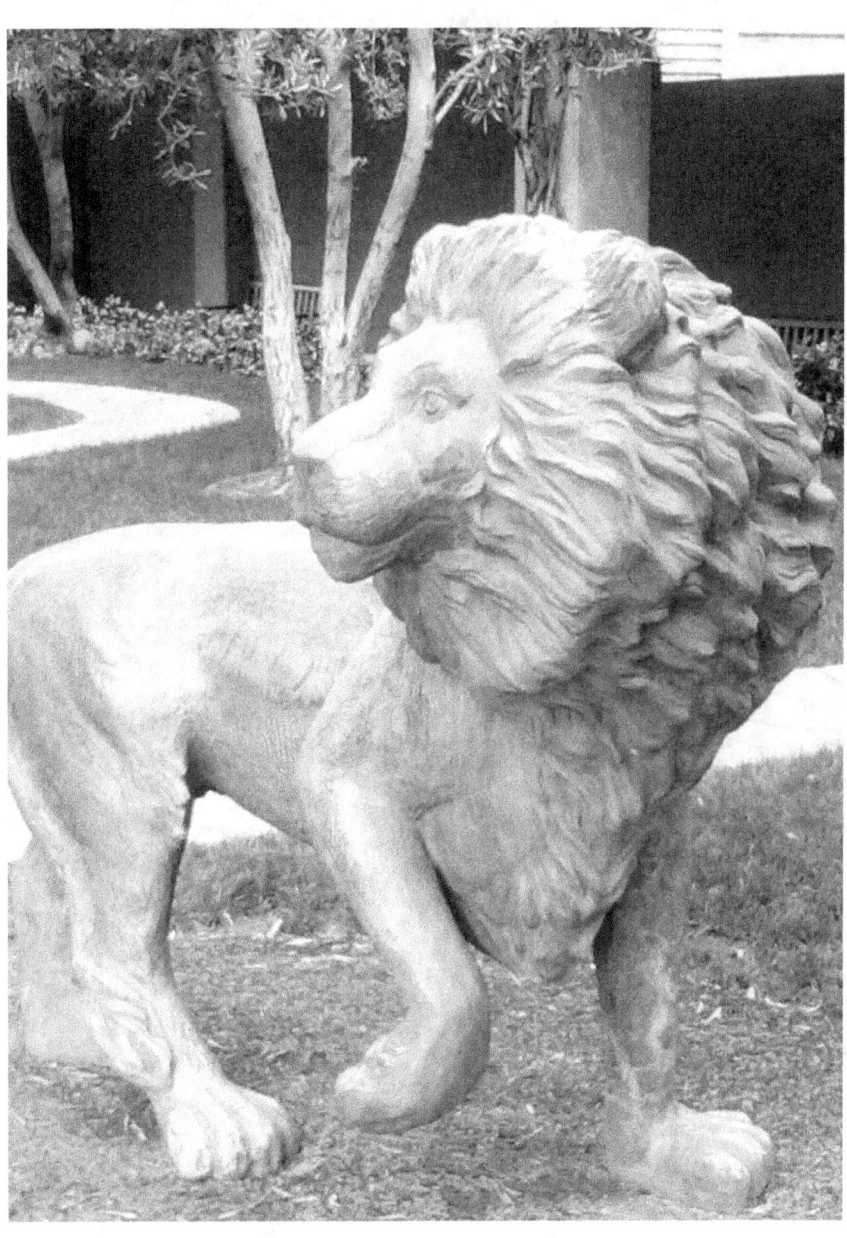

*Massive bronze doors, intricately carved with religious symbols and icons, greet visitors who enter via the front door. The doors were designed by Robert Graham.*

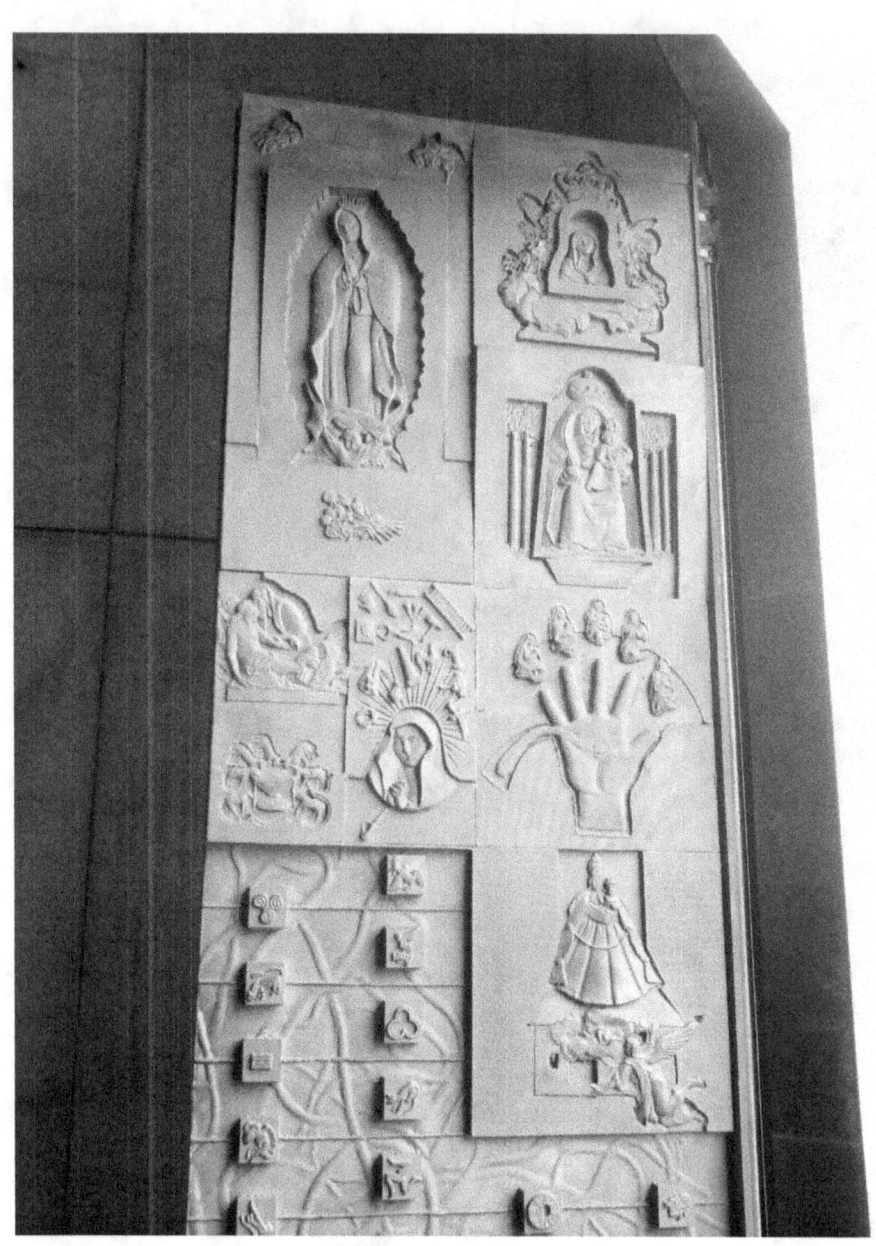

# CATHEDRAL OF OUR LADY OF THE ANGELS

555 W. Temple Street

*Designed by architect Rafael Moneo, the cathedral is a striking building, at once modern and timeless. Narrow channels like the one pictured below lead visitors into the light and spaciousness of the nave.*

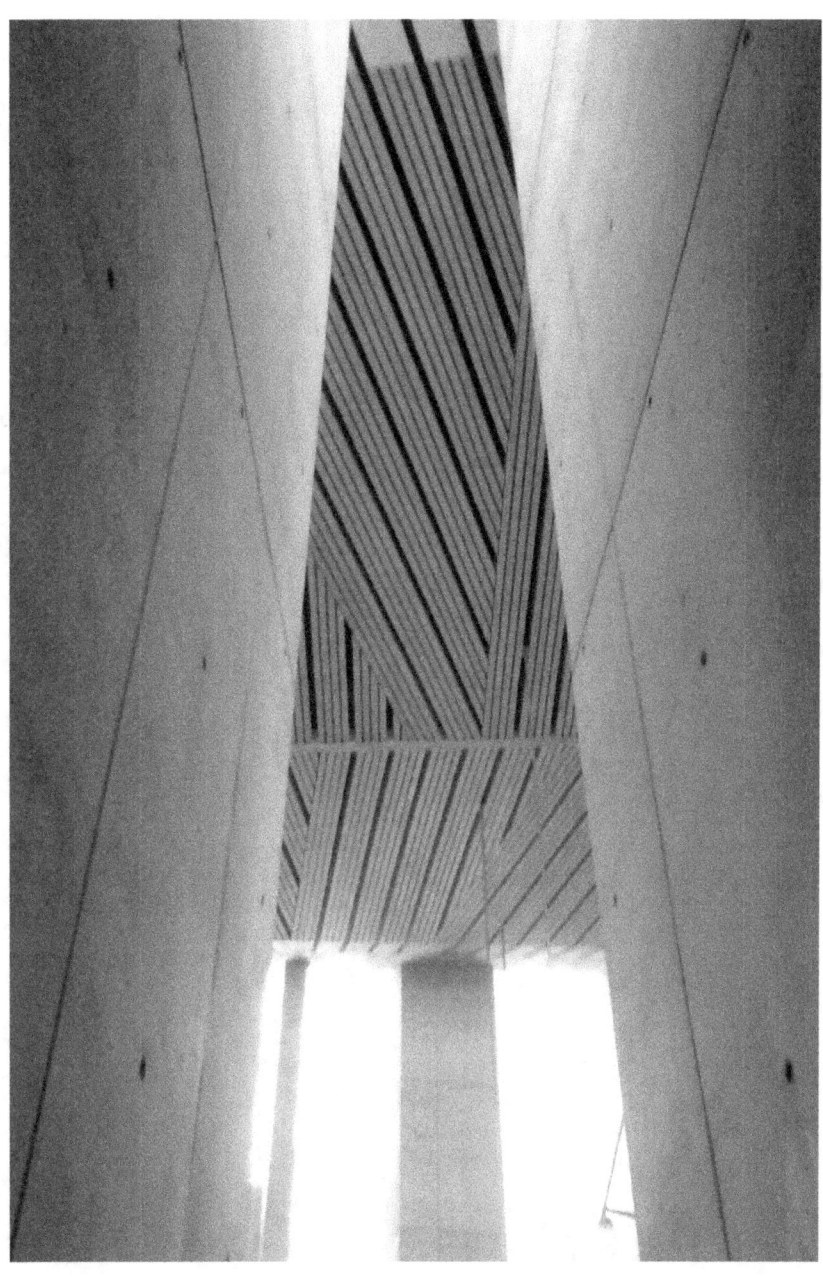

555 W. Temple Street

*Tapestries lining both sides of the nave were designed by artist John Nava. They portray saints such as Joan of Arc (far right) as well as regular people, including children wearing sneakers. The concept behind the unusual and moving combination? Anyone of us can become a saint.*

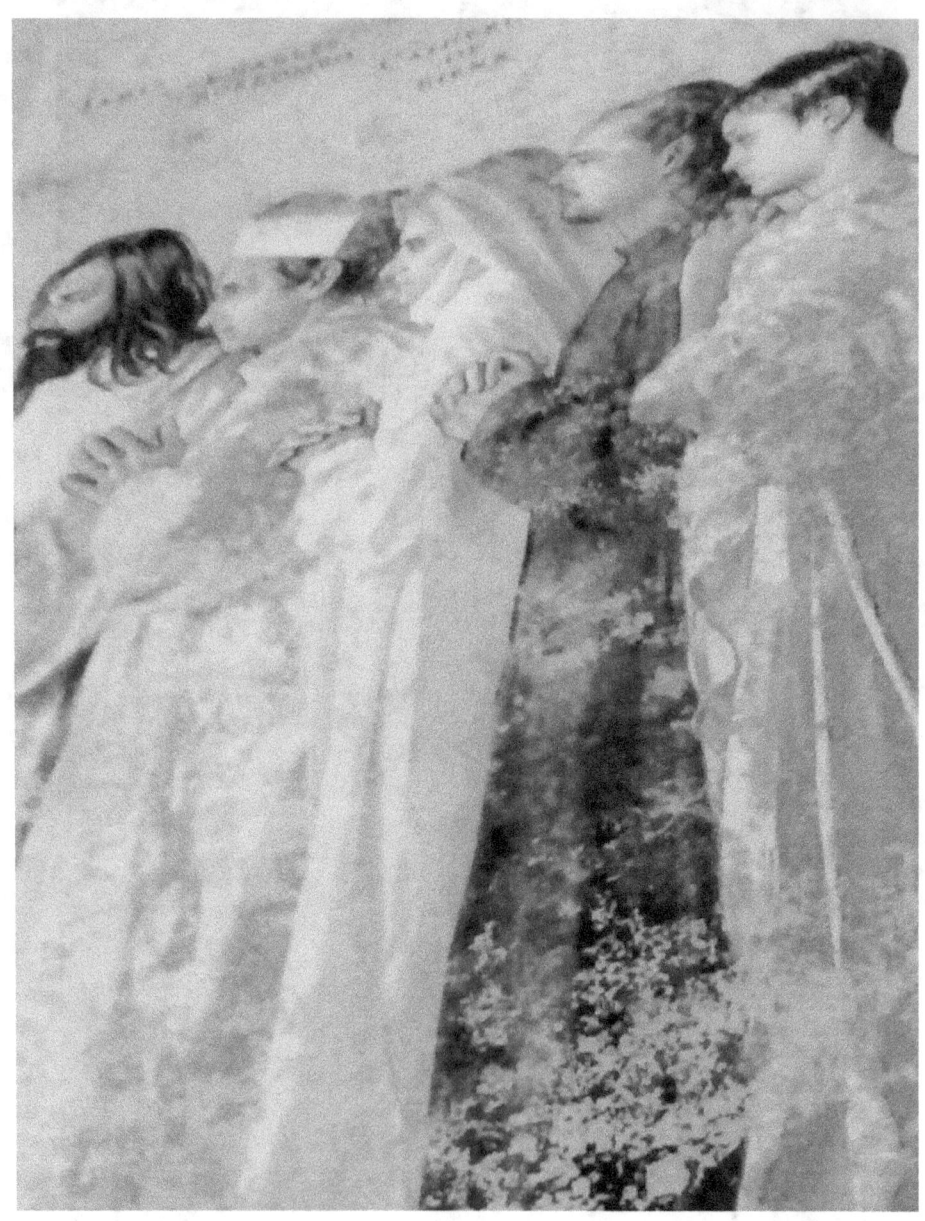

# CATHEDRAL OF OUR LADY OF THE ANGELS

555 W. Temple Street

*On the reredo against the southeast wall, a carved figure seems to contemplate the sunlight.*

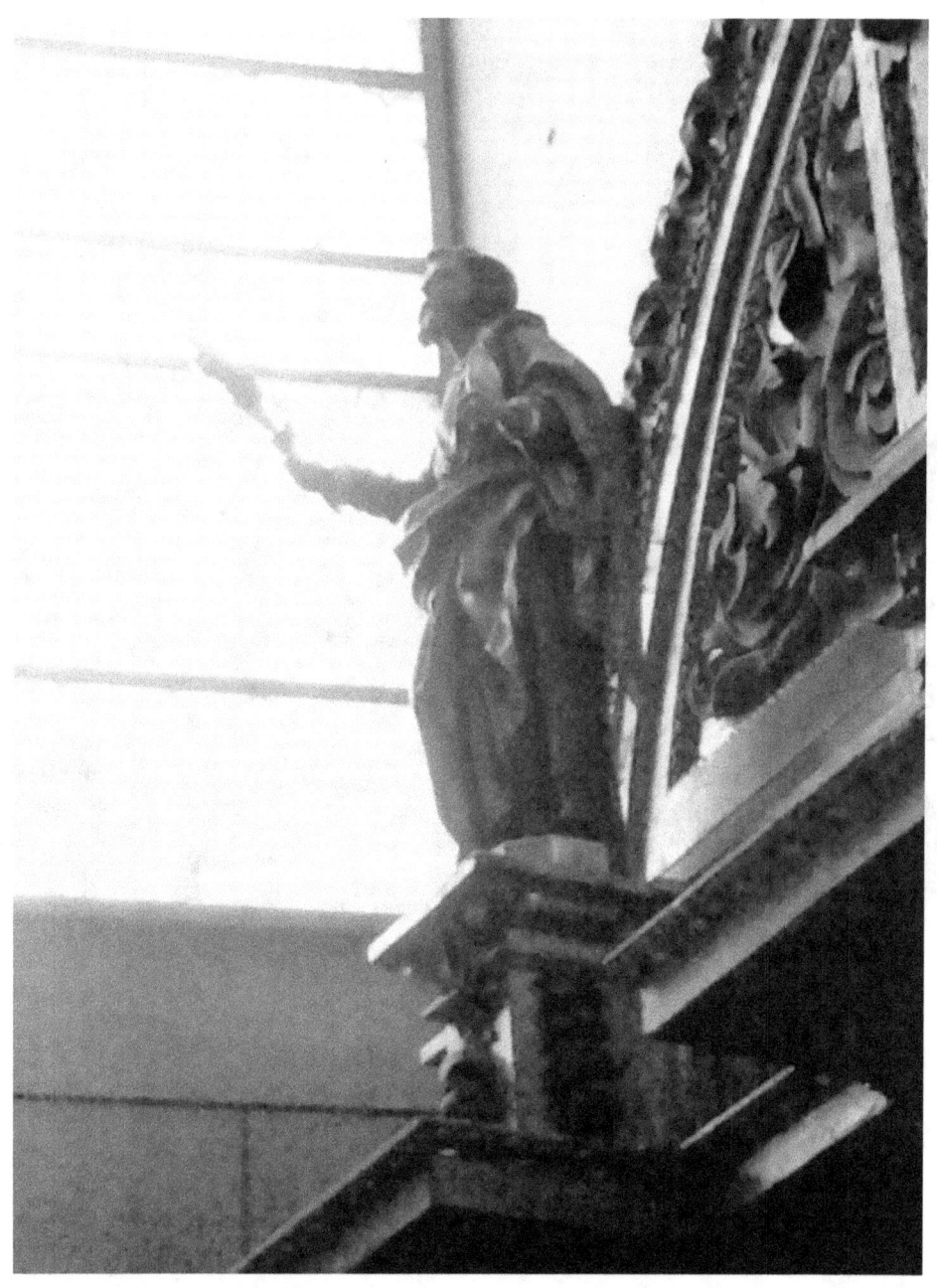

## CATHEDRAL OF OUR LADY OF THE ANGELS

555 W. Temple Street

*In the nave, where the ceiling rises 100 feet above the altar, the cathedral's majestic whole is even greater than the sum of its majestic parts.*

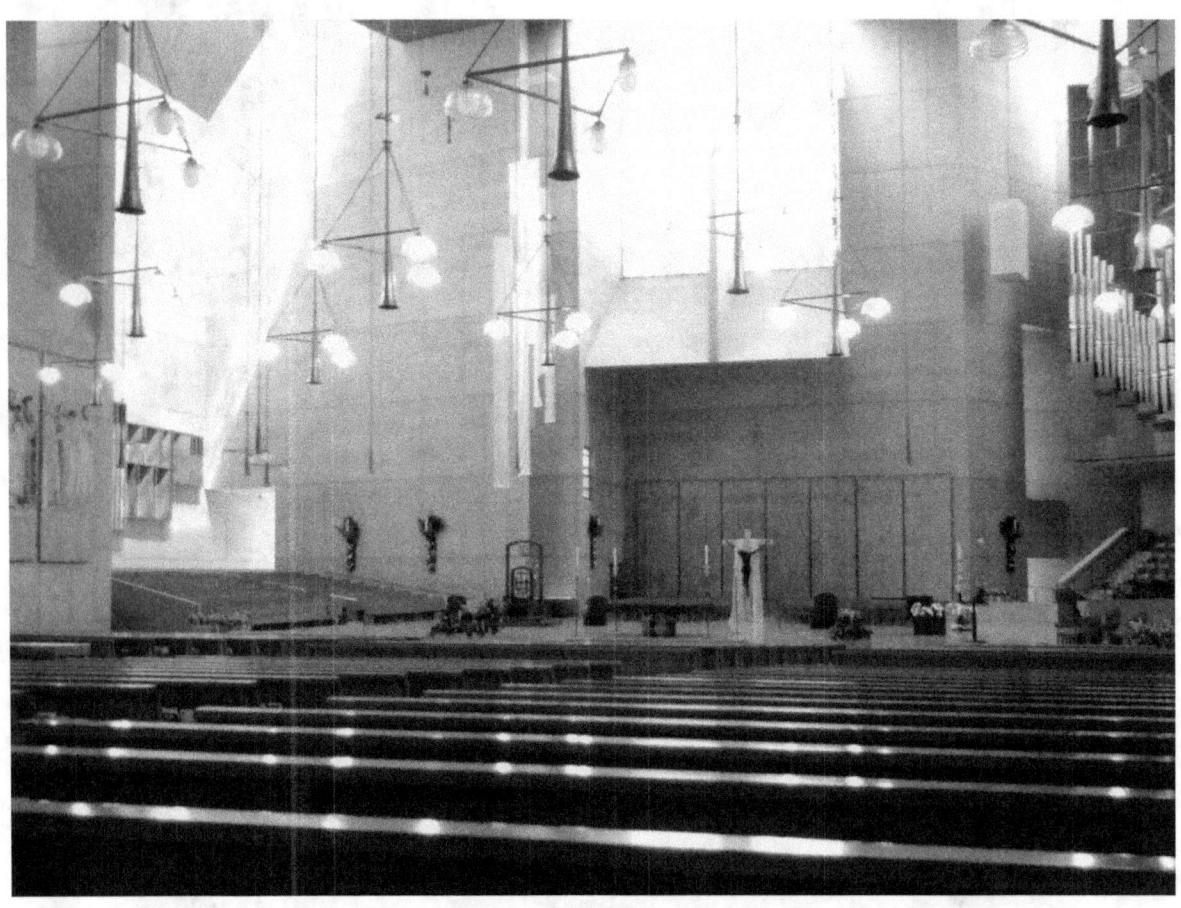

## GRAND PARK

Civic Center

*Stretching from the Music Center on Grand Avenue, all the way east to City Hall on Spring Street, Grand Park opened in 2012 to give Angelenos and tourists a clean, safe, green, and entertaining refuge in the middle of the civic area. It is intended to be "The Park for Everyone". In the photo below, the perspective is looking east from the Community Terrace (the section of park between Hill Street and Broadway). It turns out that views at Grand Park are, indeed, quite grand.*

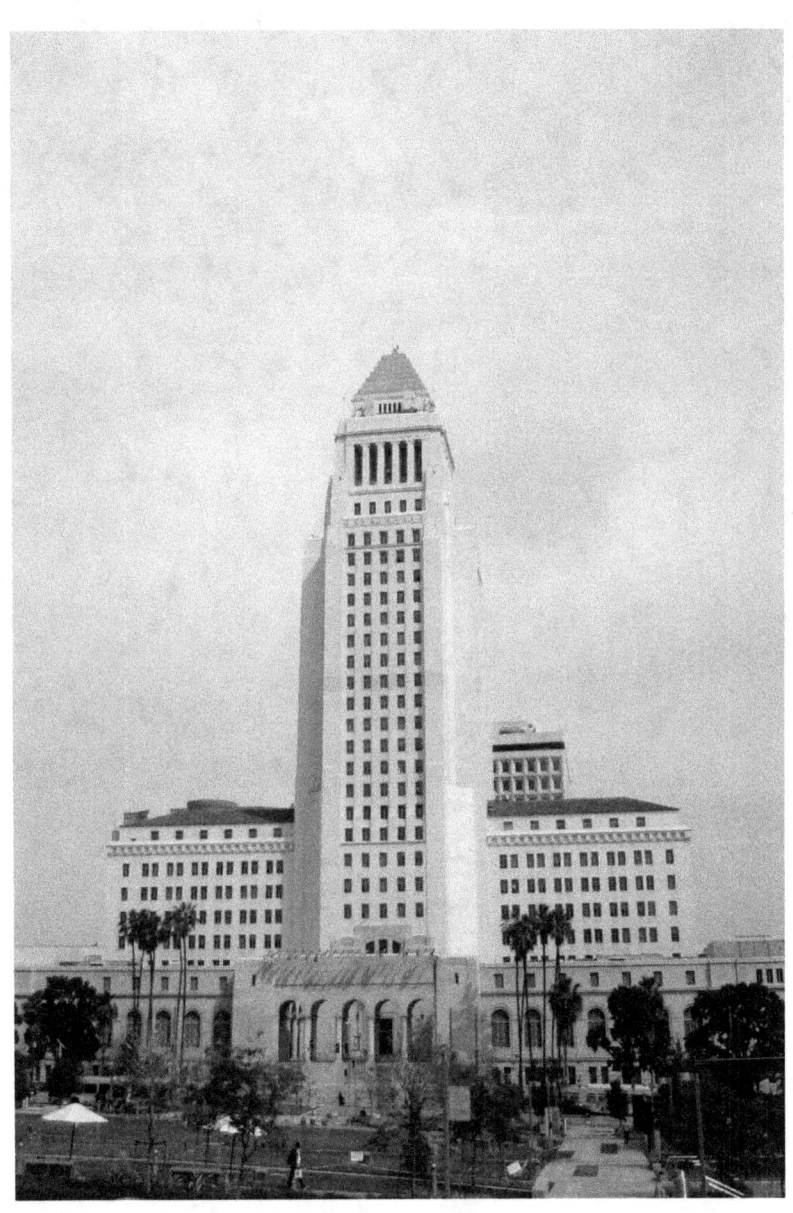

## GRAND PARK

Civic Center

*Visitors to Grand Park enjoy concerts, coffee, and food-truck feasts while sitting at whimsical magenta tables designed to withstand the elements.*

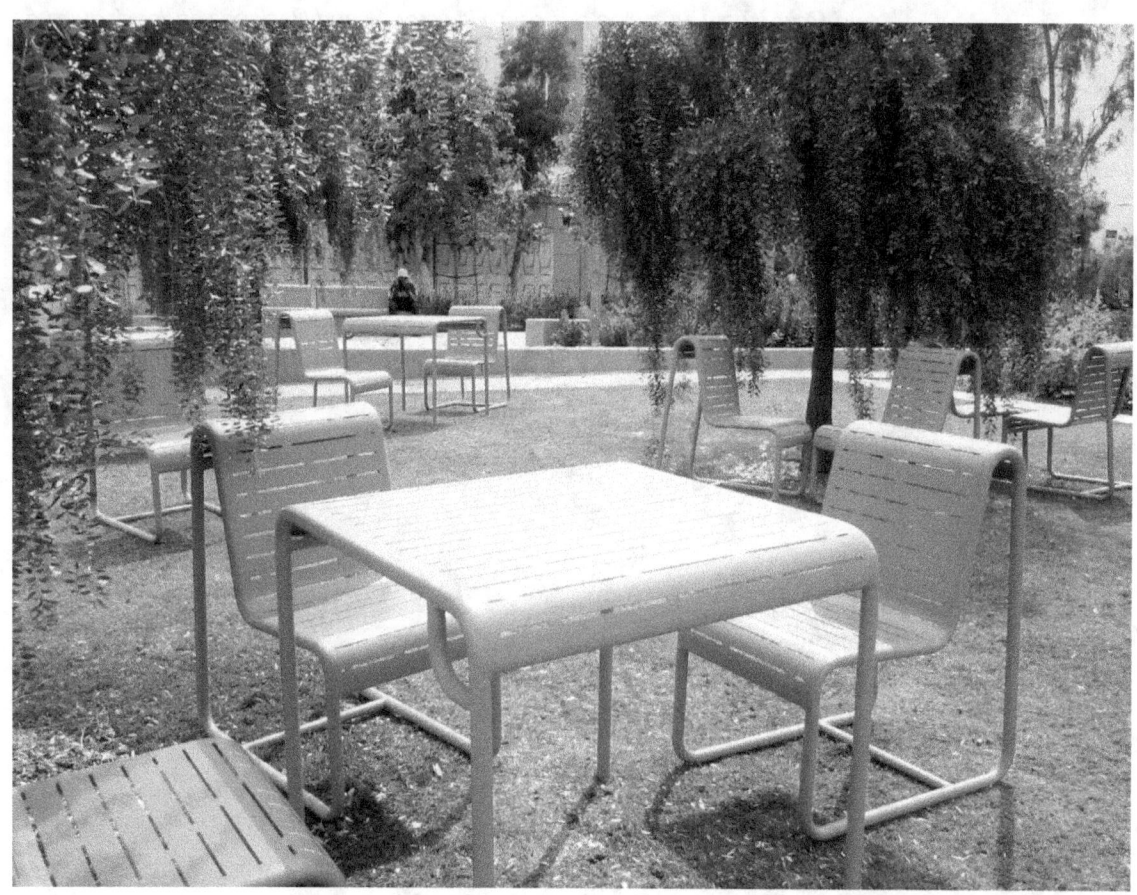

# GRAND PARK

Civic Center

*A view of the Los Angeles Times building from the Broadway Steps that lead from the Community Terrace to Event Lawn sections of Grand Park. This L.A. Times building opened at 201 W. 1ˢᵗ Street in 1935. The original Times building was bombed by brothers John and James McNamara in 1910; the building was destroyed, and 21 workers lost their lives.*

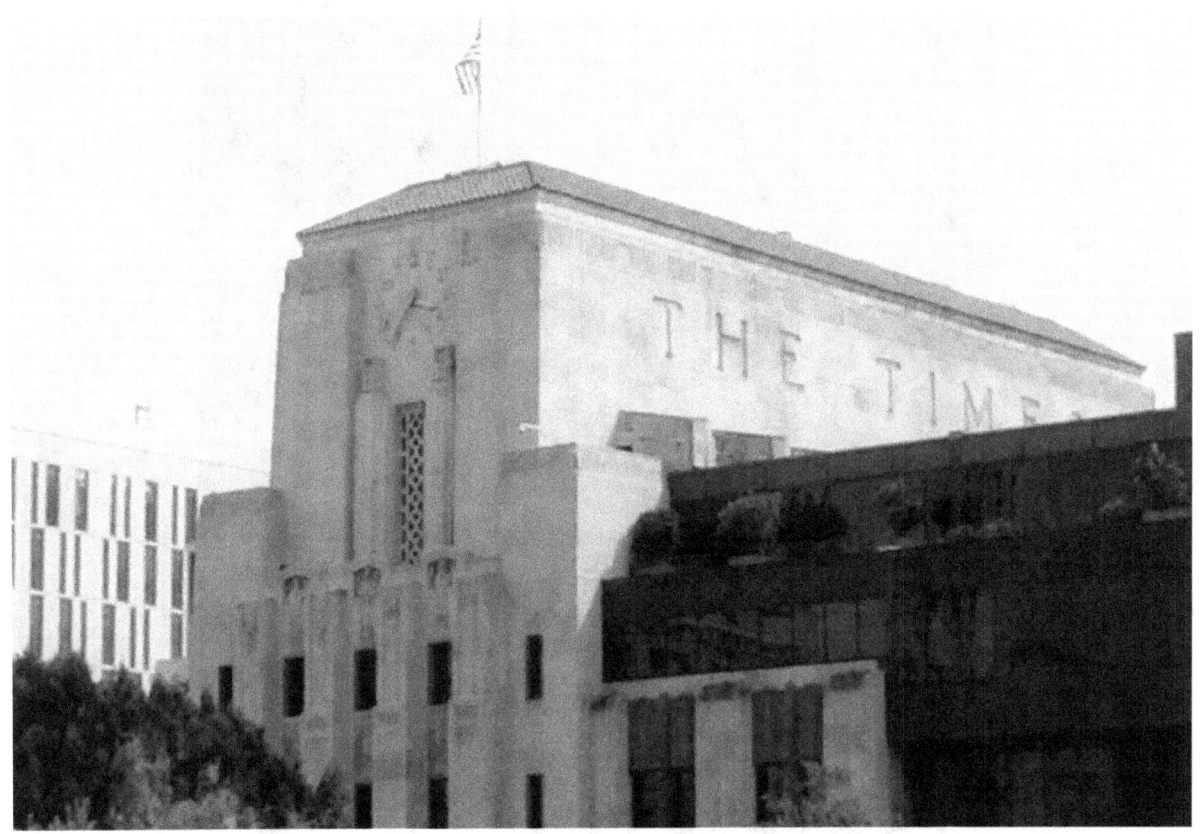

# GRAND PARK

Civic Center

*Reflection of the Arthur J. Will Memorial Fountain. Hidden by foliage and other obstructions since the 1960's, the fountain is now one of the key attractions of the Fountain Plaza between Grand Avenue and Olive Street. Will was Chief Administrative Officer of L.A. County during the 1950's.*

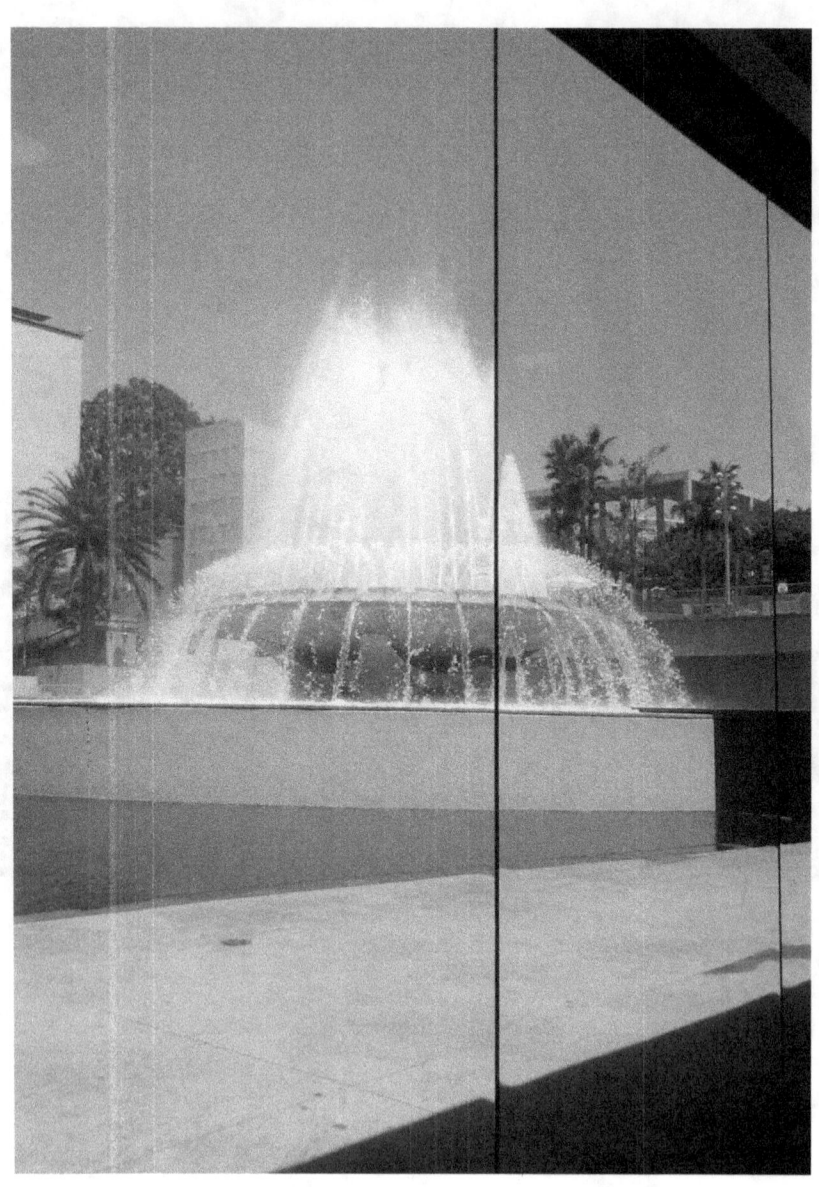

# GRAND PARK

## Civic Center

*The Arthur J. Will Memorial Fountain can shoot a jet of water fifty feet into the air. When the waters are quiet, park-goers have a clear view of City Hall to the east.*

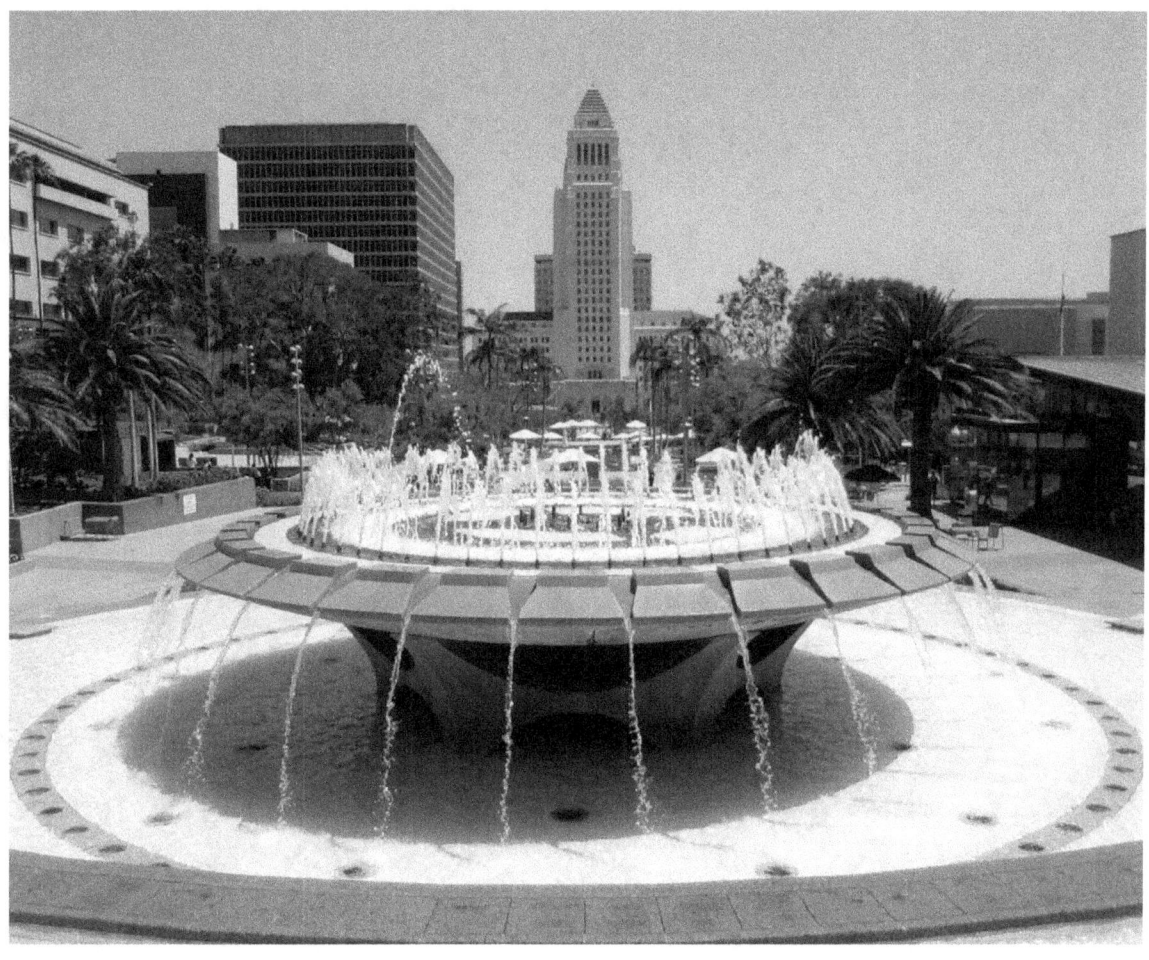

## WALT DISNEY CONCERT HALL

### 111 S. Grand Avenue

*Designed by architect Frank Gehry, the striking Walt Disney Concert Hall is home to the Los Angeles Philharmonic. A gift from Walt Disney's widow, Lillian Disney, sparked the center's construction. After years of delay, and the tireless efforts of Walt Disney's eldest daughter, Diane Disney-Miller, the music center opened in 2003. Unique and flowing, there is nothing else like it in L.A.*

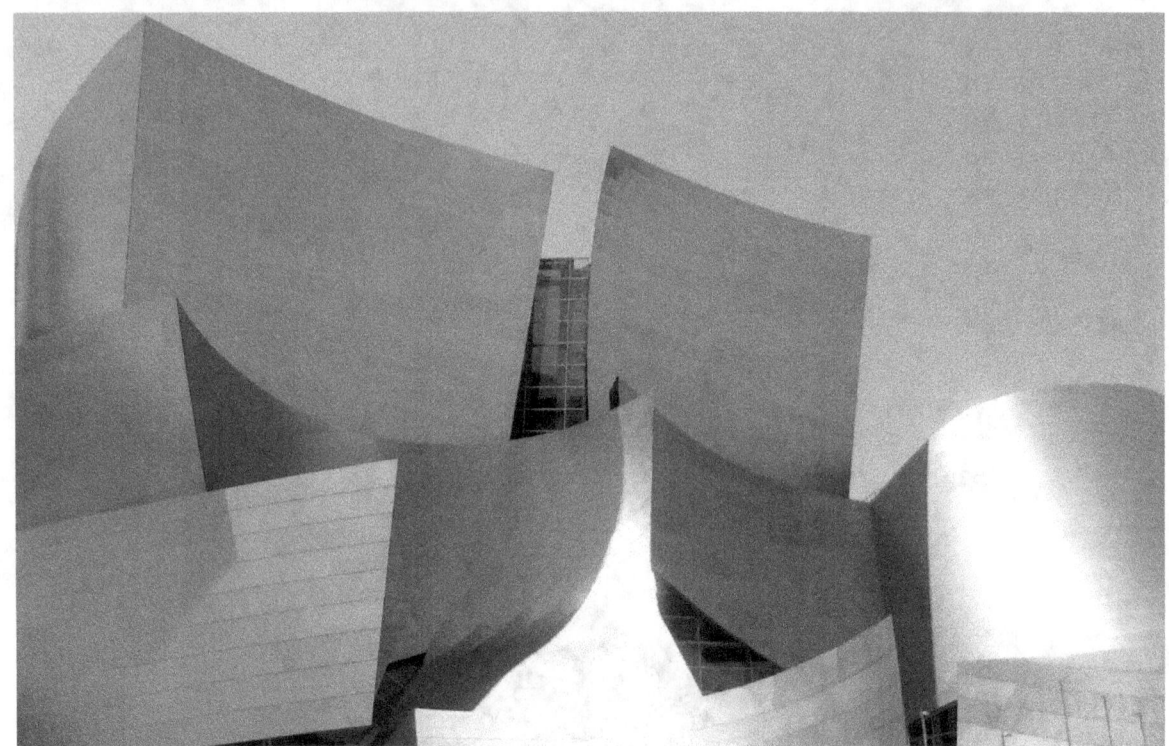

## GRAND AVENUE

333 S. Grand Avenue

*Just south of the Walt Disney Concert Hall, at the top of Angel's Flight, along Grand Avenue, L.A.'s district of towering skyscrapers – mostly financial buildings – commences. The view here is looking upward near the Wells Fargo building, which appears in the upper left of the photo. The Wells Fargo Plaza and the California Plaza across the avenue feature a myriad of restaurants and shops on the ground and sub-levels. This is a popular lunch-time destination for local business people and tourists.*

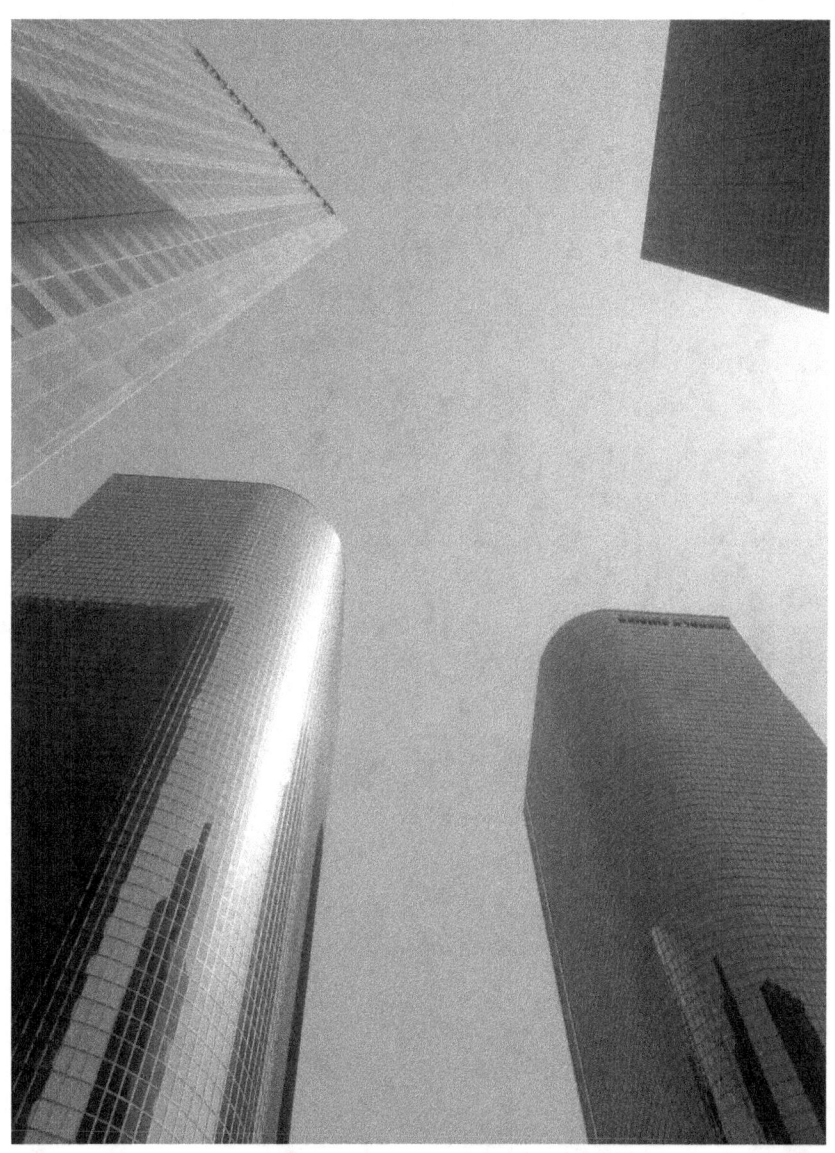

## WELLS FARGO MUSEUM

### 333 S. Grand Avenue

*The towering Wells Fargo complex might look intimidating, but it holds a charming secret, a modest little museum on the ground floor dedicated to the old west. View exhibits, authentic artifacts, and (as seen in this 2012 photo) old-time stage coaches – free of charge. This experience is great for tourists, children, and locals who never knew this museum existed.*

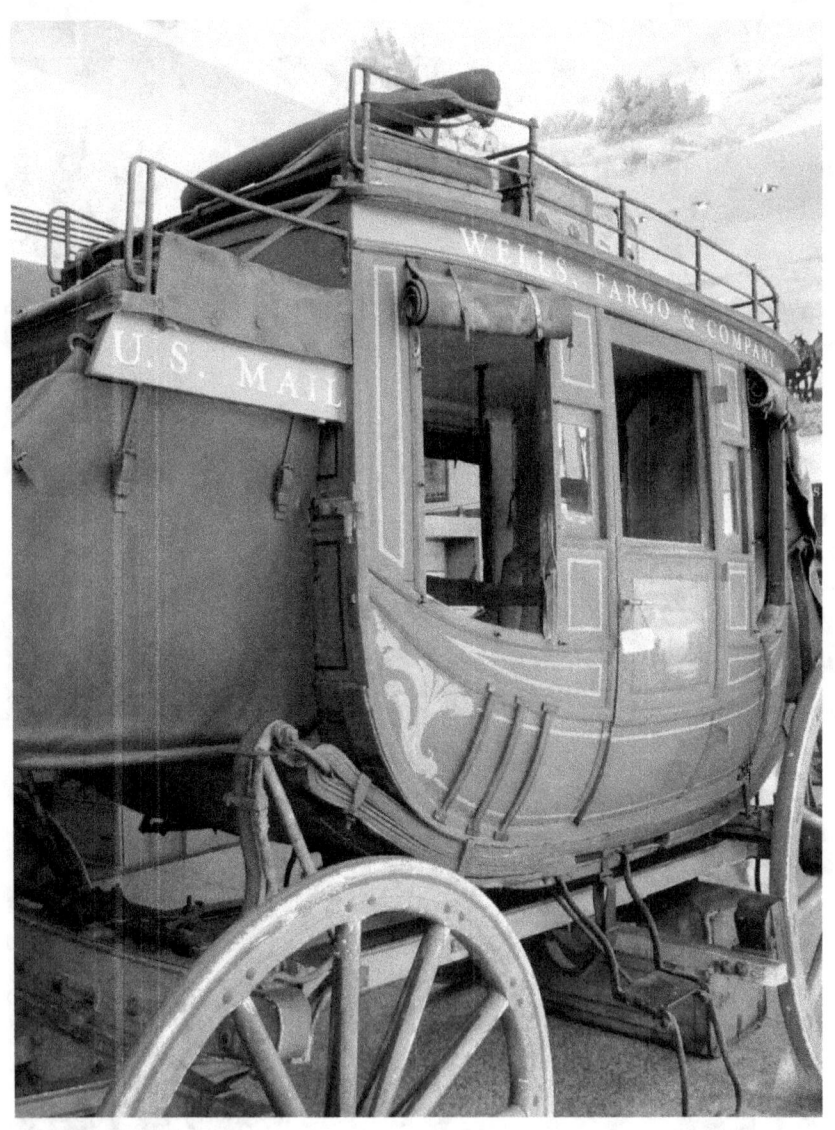

## EDISON BUILDING

One Bunker Hill (601 W. 5ᵗʰ Street)

*The great skyscrapers of Grand Avenue flow west from the Wells Fargo Plaza, down to 5ᵗʰ Street, where the terra cotta, limestone, and marble So Cal Edison Building (left) has proudly anchored the intersection's northwest corner since 1931.*

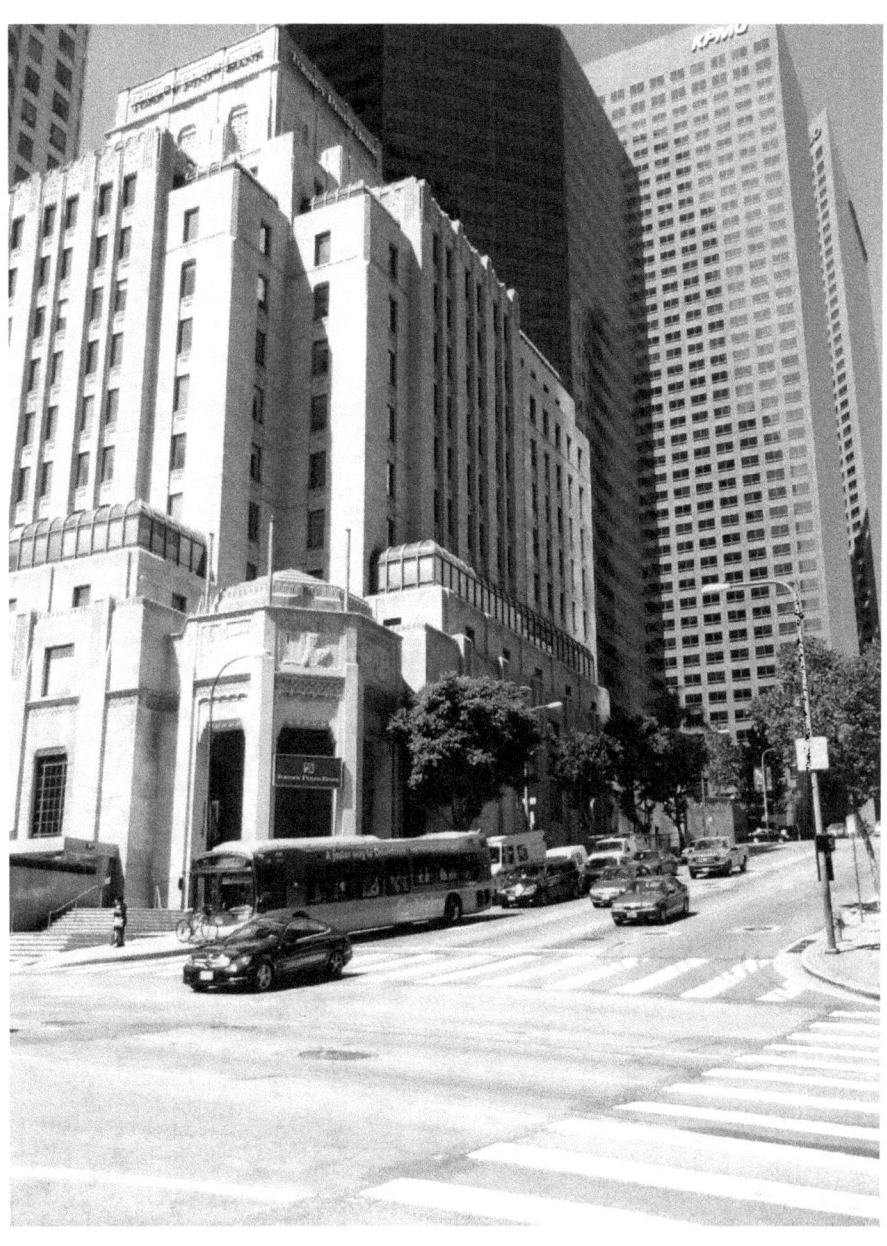

# EDISON BUILDING

601 W. 5ᵗʰ Street (One Bunker Hill)

*The Art Deco Edison Building (center) is flanked by the U.S. Bank Tower (left), the tallest building west of the Mississippi, and the Gas Company Tower (right). Though much smaller than its neighbors, the Edison Building, with its substantial mass and striking design, more than holds its own visually.*

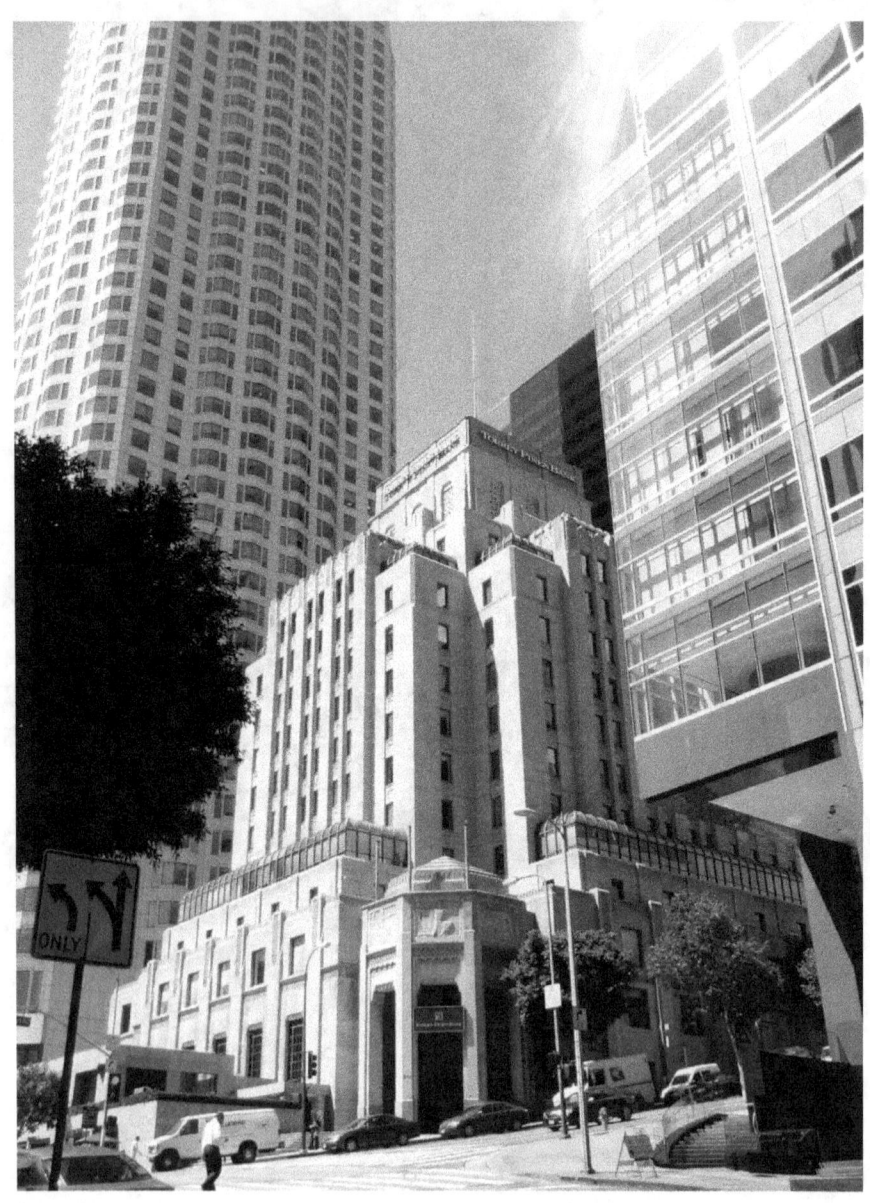

## U.S. BANK TOWER

633 W. 5th Street

*The U.S. Bank Tower looms more than 1,000 feet tall. It was constructed in 1989. It has had multiple owners and multiple names, but locals often refer to it simply as Library Tower. Why? L.A.'s central library sits directly across 5th Street, and the skyscraper was constructed as part of the revival of the library and its surroundings. Originally the tower was known as "Library Tower," and that is how many Angelenos continue to think of it. Because of its height and its status as an L.A. icon, this skyscraper was originally a target for the 9/11 terrorists.*

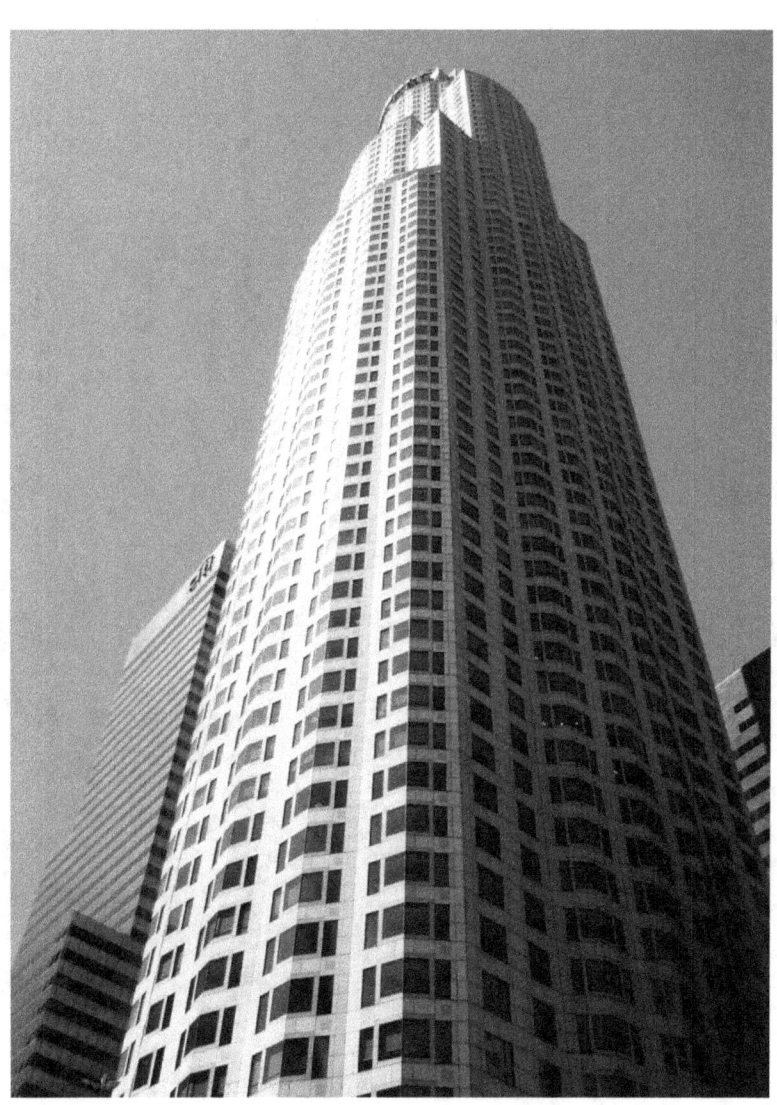

## PERSHING SQUARE

5th Street & 6th Street / Hill & Olive

*L.A.'s elegant Millennium Biltmore Hotel (the three connected Beaux-Arts buildings in the left and center of the photo, and the peaked tower in the top center) is fronted by Pershing Square (1918) on its Olive Street side. Although the park's name has changed many times over the years (it was finally named Pershing Square for General Pershing of WWI renown), the space has been a public park or plaza since 1866. From a distance, the shady trees and unique art installations give Pershing Square a cheerful air, and in its heyday it was indeed a beautiful and much-utilized public park and plaza. At present it is the refuge of many of L.A.'s homeless, and the park center is closed to the public. In a subway station deep underground, trains carry riders to Wilshire, Hollywood, and Union Station.*

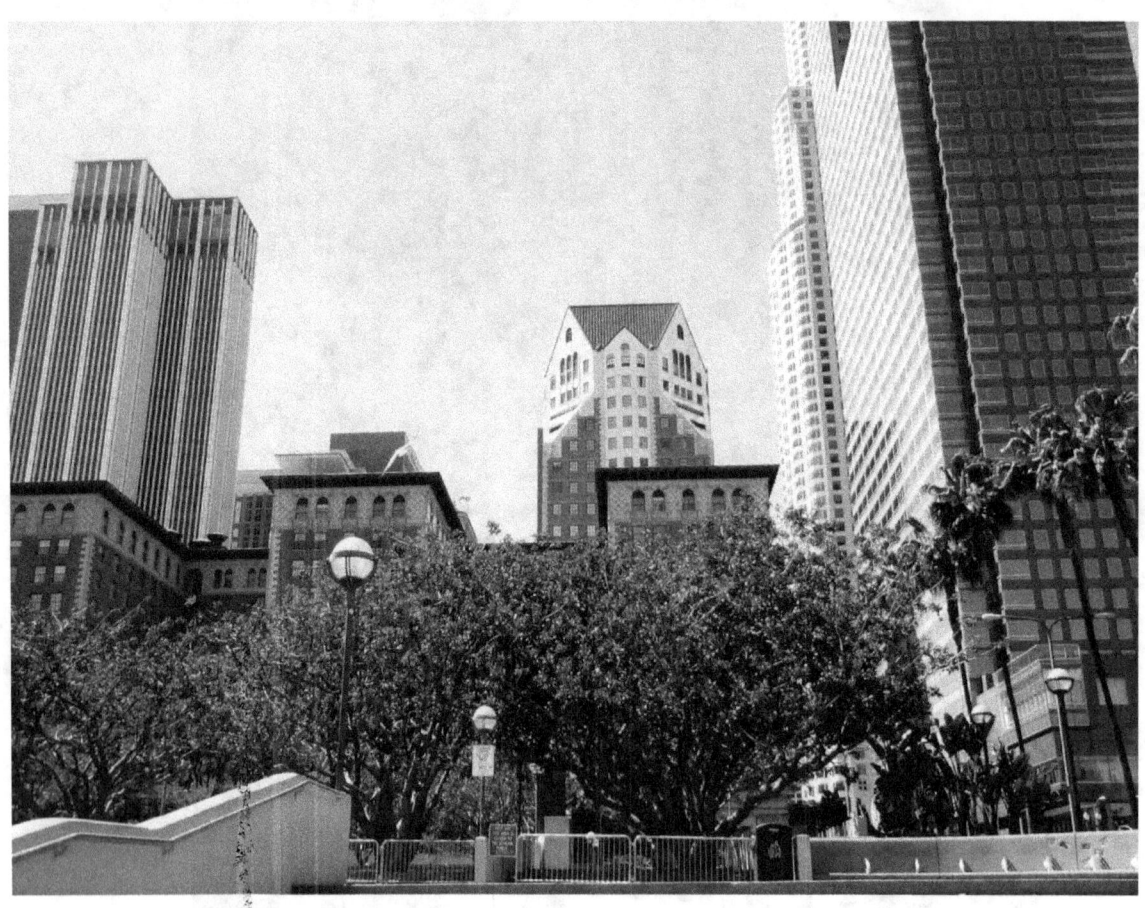

## MILLENNIUM BILTMORE HOTEL

506 S. Grand Avenue

*Seen here from its Olive Street side, the Biltmore opened in 1923 and quickly surpassed and replaced L.A.'s other grand hotels (like the Alexandria at 5ʰ and Spring).*

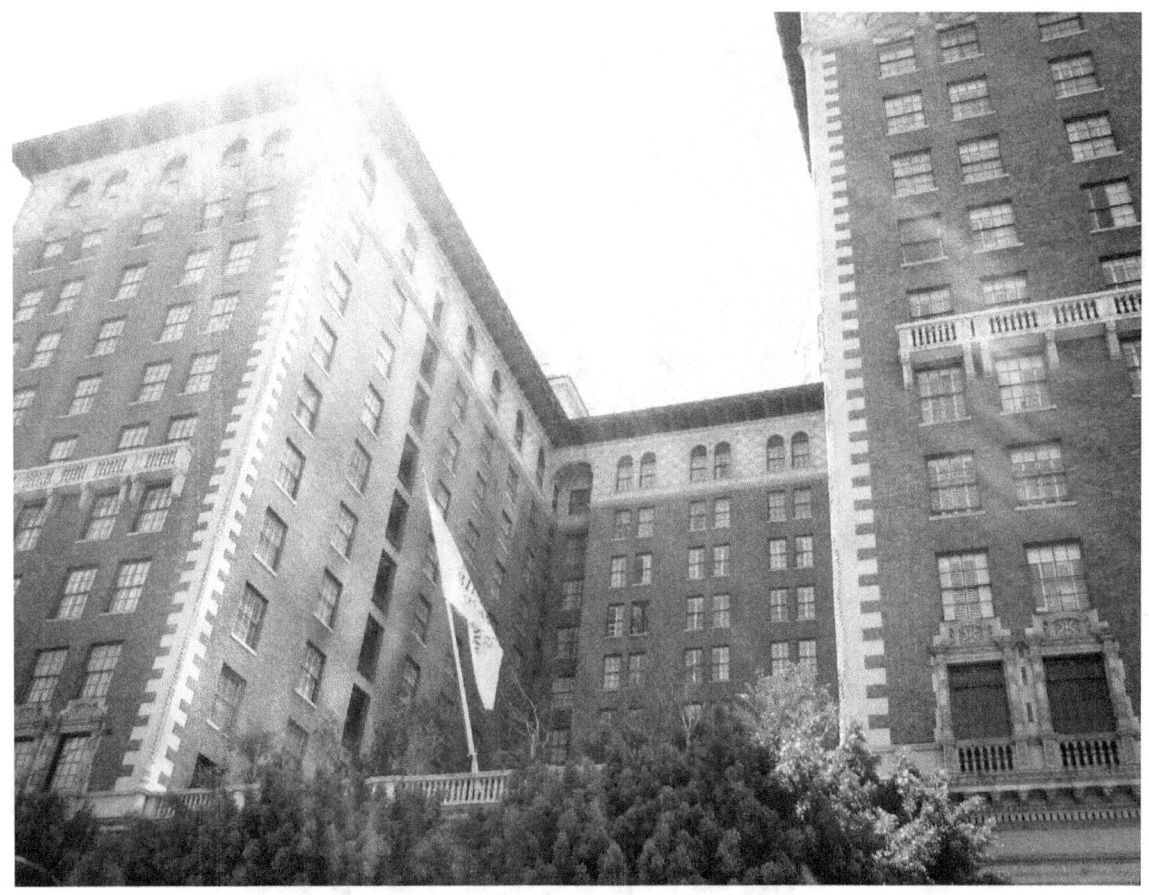

# MILLENNIUM BILTMORE HOTEL

506 S. Grand Avenue

*The Biltmore (1923) was constructed in the Beaux-Arts style, with Mediterranean touches.  Although ownership was assumed by the Millennium hotel chain in 2009, the hotel's classic luxurious ambiance remains intact – witness the beauty of the Olive Street entrance.*

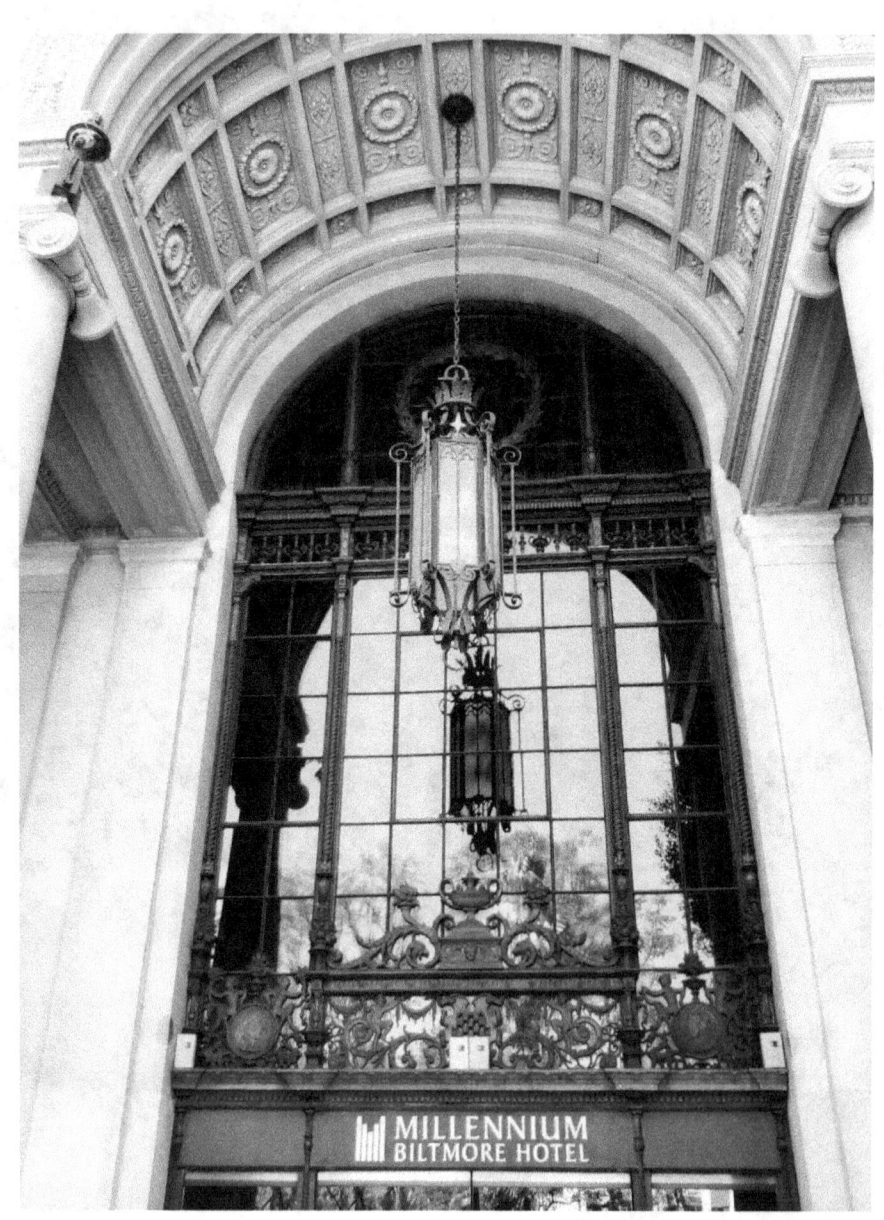

## SUBWAY TERMINAL BUILDING

417 S. Hill Street

*Looking north from Pershing Square and the Millennium Biltmore Hotel, one sees the old Subway Terminal Building in the near distance.  For thirty years (1925 – 1955) the Subway Terminal Building housed a complex underground rail station that served up to 65,000 riders daily.  It closed in the mid-1950's as Los Angeles became an automobile-centered culture.  Presently, the Subway Terminal Building is a luxury apartment house called "Metro 417".*

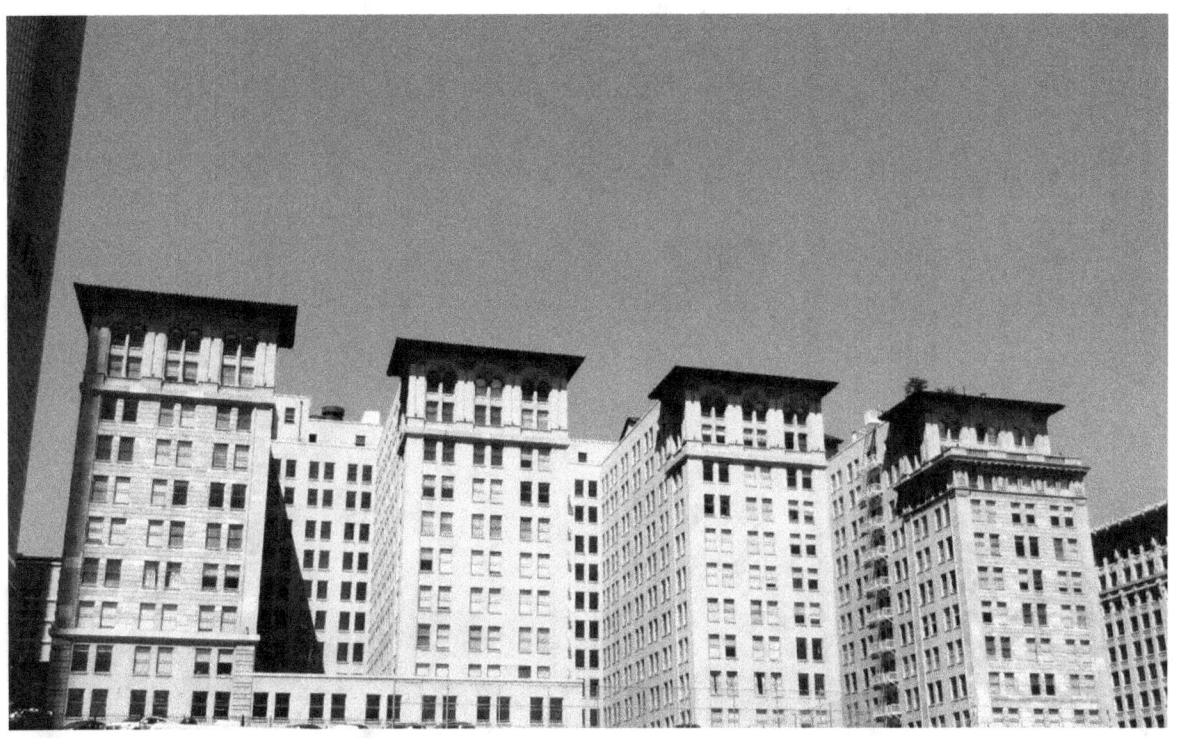

## LOS ANGELES CENTRAL LIBRARY

630 W. 5th Street

*A block west of the Millennium Biltmore, we find the Los Angeles Central Library just across 5th Street from the Edison Building and the U.S. Bank Tower. Pictured here: the 5th Street entrance.*

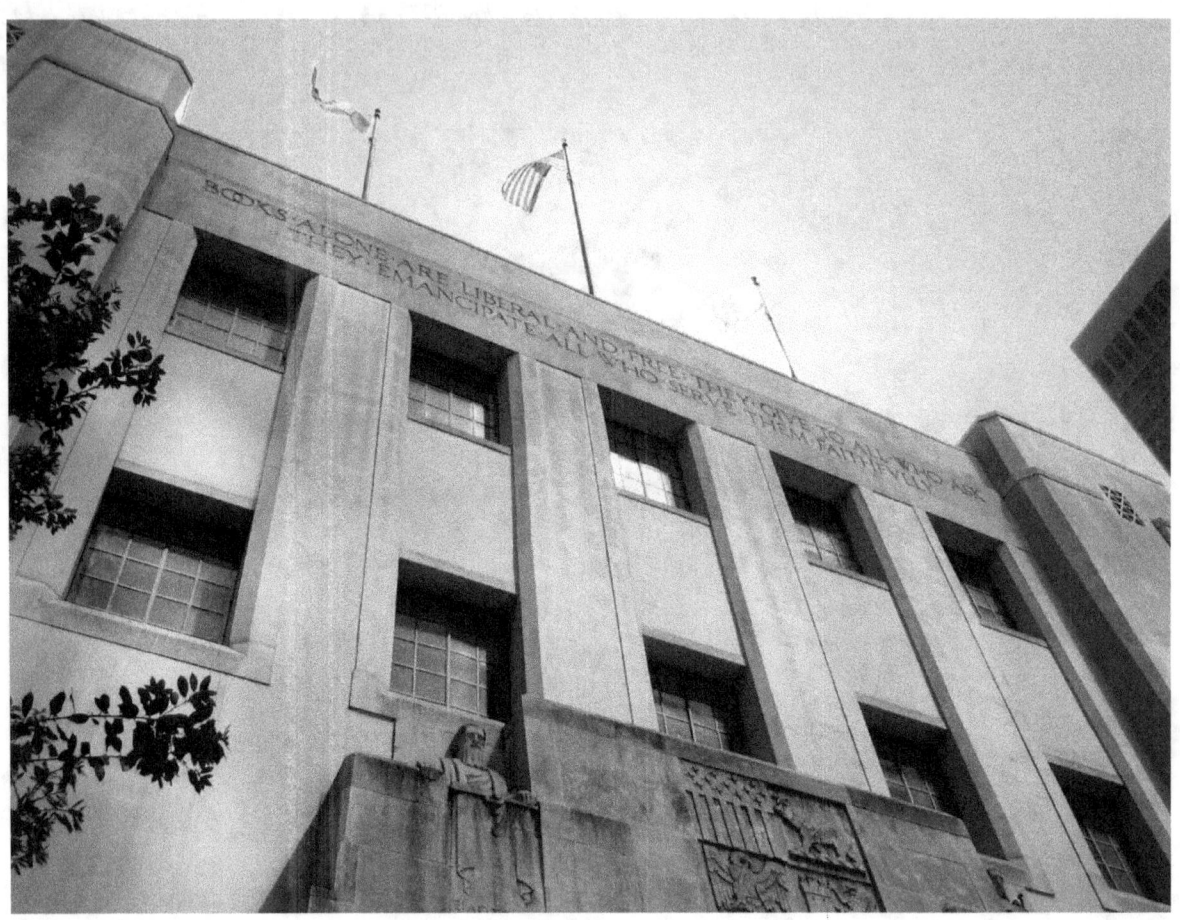

## LOS ANGELES CENTRAL LIBRARY

630 W. 5ᵗʰ Street

*The Central Library was completed in 1926, and was constructed on the site of the former State Normal School (1882). The normal school educated teachers who practiced what they learned at an elementary school on campus. The Central Library continues to foster children's education via a lovely children's library. The children's library is accessible through this ornate lobby on the 2ⁿᵈ floor. Note the dome's elaborate designs; images of light - flames, radiance, suns, and stars – are prevalent throughout the library, and symbolize the light of knowledge.*

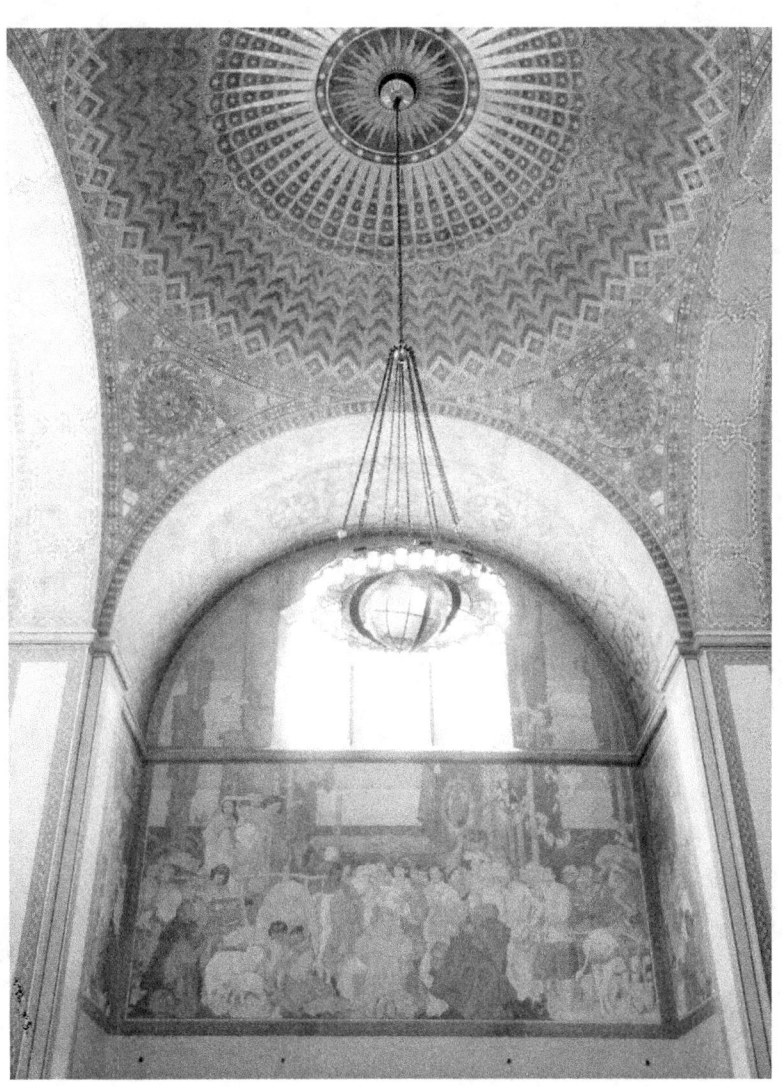

# LOS ANGELES CENTRAL LIBRARY

630 W. 5ᵗʰ Street

*One of the library's most striking features is this atrium, decorated with whimsical sculptures.*

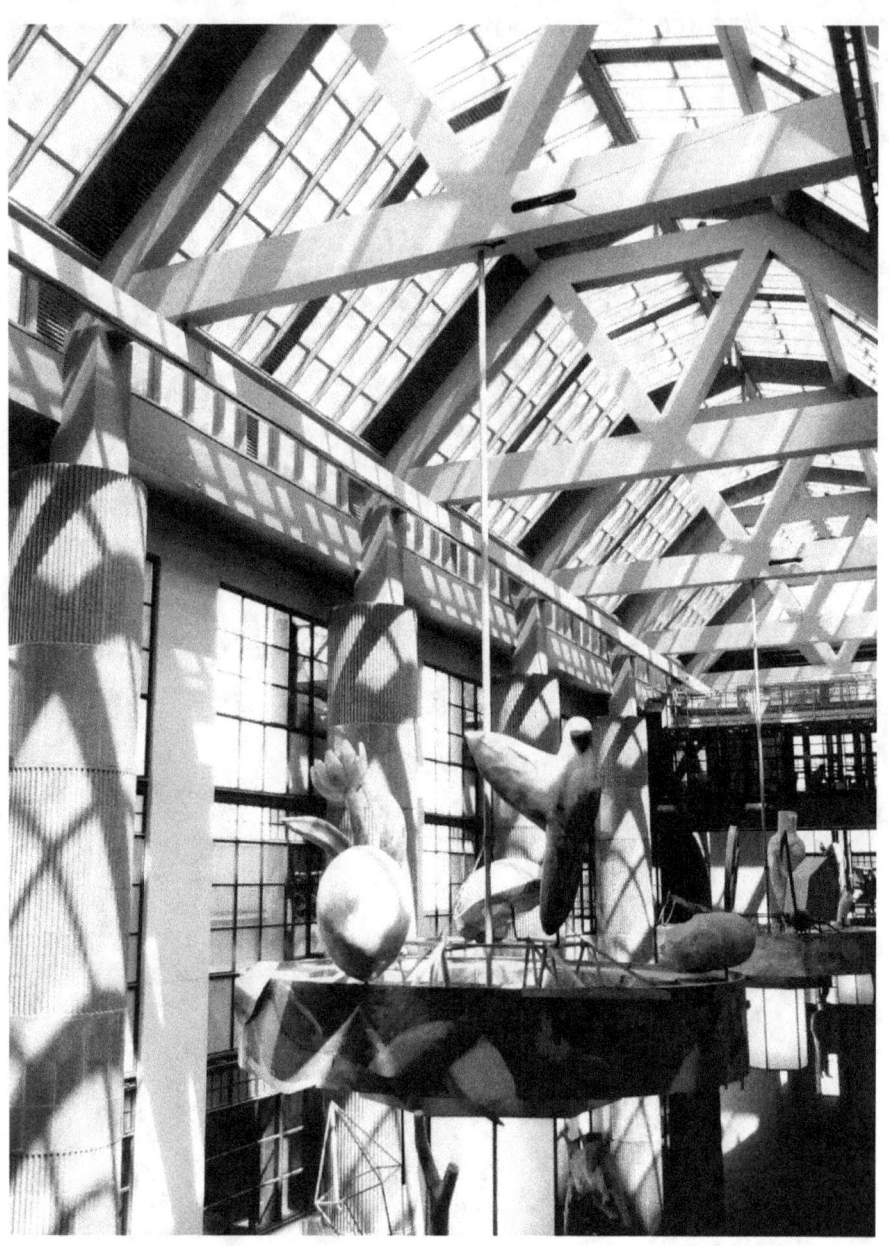

# LOS ANGELES CENTRAL LIBRARY

630 W. 5<sup>th</sup> Street

*Tiered escalators transport library visitors from the top of the eight-story atrium deep underground. Much of the library's vast collection is housed in the building's depths.*

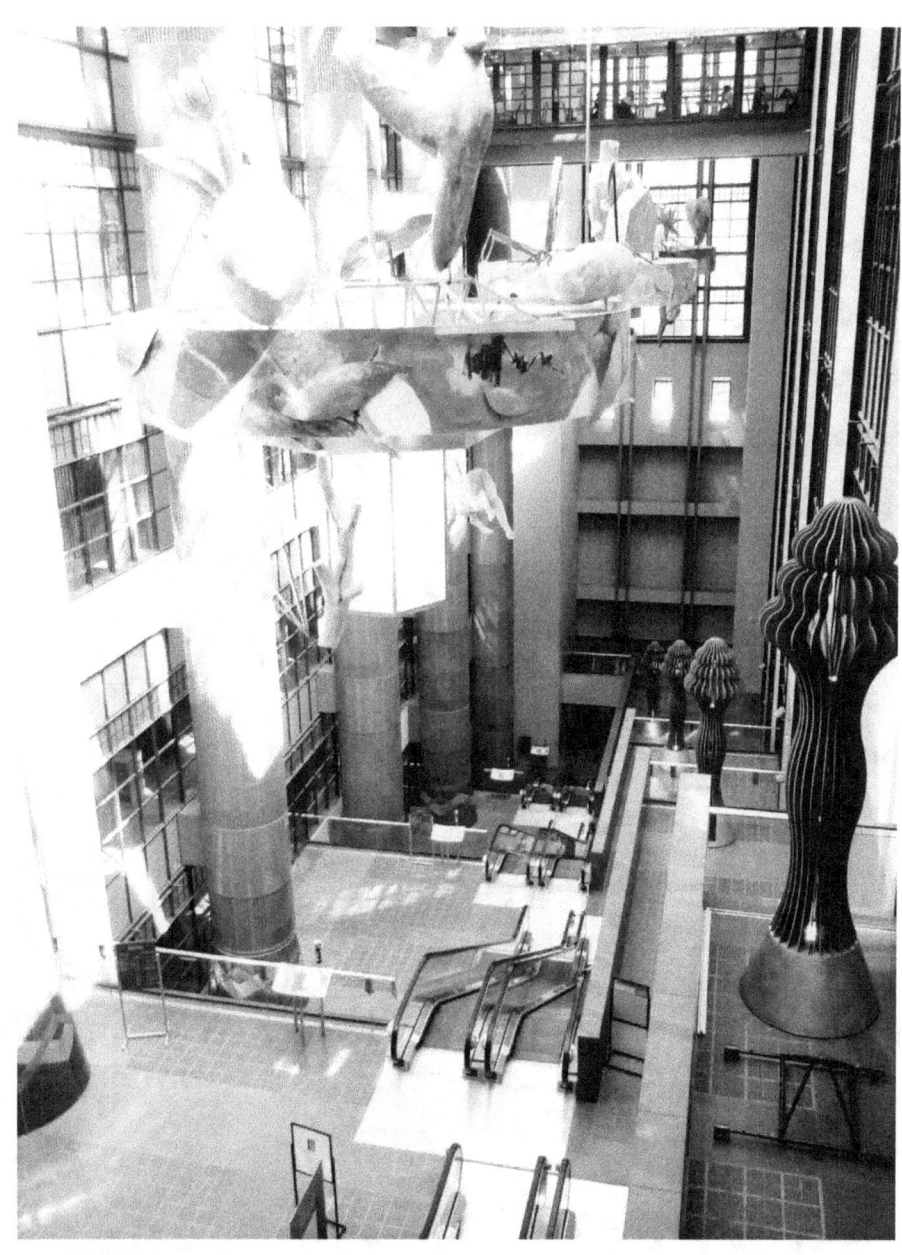

*The library's exterior has an Egyptian flavor, from the pyramid at the top, to the pharaoh-like Art Deco statues flanking the western entrance (Phosphor the morning star on the left, Hesper the evening star on the right). The Latin quote above the door, "Et Quasi Cursores Vitai Lampada Tradunt," means "And, like runners, they pass the torch of life" – a quote from Lucretius. The golden spire gleaming atop the pyramid is a hand holding the "Light of Learning".*

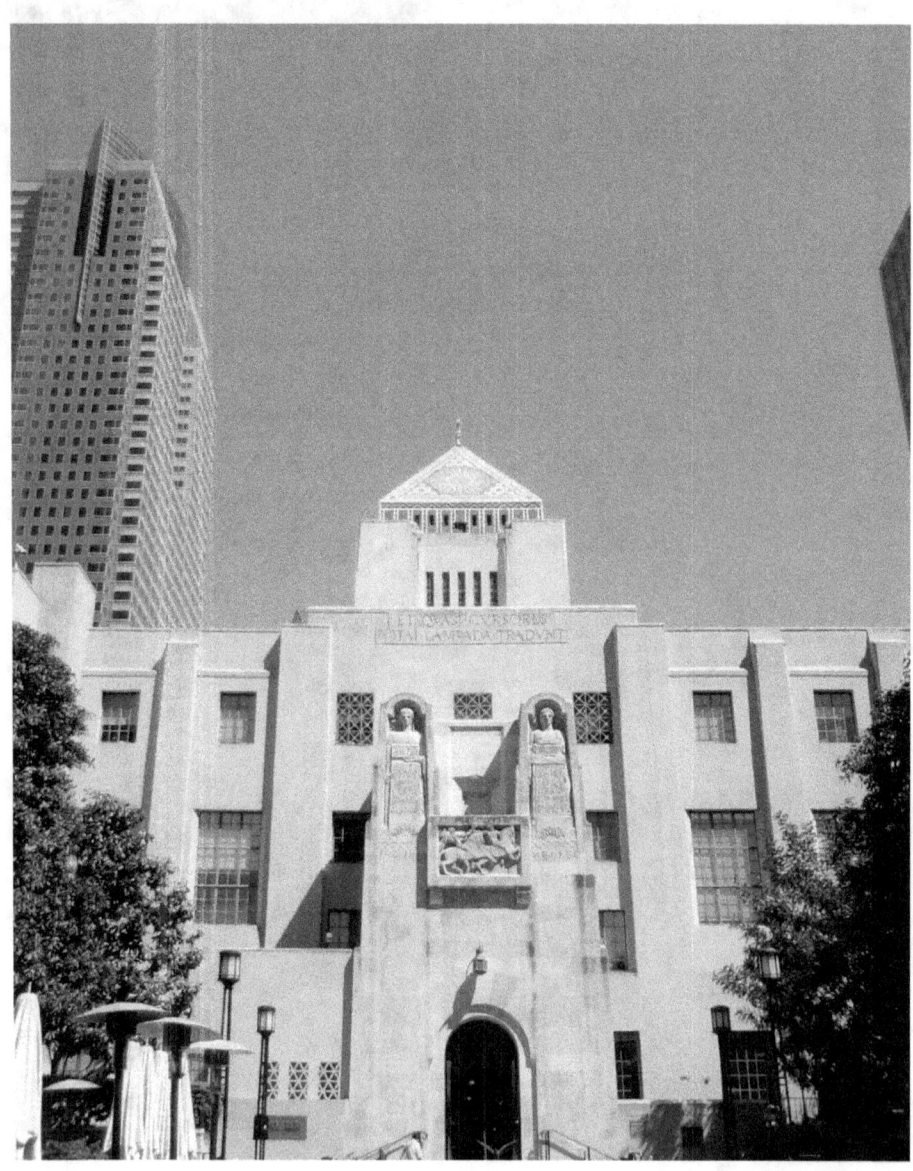

*The library's western façade is mirrored in one of the reflecting pools ...*

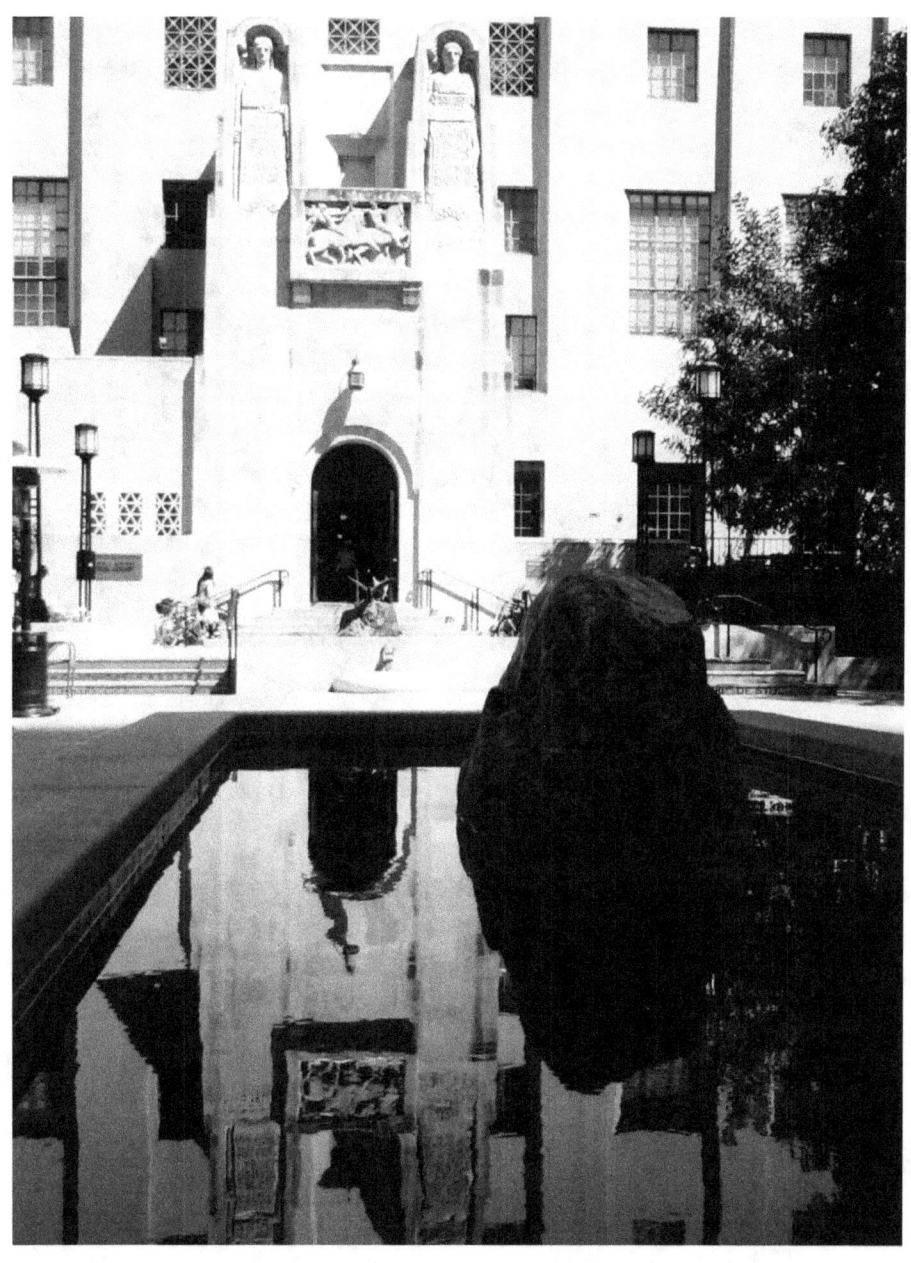

# LOS ANGELES CENTRAL LIBRARY

630 W. 5th Street

*... And reflected in the glass windows of a Flower Street bank.*

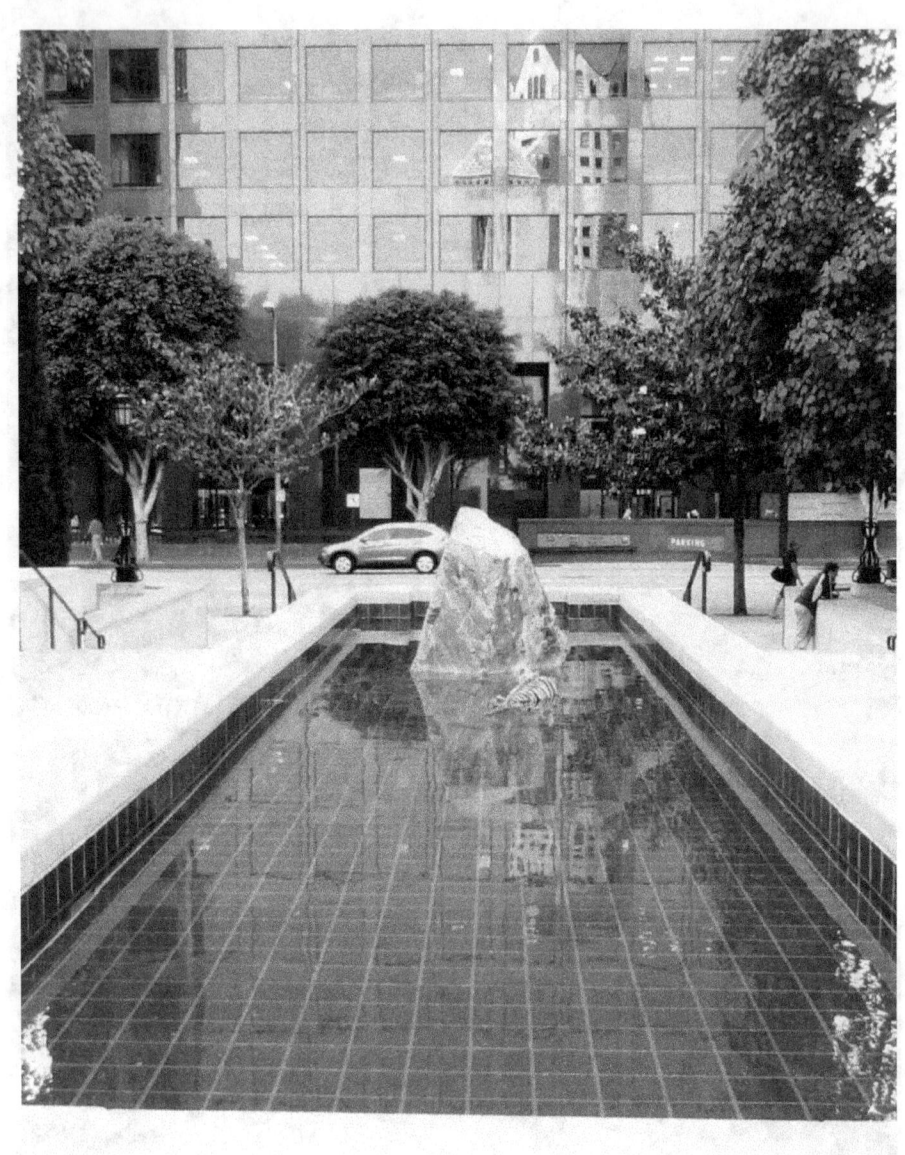

Broadway

*Now we backtrack somewhat, heading northeast to Broadway. The contrast between L.A.'s modern and historic districts could not be more dramatic. The financial district is electric with activity and prosperity, but down the hill and several blocks east stretches the north-south corridor of Broadway, a living time capsule. Once a thriving thoroughfare, particularly known for its movie theaters, as the movie palaces and other businesses closed, Broadway lapsed into crime and decay for many decades. Although some of its buildings have been lovingly restored in recent years, most now host pawn shops and bargain electronic and clothing stores. Some are abandoned. Pictured here is the Metropolitan Water District Building (1918) at 301 – 313 S. Broadway, with the Deloitte & Touche tower at Two California Plaza looming to the west.*

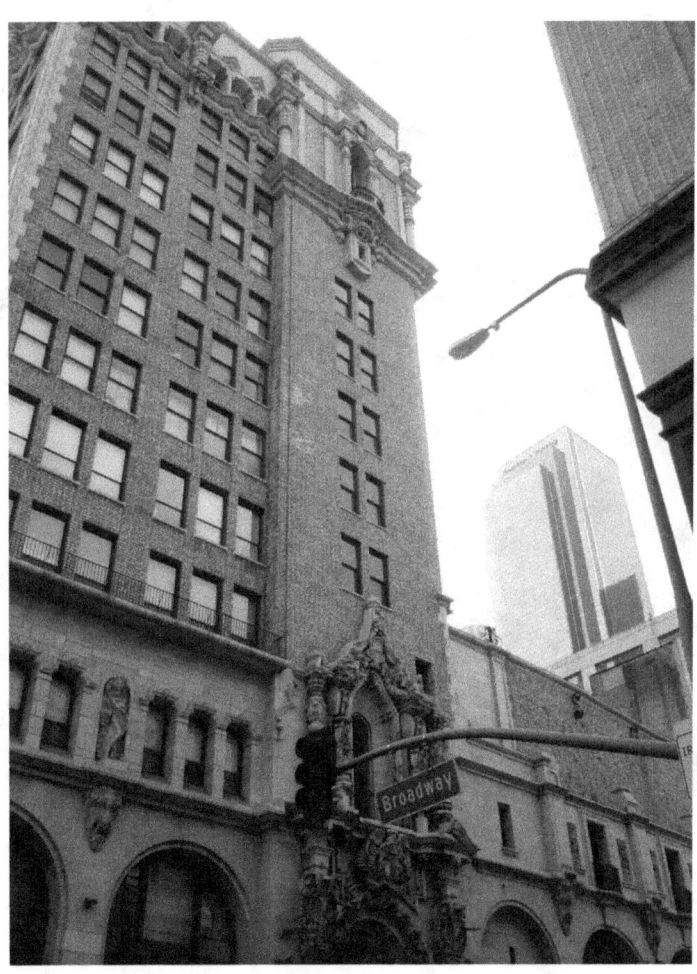

# FINANCIAL DISTRICT – FROM A DISTANCE

Financial District

*In the background:  A view of some of L.A.'s. tallest buildings, most of them banks and financial institutions.  The empty lot at Broadway and 1$^{st}$ Street is in the foreground.  General rule of thumb when downtown:  The further southwest one moves, the taller and more modern the landscape becomes.  What once occupied this empty lot?  The Junipero Serra State Office Building, which was torn down in 2007 due to earthquake damage.  What is planned?  A new federal courthouse.*

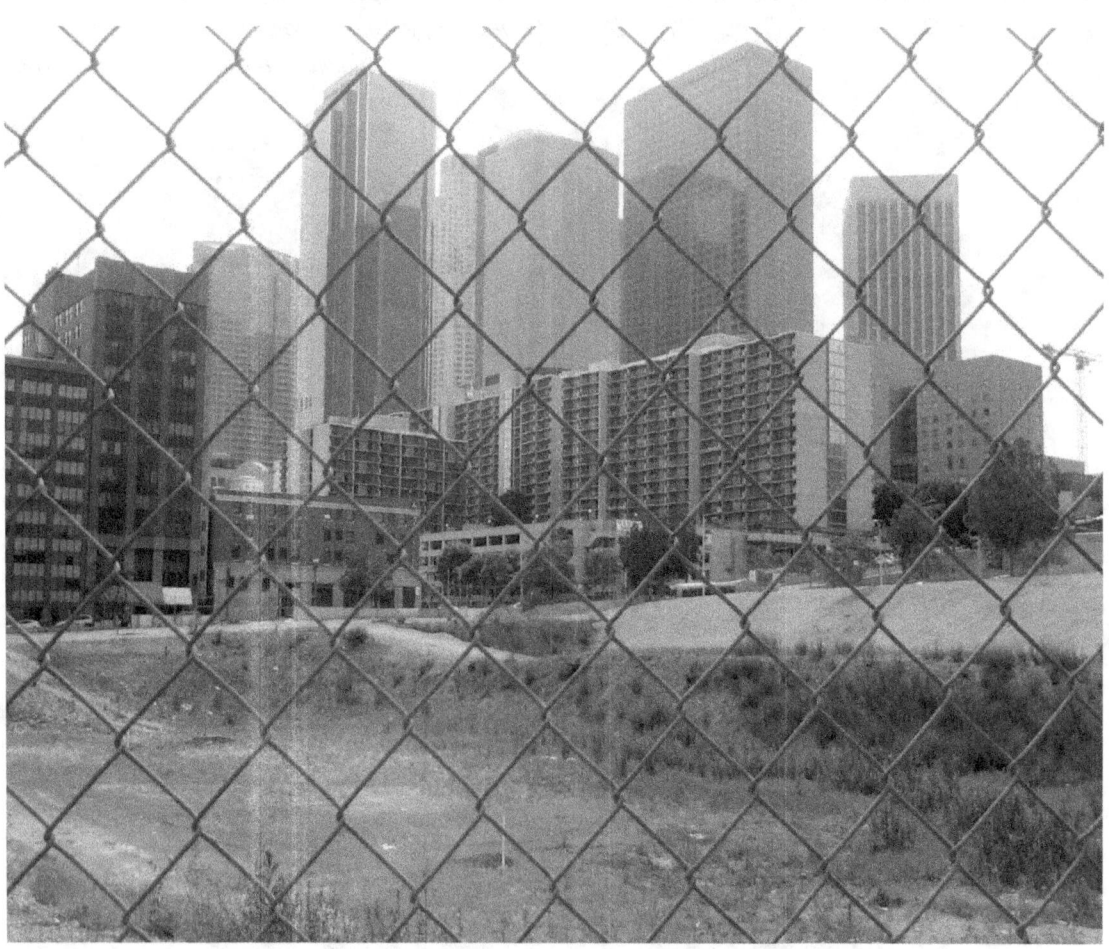

# VICTOR CLOTHING

242 S. Broadway

*A view looking south down Broadway. Note Victor Clothing, and the mural on its north wall. With its classic buildings and low skyline, Broadway retains much of its early 20th century appearance. Aside from the modern vehicles, this photo could have been taken in the early decades of the last century. Victor Clothing occupies the Hosfield Building, built in 1914. The structure is known for its vivid murals that catch the attention of passers-by. Colorful, skillfully executed murals are a Los Angeles art form.*

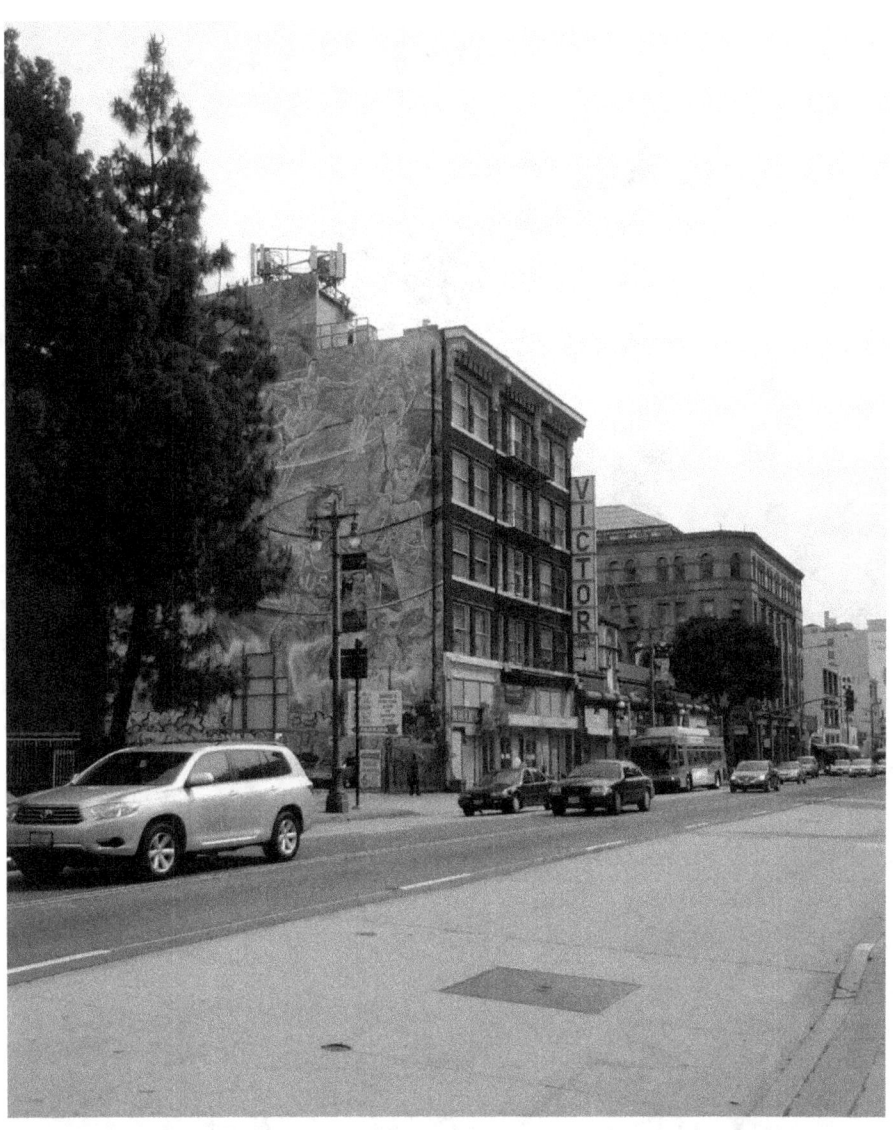

## VICTOR CLOTHING

### 242 S. Broadway

The Hosfield Building was constructed as an annex for L.A.'s City Hall, which at the time was a grand building next door at 226 – 238 S. Broadway. The old City Hall was torn down in the late 1920's after the present City Hall on Spring Street opened. The Hosfield annex still stands. The murals on its walls are a form of Los Angeles street art, which takes many forms, from the accomplished to the amateur. Note the bus bench in front of the Basic Flowers shop. The bench ad urges people to "VOTE" in the May 21, 2013 election. You can just discern that the "O" in "VOTE" has been replaced by a carefully painted face, which appears to be the visage of a model or glam-rock star. It's graffiti – but with style.

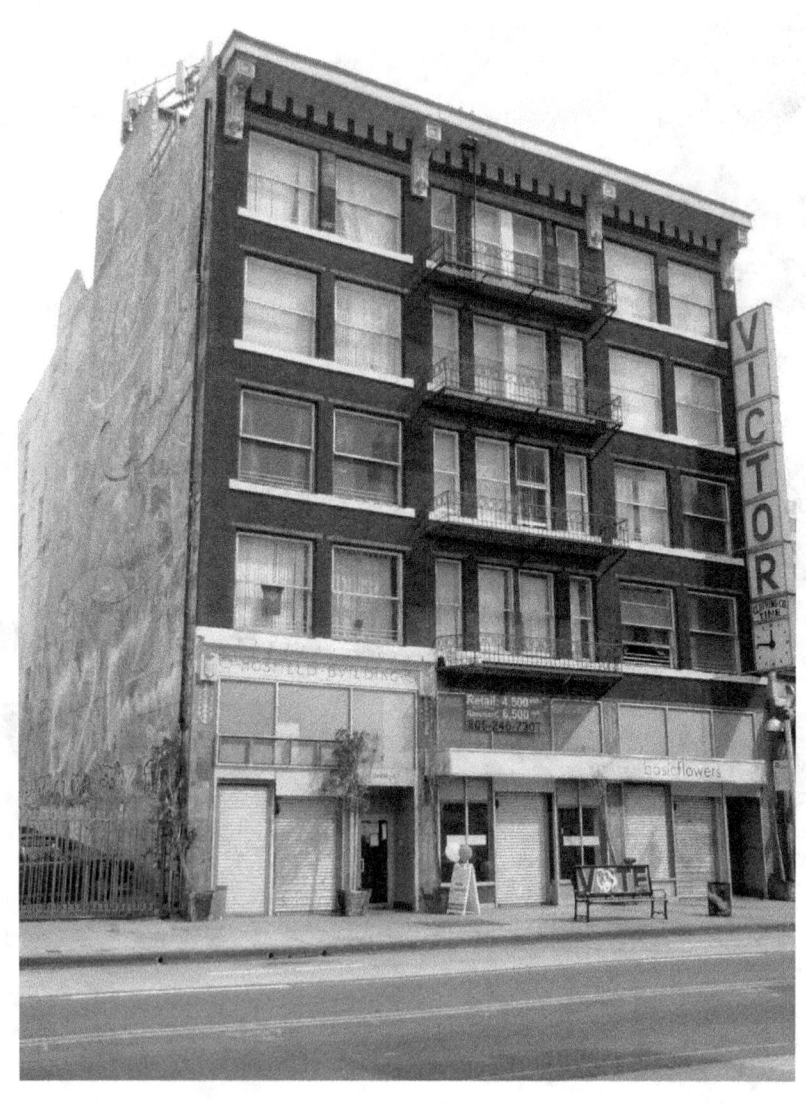

# METROPOLITAN WATER DISTRICT BUILDING

301 – 313 S. Broadway

*Completed in 1918, the Metropolitan Water District Building had multiple tenants, including, for many years, the headquarters of Los Angeles' Metro Water District (MWD). The busy Churrigueresque exterior by Joseph Mora gives this building a unique appearance. In 1918, the Million Dollar Theater opened at this location (307 S. Broadway). The theater was built by Sid Grauman (of Egyptian Theatre and Chinese Theatre fame) during a time when L.A.'s movie palaces were concentrated along Broadway. From the 1950's through the 1990's, the theater became a leader in providing entertainment for L.A.'s Spanish-speaking residents. After a stint as a church, the theater once more hosts Spanish-language productions.*

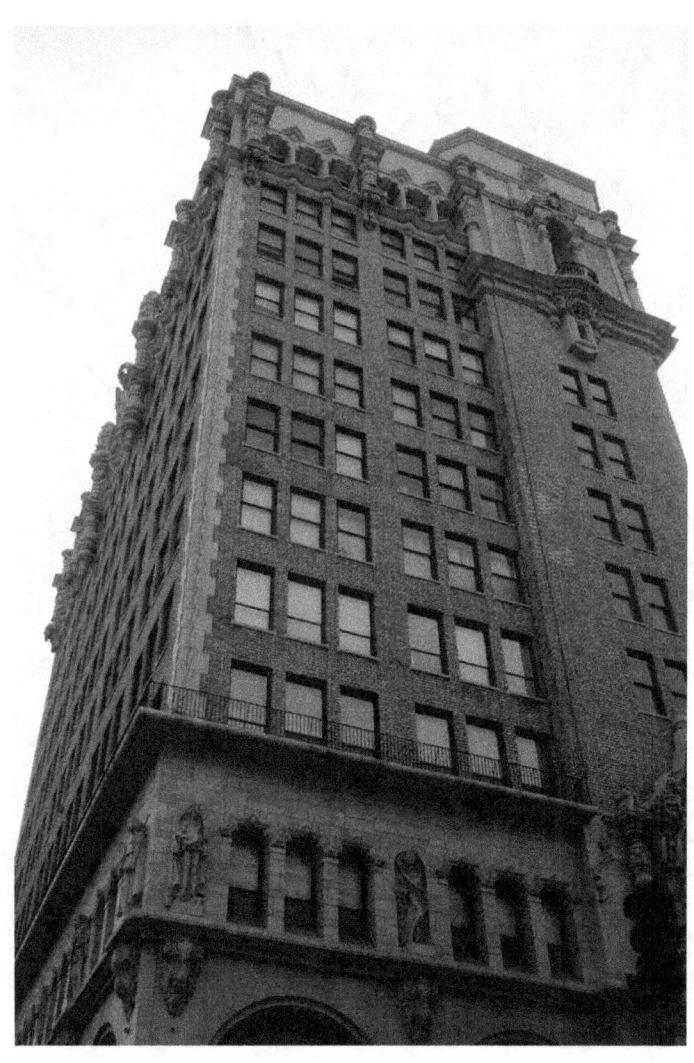

# BRADBURY BUILDING

304 S. Broadway

*The famous Bradbury Building was designed by George Wyman, who said he was told to take the commission during a spirit conversation with his deceased brother. Completed in 1893, this was the first building Wyman ever designed. Sometimes the first time is the charm; Wyman never again matched the success of his first commission. The Bradbury Building is a unique architectural gem.*

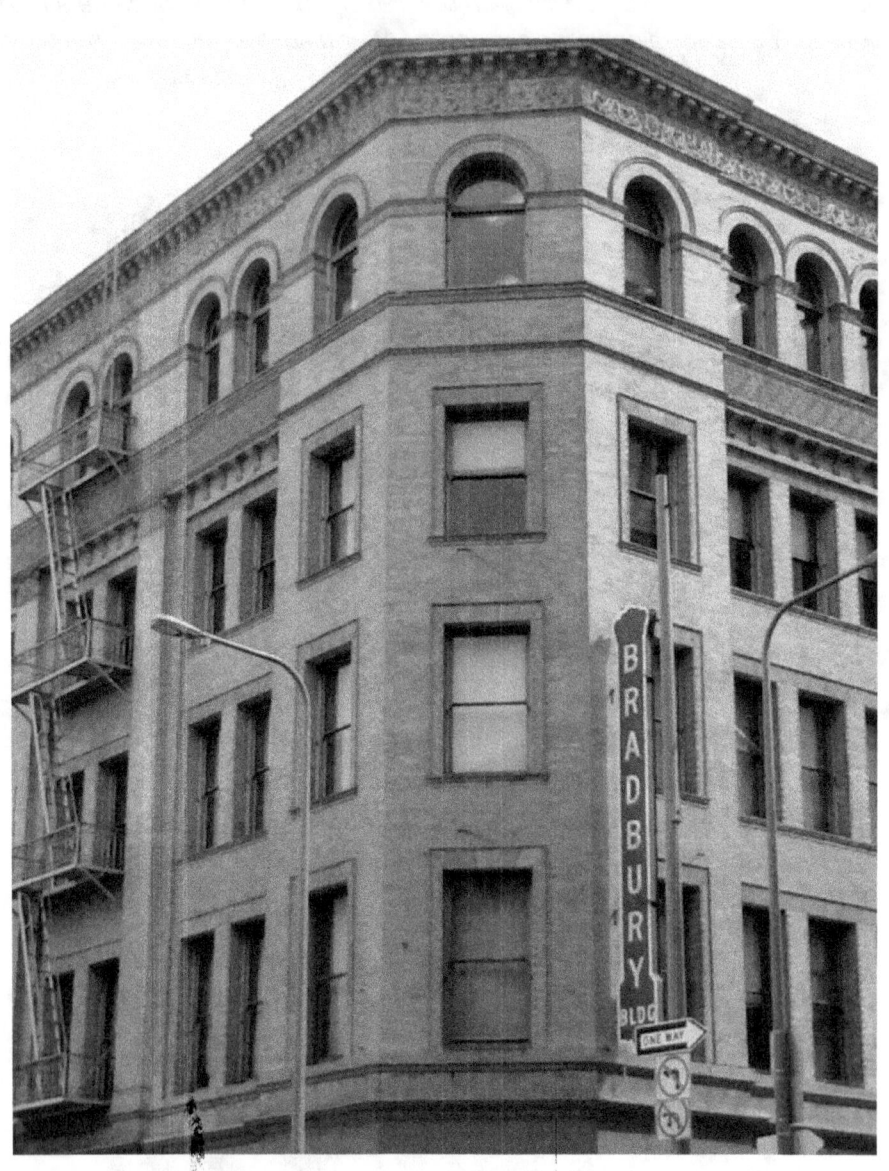

## BRADBURY BUILDING

304 S. Broadway

*This snapshot from 2012 shows the ornate western entrance arch. Lewis L. Bradbury, who commissioned the building, was a millionaire who made his fortune in mining. He had a grand vision for the building, which Wyman's unique and ambitious design fulfilled.*

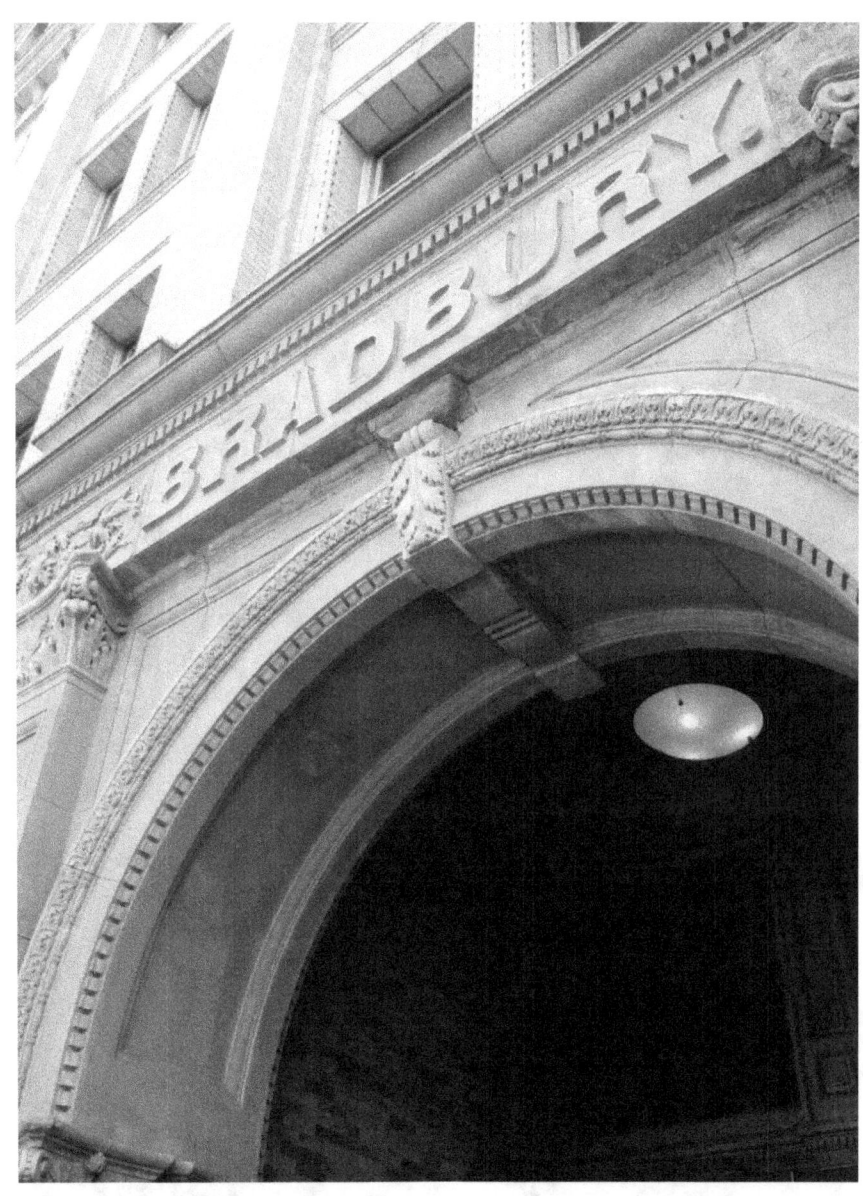

## BRADBURY BUILDING

304 S. Broadway

*The Bradbury Building's interior has been used for scenes in TV shows, and movies as varied as "Wolf" and "Blade Runner". As seen in this 2012 photo, the Bradbury's narrow, open interior, with its glazed tiles, marble, wrought-iron Escher stairs, and skylights, creates a noir atmosphere of dreamlike shadows and lights. Wyman's design of the unusual interior was inspired by a late-1800's sci-fi novel.*

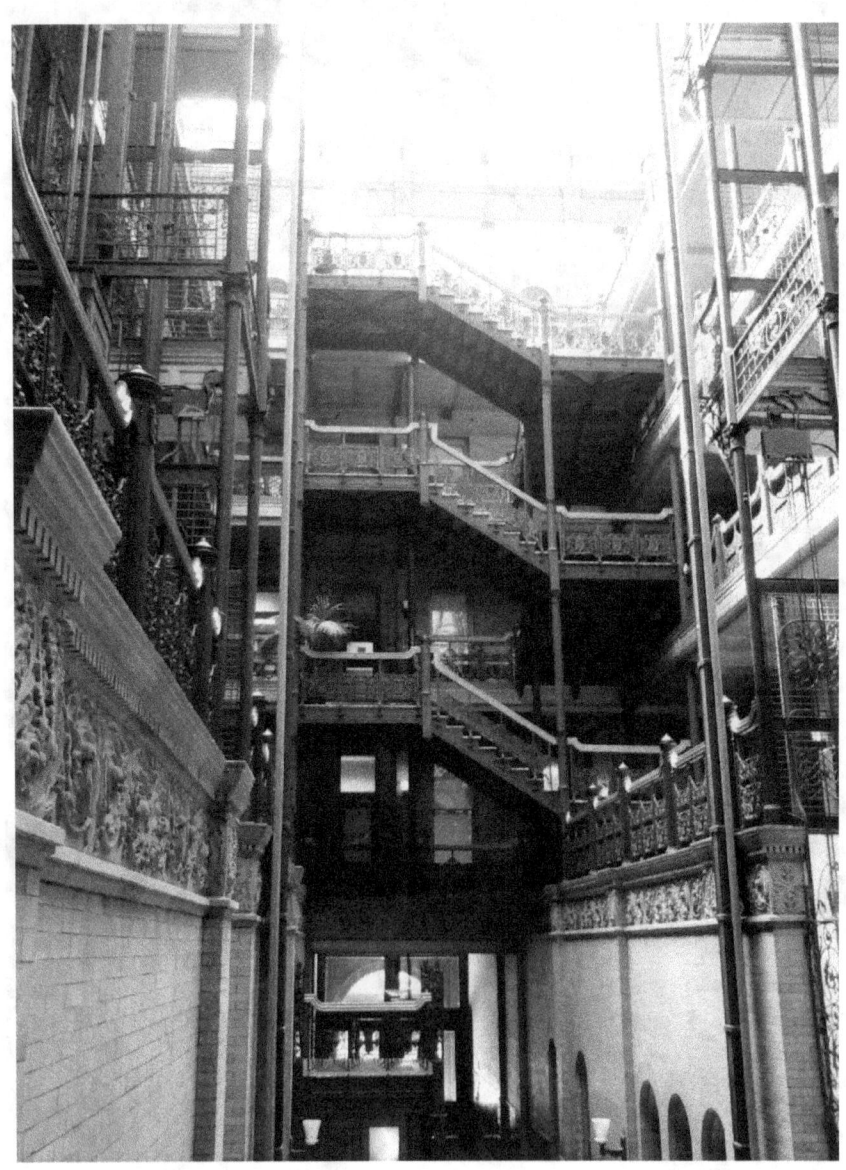

# BRADBURY BUILDING

304 S. Broadway

*Presently the interior of the Bradbury Building is used as office space, and retail stores (like Subway) occupy the ground floor exterior. Visitors are welcome to explore the lobby and snap photos free of charge – although donations are appreciated. The building is open 9 a.m. to 5 pm. Monday – Friday, and closed to the public on Saturdays and Sundays.*

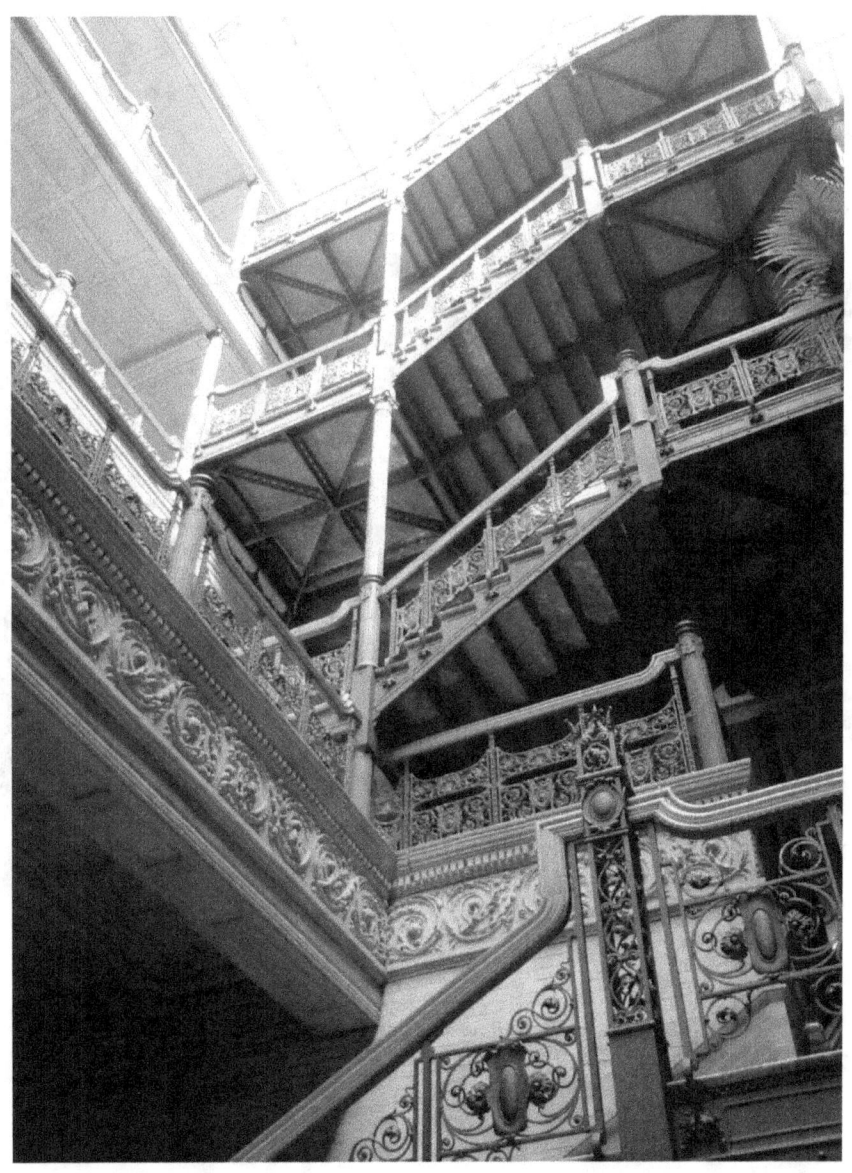

# GRAND CENTRAL MARKET

317 S. Broadway

*Bordered by Broadway and Hill Street to the east and west, 3ʳᵈ and 4ᵗʰ Streets to the north and south, L.A.'s Grand Central Market has been selling produce, meats, and treats since 1917. Locals swing by to pick up ingredients for their evening meals. Tourists pass through for historic photo opportunities and a quick snack. The Grand Central Market is open from 9 a.m. – 6 p.m. daily.*

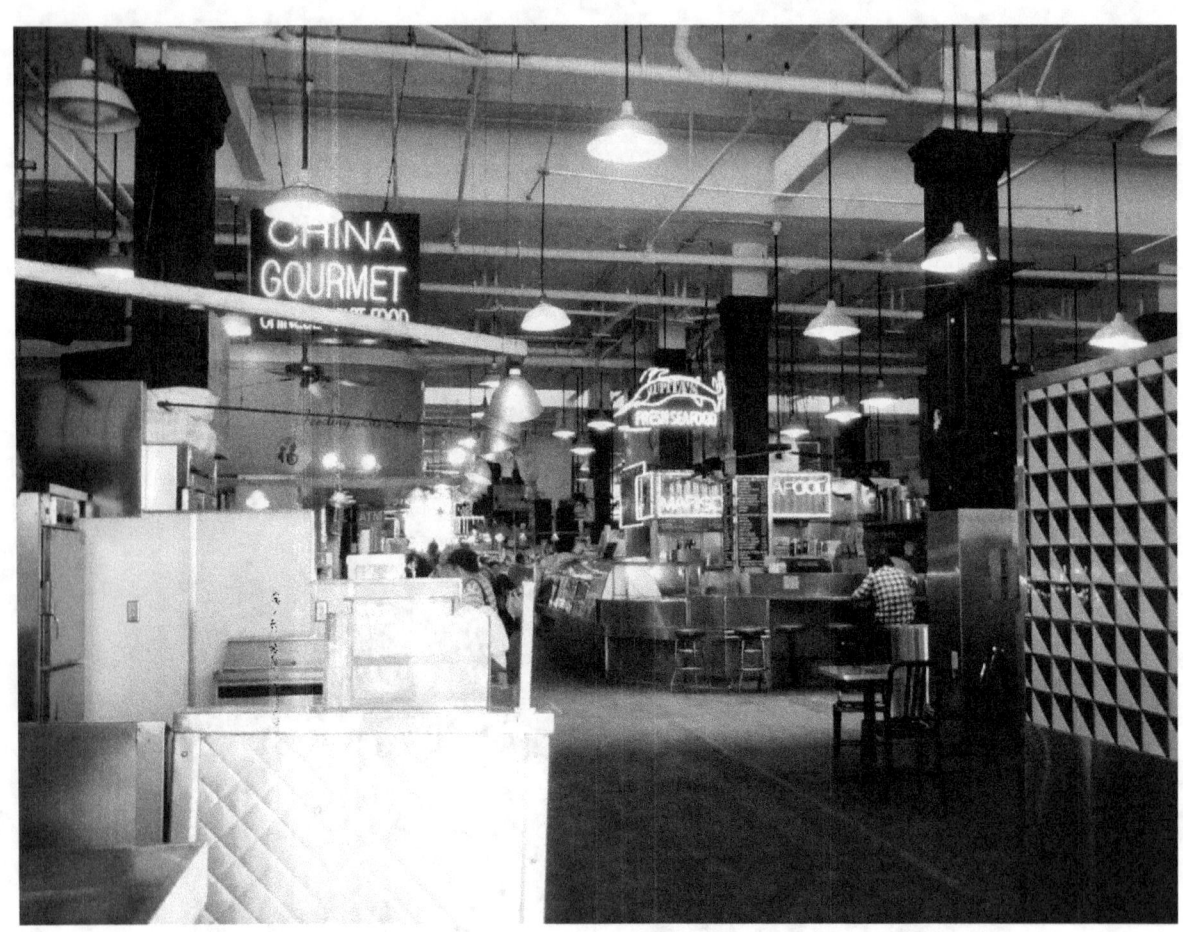

# GRAND CENTRAL MARKET

317 S. Broadway

*Grand Central Market is a maze of counter restaurants, bakeries, butchers, and produce vendors. This snapshot, taken in 2012, shows a selection of fruits for sale, including oranges and pineapples. The Grand Central Market is housed in the Homer-Laughlin Building, which was constructed around the turn of the 20th century.*

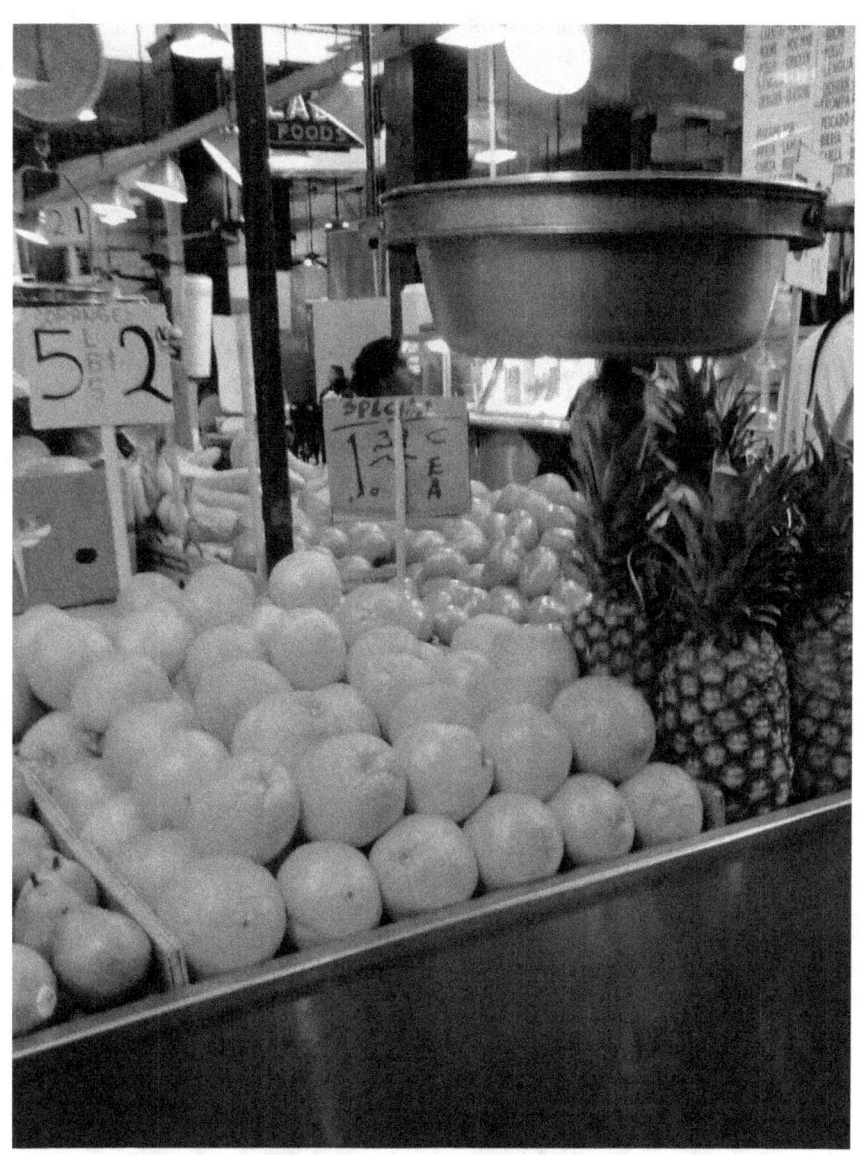

## ANGEL'S FLIGHT

355 S. Hill Street

*Originally located at Hill Street and 3$^{rd}$ Street, Angel's Flight operated from 1901 to 1969 before being discontinued. The railway reopened at its present location at Hill and 4$^{th}$ Streets in 1996, was closed in 2001 due to an accident, and then reopened in 2010. It stands across the street from Grand Central Market's Hill Street entrance. It is to be hoped Angel's Flight will continue to run for many years. Trips cost a modest 50 cents each way. This scenic and beautifully restored railway lifts riders from Grand Central Market up to the soaring skyscrapers of Grand Avenue at the top of the hill. In this 2012 snapshot, an unknown rider descends the tracks toward Grand Central Market. The original Angel's Flight transported Bunker Hill ladies to and from church.*

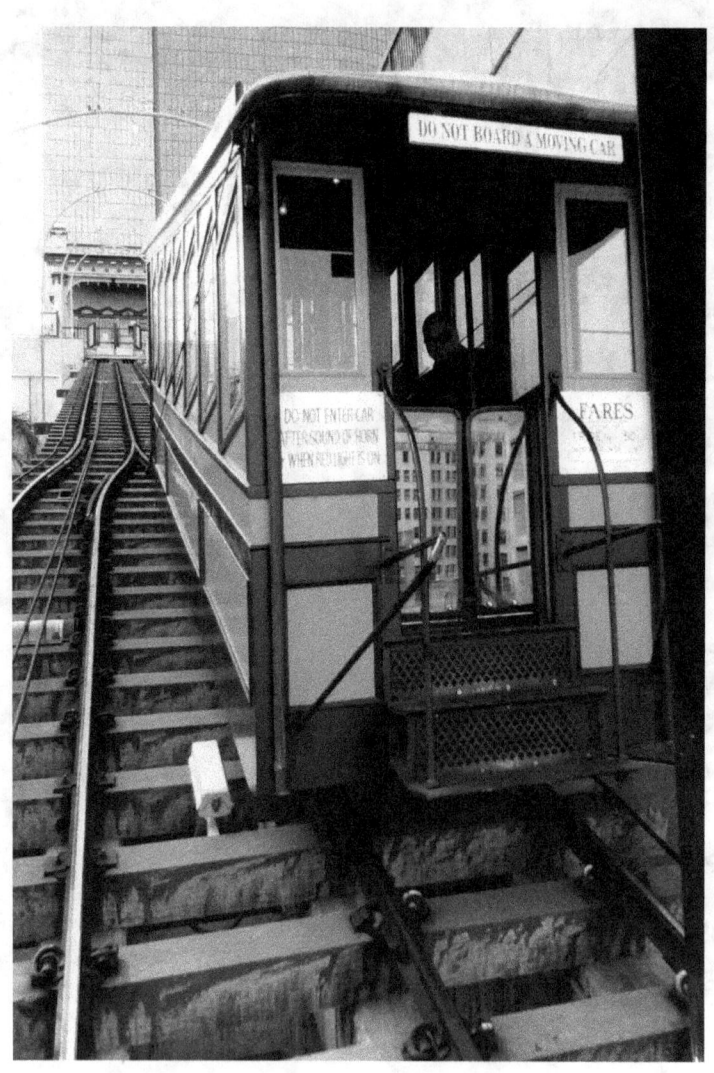

Broadway & 5th Street

*Looking south down Broadway at 5th Street. Signs in the top right of the photo direct travelers to Bunker Hill, the Downtown Center, and the Jewelry District. A radio tower for KRKD is visible in the distance. Religious leader Aimee Semple McPherson once owned and broadcast services via KRKD.*

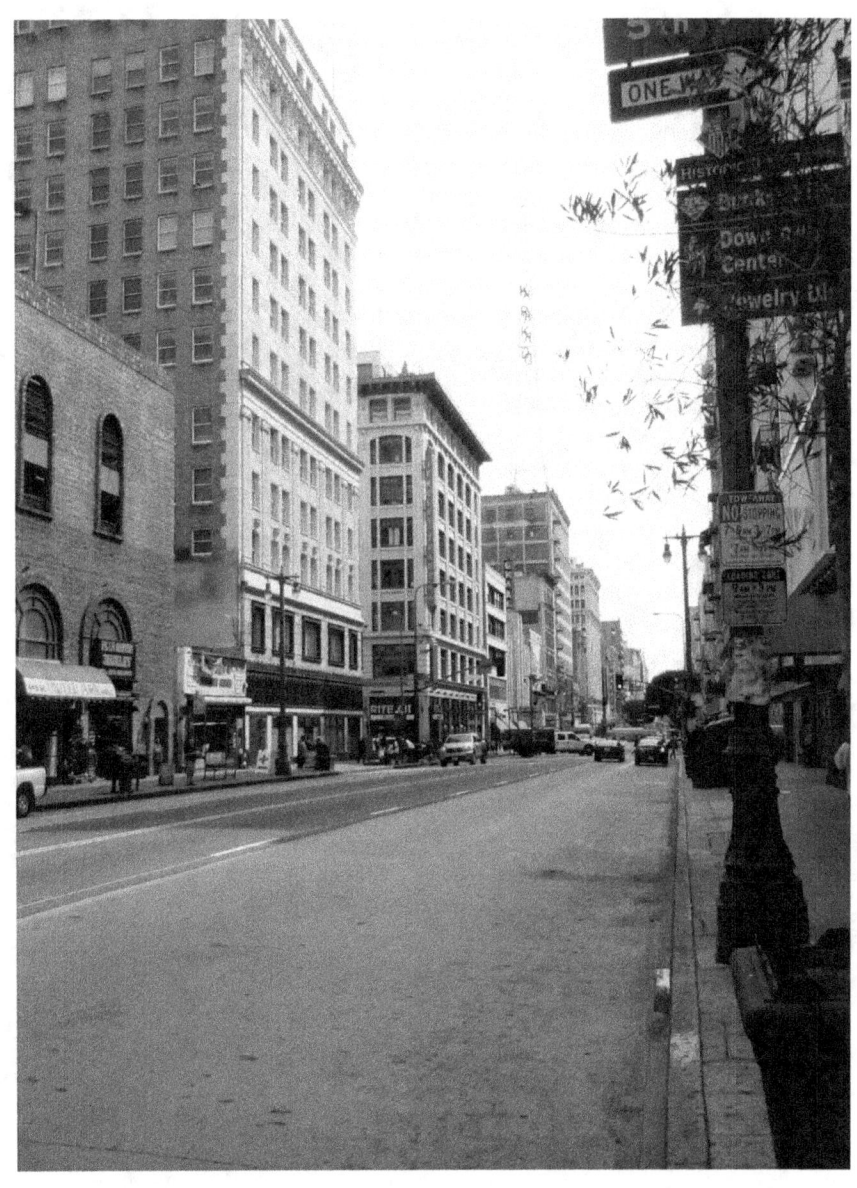

# BROADWAY

Broadway Between 4$^{th}$ & 6$^{th}$ Streets

*For every preserved and/or restored architectural treasure along Broadway, there are numerous blighted wrecks like the one pictured below.*

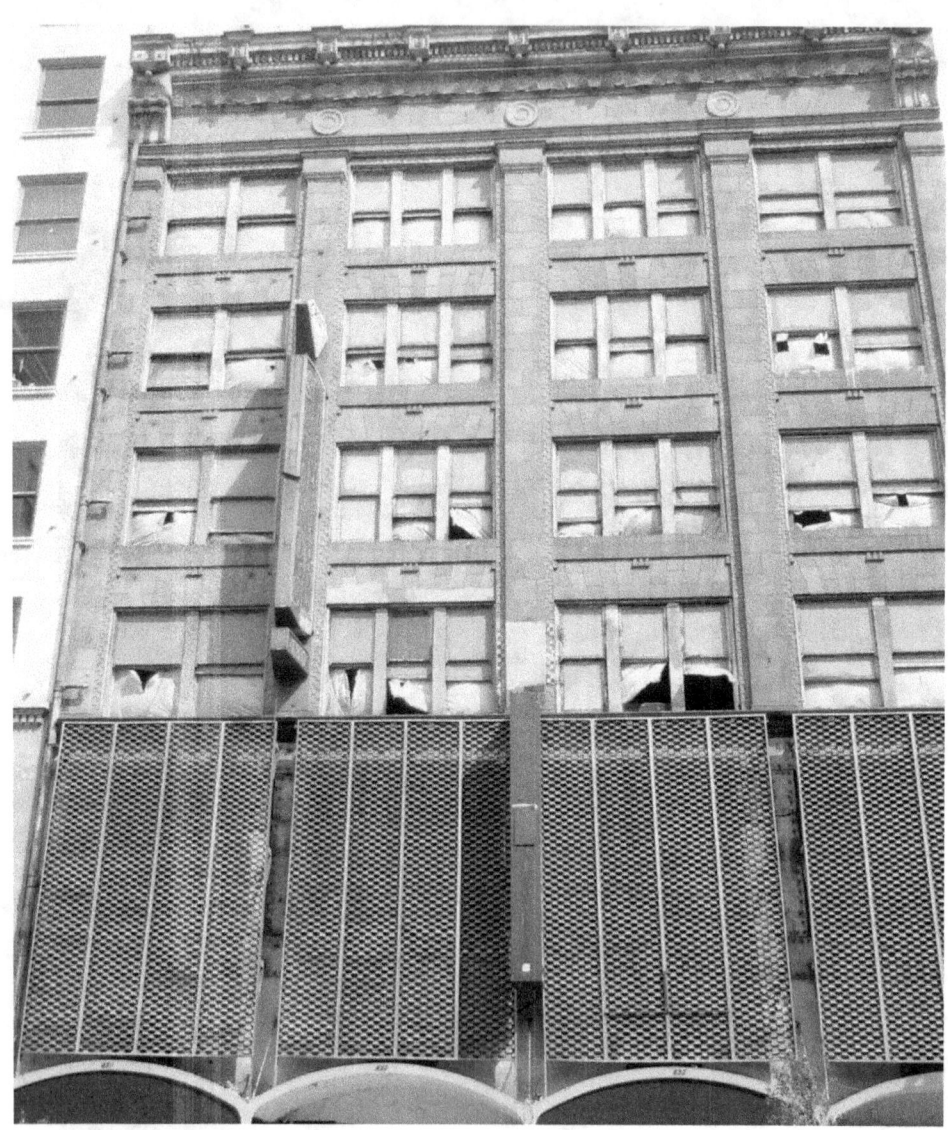

## J.J. NEWBERRY'S

449 S. Broadway

*Broadway's Metropolitan Building was completed in 1913. J.J. Newberry opened at this location in 1939 and closed in the mid-1990's. A bustling five-and-dime store in its heyday, this property now hosts a modern bargain apparel shop. Hints of former grandeur remain, like this terrazzo "Newberry's" sign on the pavement outside the Broadway entrance.*

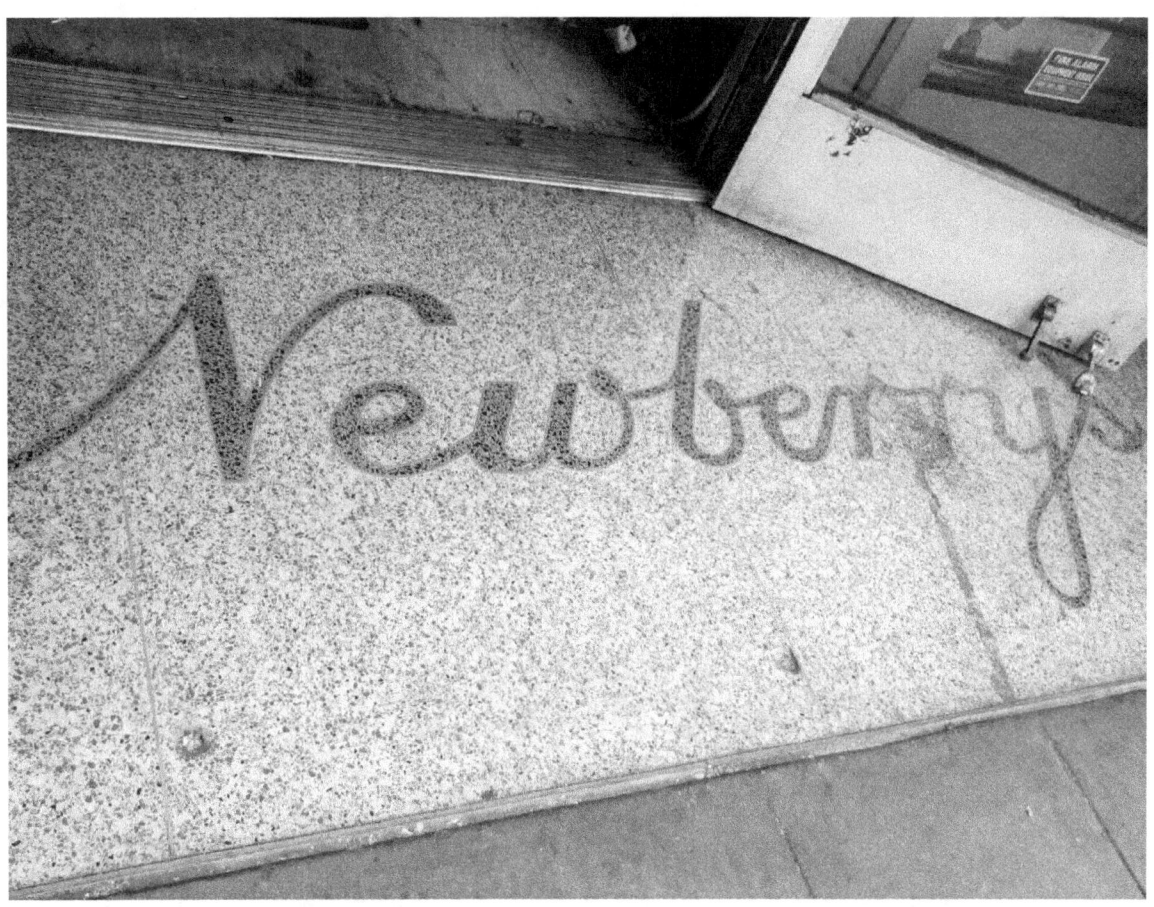

Broadway Between 5ᵗʰ & 6ᵗʰ Streets

*Moving south on Broadway, we get a better view of the KRKD radio tower.  Aimee Semple McPherson, whose organization once owned and operated KRKD, was the founder of the Foursquare Church.  Just visible on the left side of this photograph are the strong Art Deco lines of the old Roxie Theater façade at 518 S. Broadway.  The Roxie was late to the party; it opened in 1932, the last movie theater built on Broadway; the movie theater district was already moving to nearby Hollywood.*

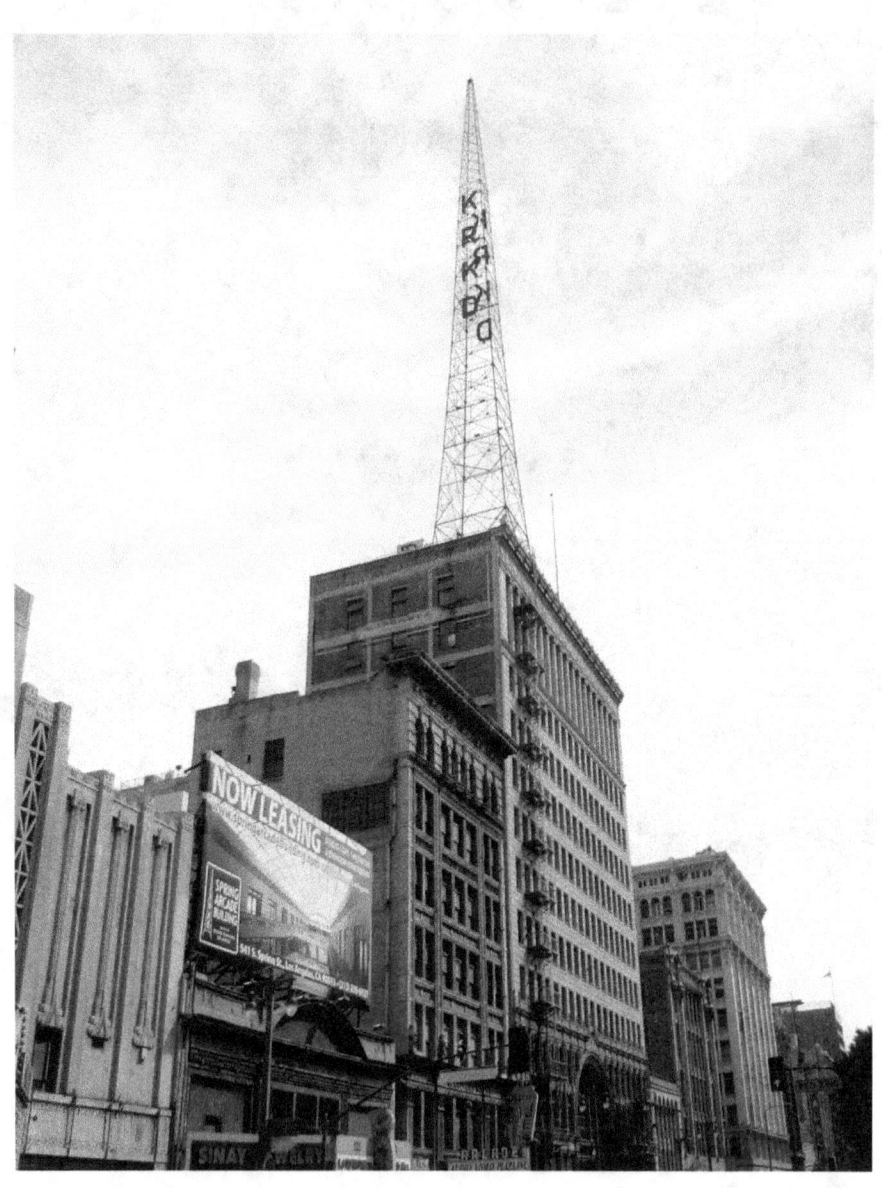

## BROADWAY ARCADE BUILDING

### 540 S. Broadway

The distinctive Broadway Arcade Building was completed in 1924 on a site once occupied by the Spring Street School. It is actually two steel office buildings connected by a central three-story arcade, magnificently lit by skylights. The arcade links Broadway and Spring Streets and is lined with retail spaces. Pedestrians can still navigate the arcade, but tenants like Western Union and an elegant barber shop have given way to stores hawking bargain clothing and electronics.

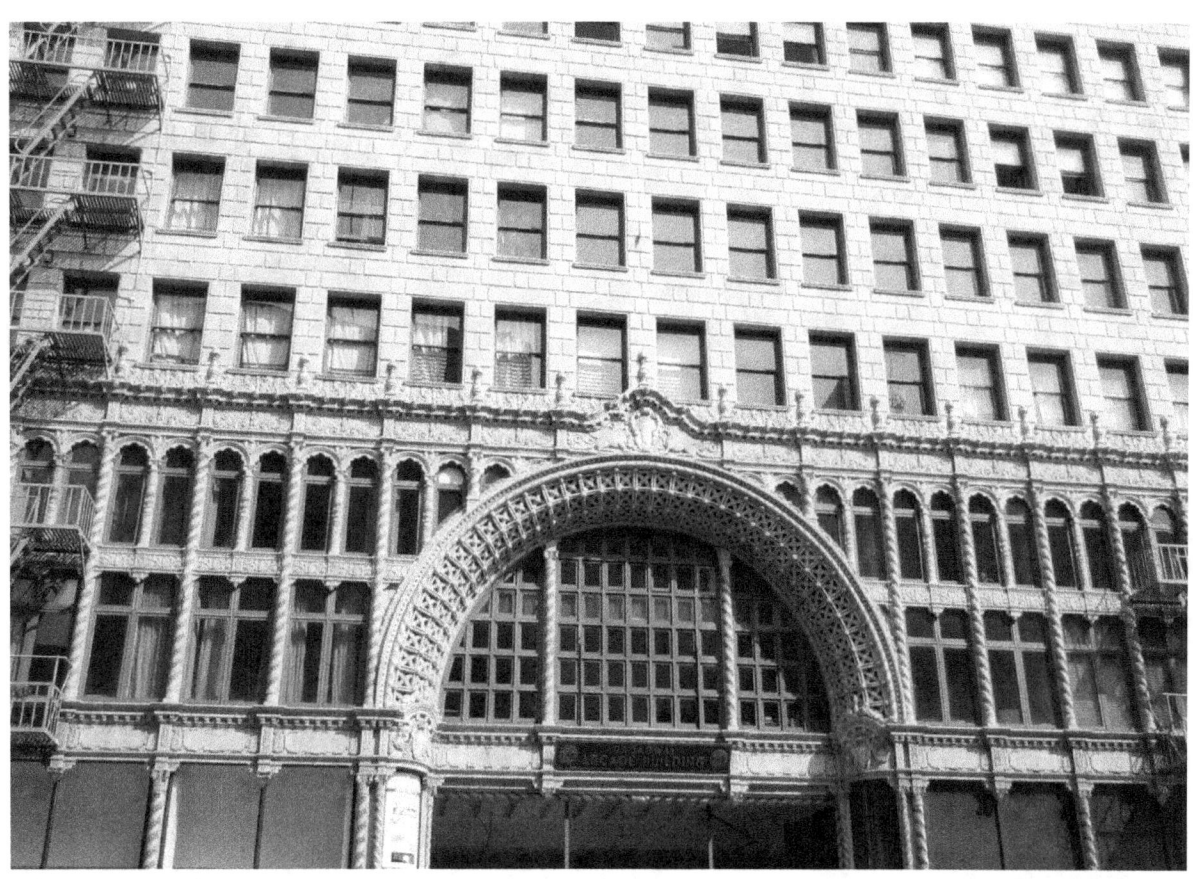

Broadway Between 6ᵗʰ & 7ᵗʰ Streets

*This photo shows how Broadway's vintage buildings, and those on Spring Street to the east, create a classic skyline.  Note the carved reliefs on all three foreground buildings.  This could be Los Angeles – or Chicago, or Manhattan – circa the early-to-mid 1900's, rather than a photo snapped in 2013.*

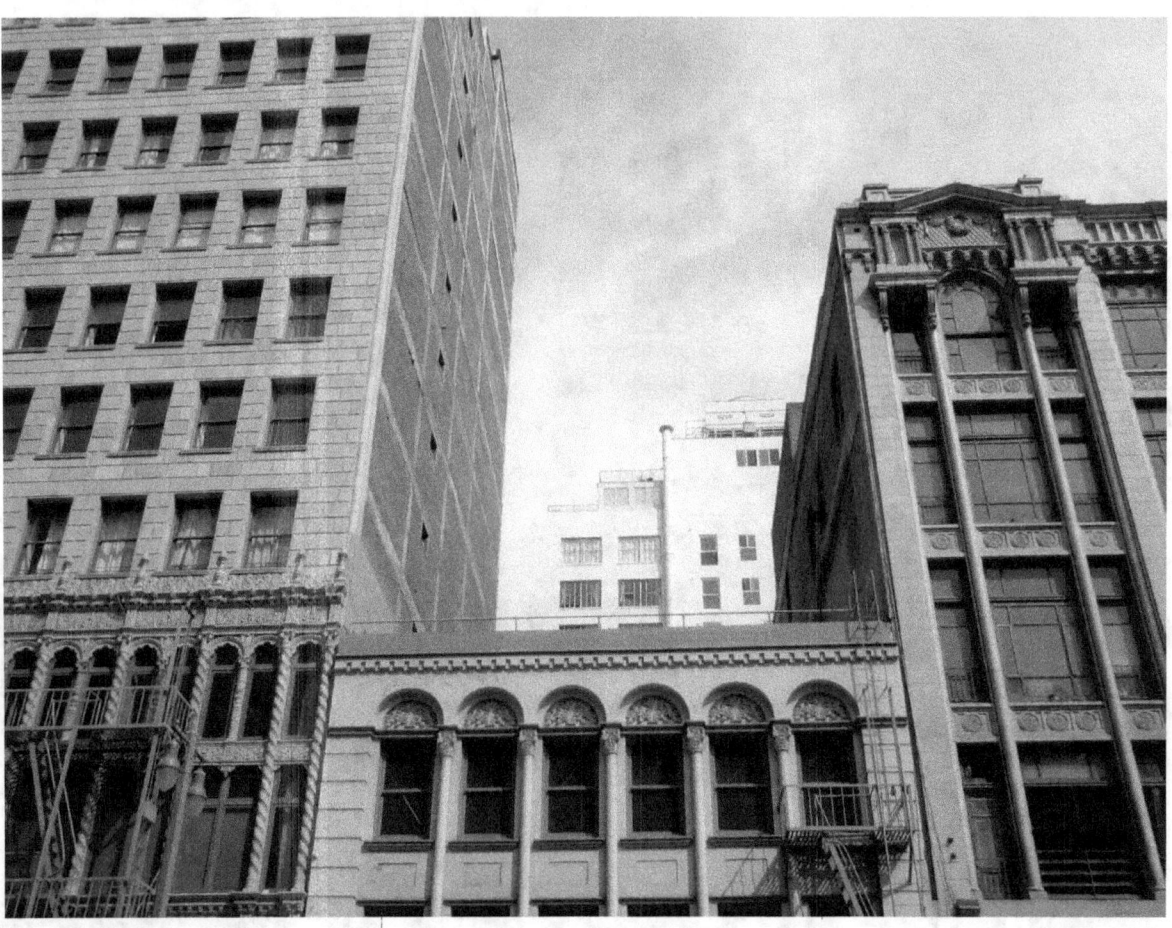

# BROADWAY

Broadway Between 6th & 7th Streets

*Along even the grittiest stretches of Broadway, expanses of lovely old terrazzo paving remain.  The small structure on the left is a magazine vendor's booth.  The marquee of the Los Angeles Theater (1931) is visible on the top center of this photo.*

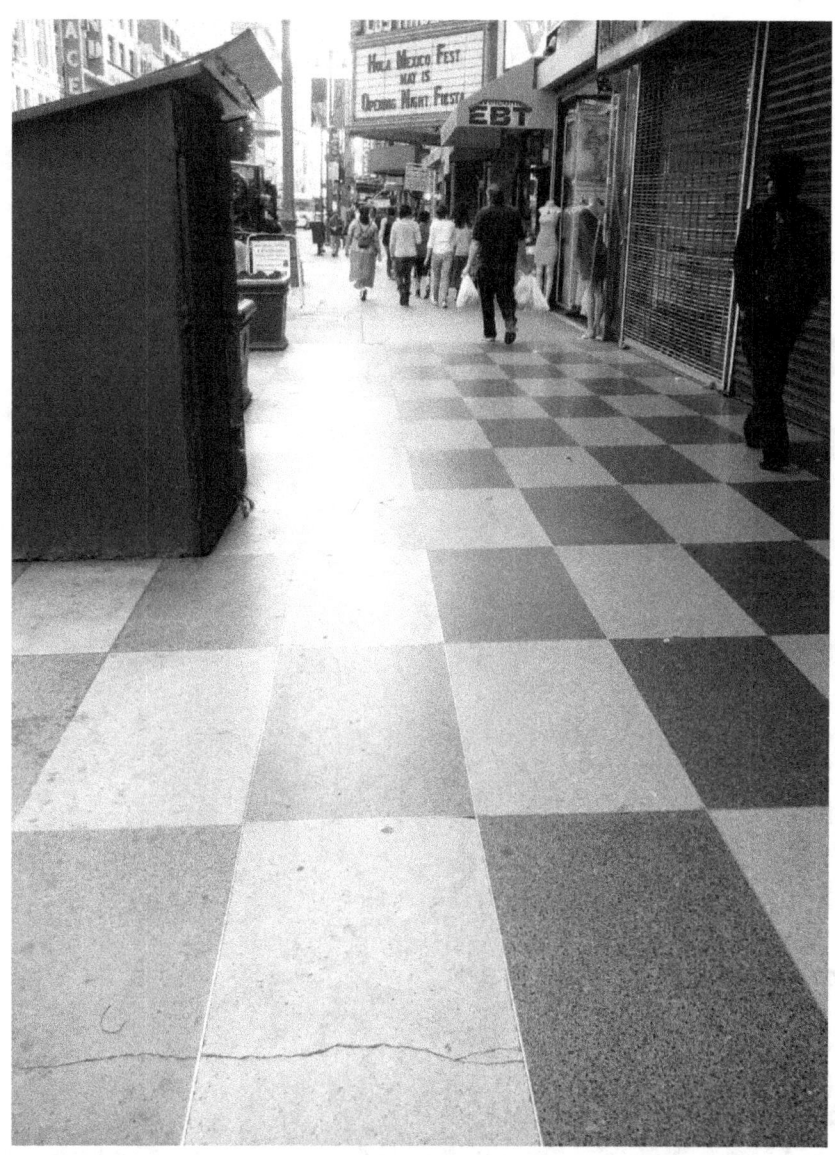

## LOS ANGELES THEATRE

615 S. Broadway

*The Los Angeles Theatre, one of the many movie palaces of Broadway's glory days, opened in 1931. It was the last word in glamour, from its elegant restaurant, smoking room, and grand staircase down to the pastel commodes. The Los Angeles Theatre is still glamorous but unfortunately is closed to the public; only attendees at special events can enjoy its beauty. Sidebar: Visitors to Disney California Adventure Park in Anaheim will note that DCA's Hyperion Theatre façade was based on the French Baroque façade of the Los Angeles Theatre.*

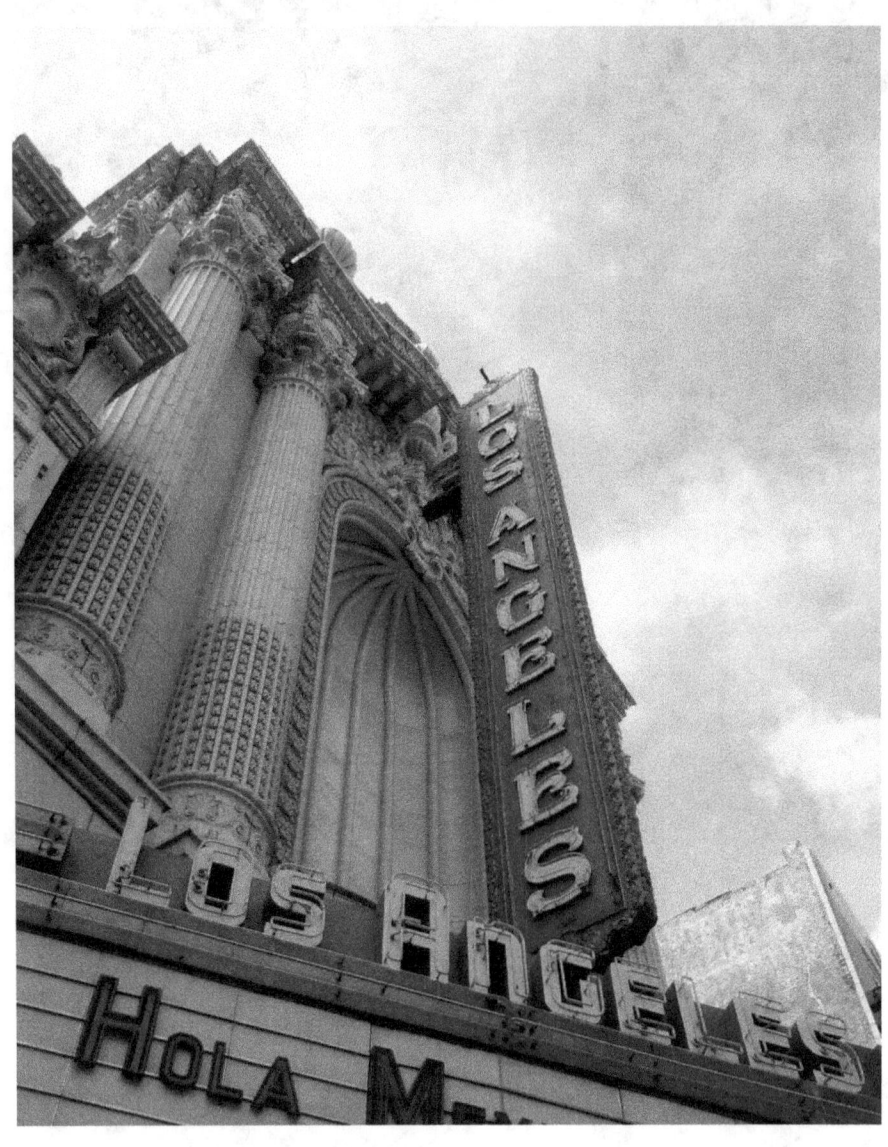

# BROADWAY

*Most of Broadway's ground-level spaces (those that aren't vacant) are occupied by fast food joints and bargain shops selling everything from electronics to perfumes and clothing. Below: Shoppers find deals on formal wear – like dresses for $99 – at one of Broadway's discount fashion outlets.*

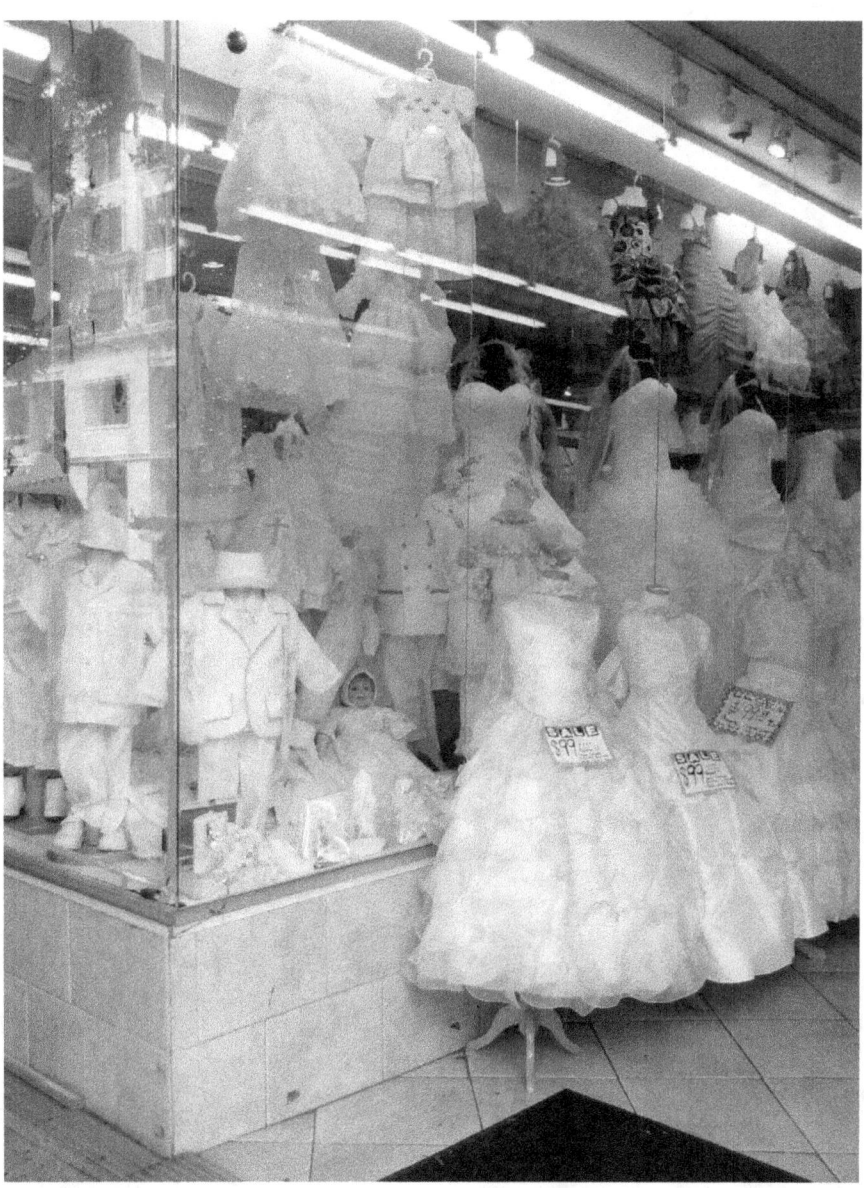

# TOWER THEATER

## 802 S. Broadway

*Pictured below: The exterior of the Tower Theater, with its stained glass and ornate terra cotta reliefs. The Tower opened in 1927, the first movie house in Los Angeles that could play "talkies" [Warner Brothers' "The Jazz Singer" premiered here]. Presently the property is used for film shoots (i.e. "The Prestige" [2006]), and church services. Note the broken windows in the structure to the right, covered with dark plastic.*

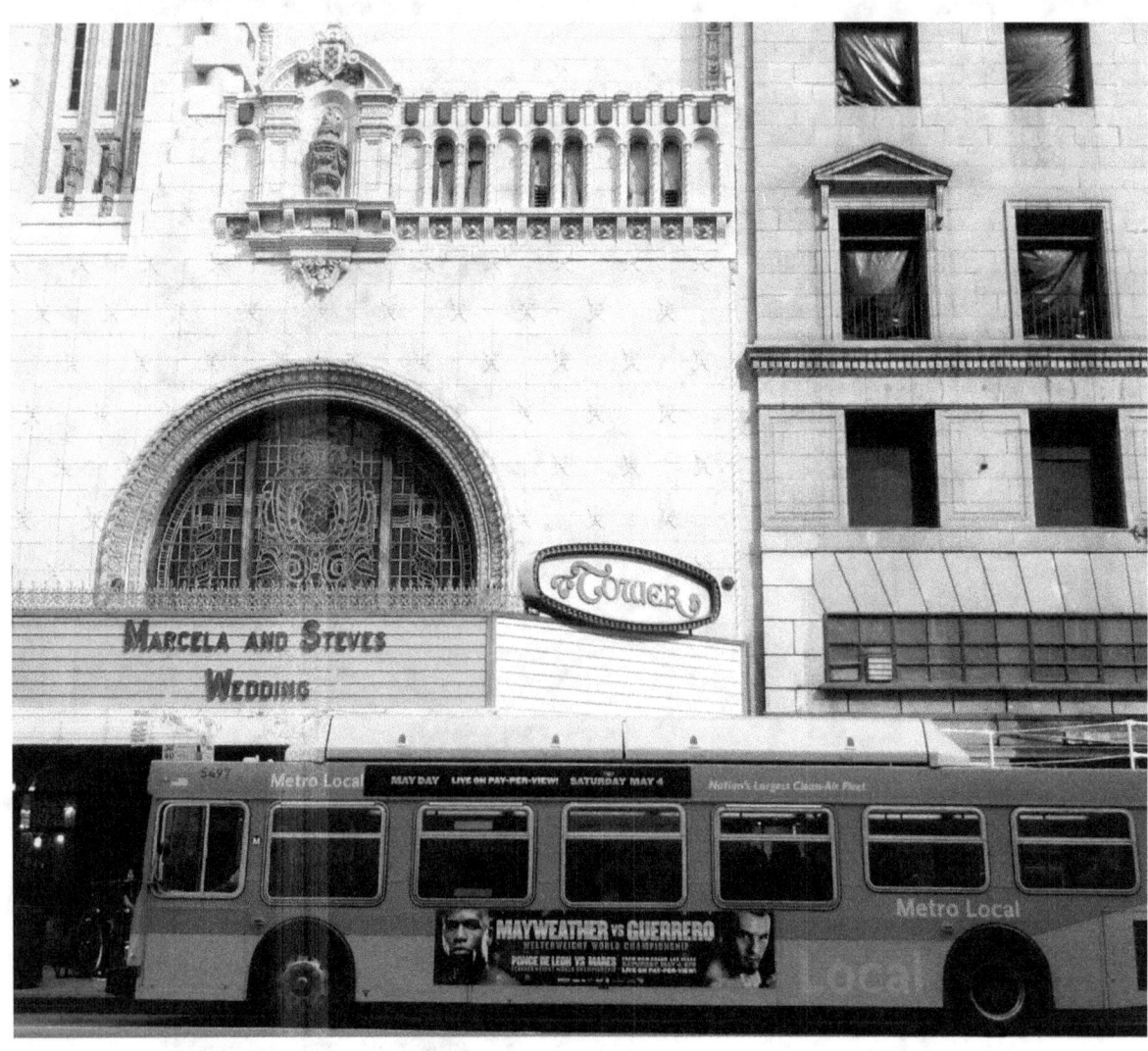

# BROADWAY & 8th

Broadway & 8th Street

*The north face of a handsome old structure on Broadway, near the corner of 8th, with its Ionic columns and ornamental rails, evokes the spirit of the early 1900's.*

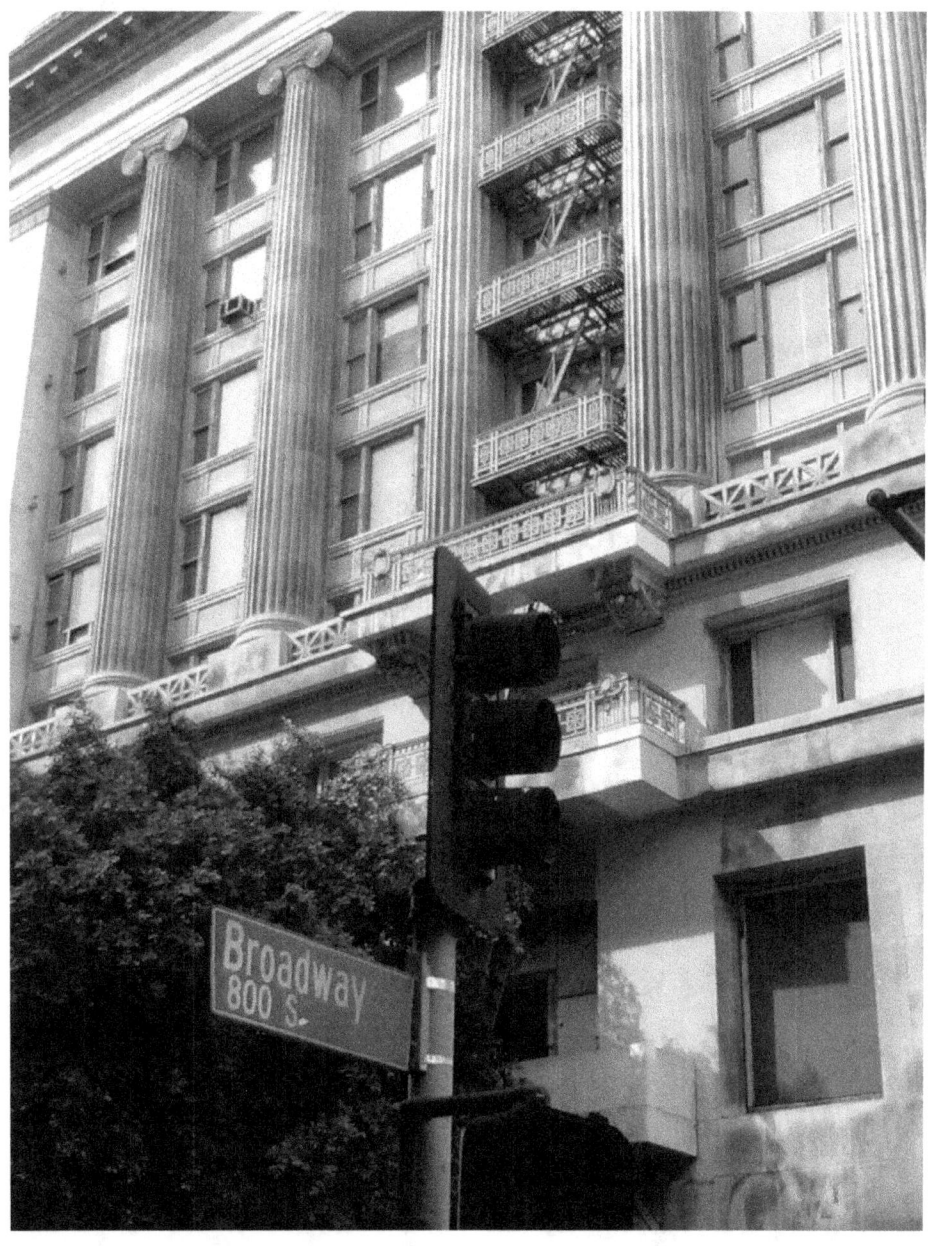

# WURLITZER BUILDING

818 S. Broadway

*Completed in 1924, the Wurlitzer Building's elaborate terra cotta ornamentation stops pedestrians in their tracks. In its heyday, Wurlitzer was billed as "The World's Largest Music House," selling musical instruments, the famous Wurlitzer organs used in movie houses, and, later, jukeboxes. Broadway was an excellent location for one of Wurlitzer's flagship buildings, in close proximity to a dozen movie palaces. Presently the Wurlitzer Building contains offices and retail spaces.*

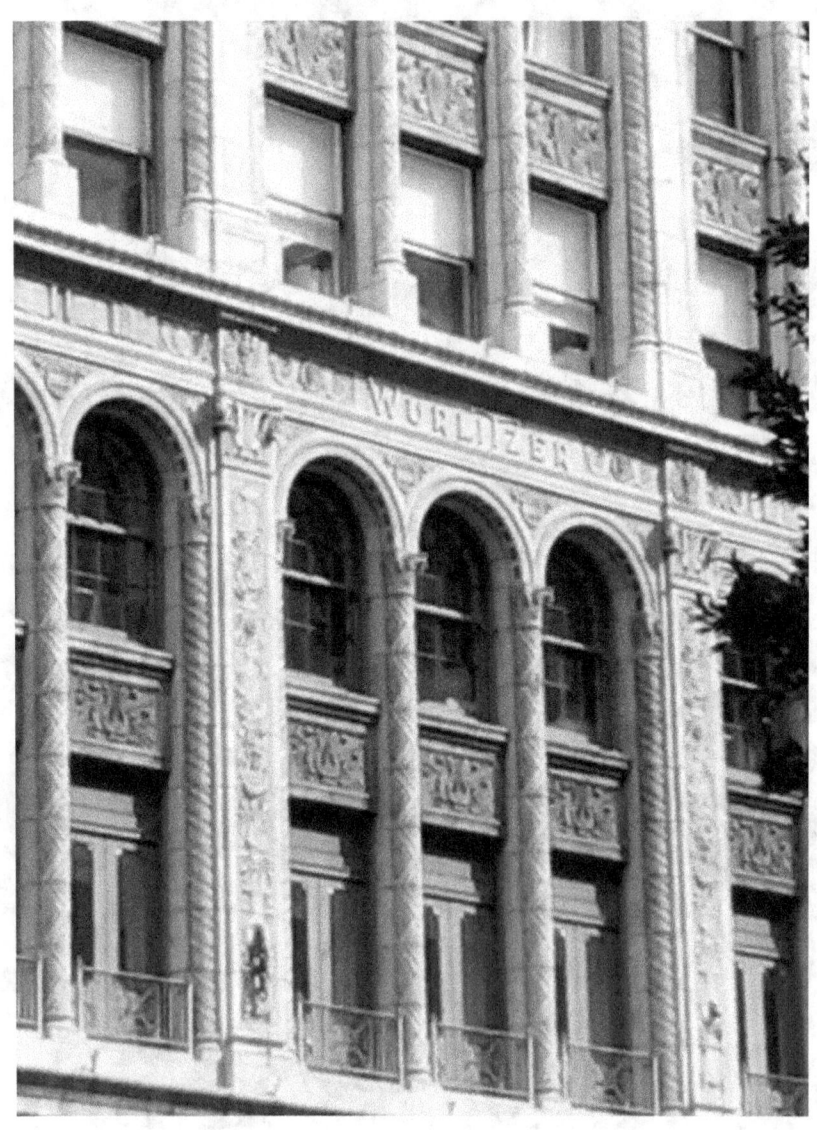

## ORPHEUM THEATRE

842 S. Broadway

*The Orpheum Theater opened in 1926 as part of the Orpheum vaudeville circuit. (Two blocks north, the Palace Theater at 630 S. Broadway was formerly known as the Orpheum (1911).) Still a gem, boasting an interior of plush reds and rich golds, the Orpheum continues to present theatrical productions and concerts, and hosts film and TV shoots, as well as special events. Everyone from Lena Horne to Jack Benny and Stevie Wonder has taken a turn on the Orpheum's stage.*

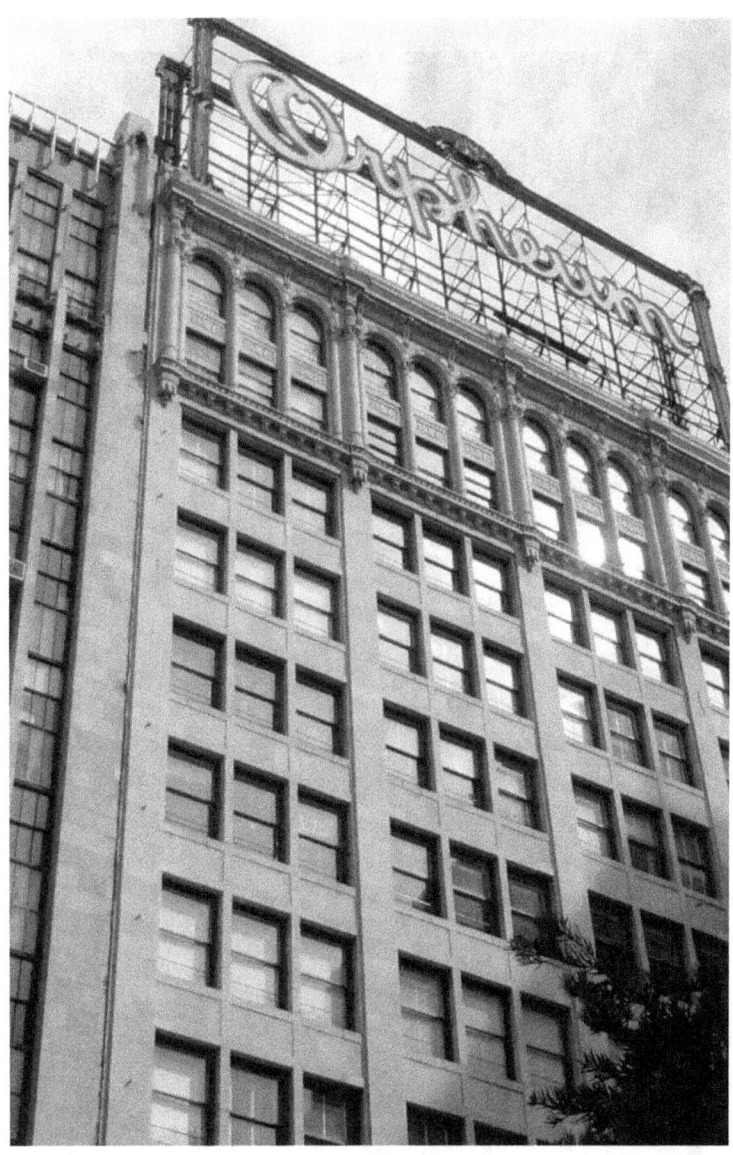

## EASTERN COLUMBIA BUILDING

849 S. Broadway

*Pictured below: Terrazzo pavement outside the main entrance to this beautiful 1930 Art Deco building on the northwest corner of Broadway & 9ᵗʰ Street. The blue-green terra cotta-clad structure with bright gold accents is an eye-catcher from blocks away, especially the neon "Eastern" signs on its clock tower. Its magnificent details, like this complex terrazzo pattern, mesmerize the pedestrian who examines it up-close. Constructed by the Eastern and Columbia Outfitter Companies, the Eastern Columbia Building now houses commercial and residential (condominium) spaces.*

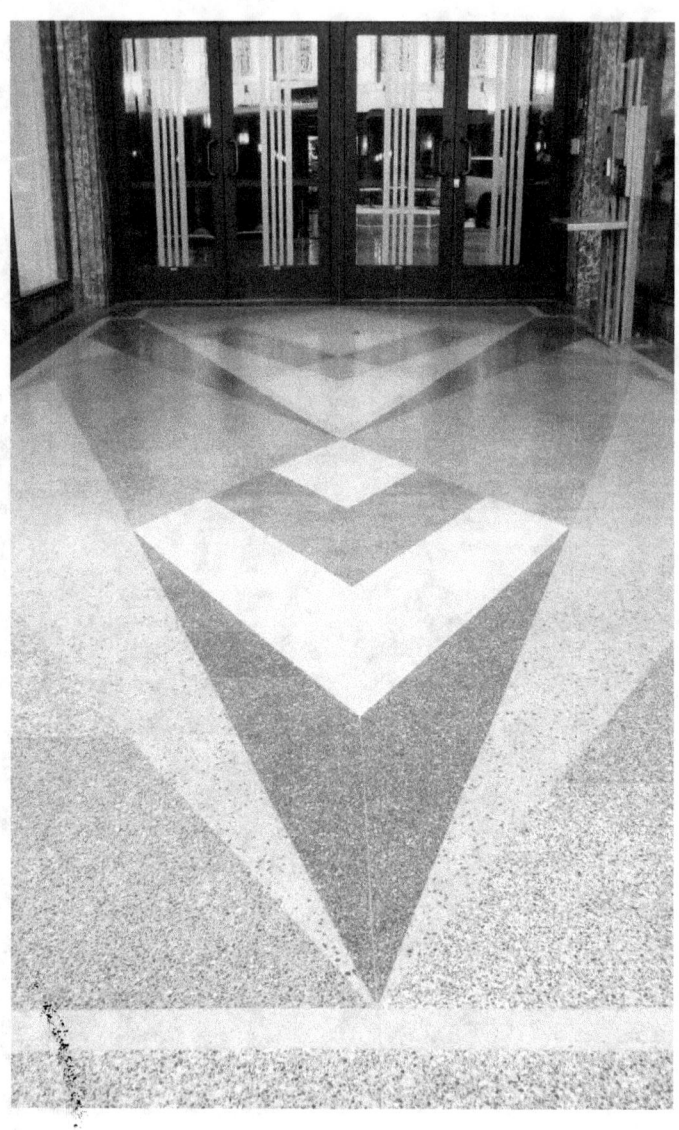

849 S. Broadway

*Above the terrazzo, the entrance vestibule is a beautiful Art Deco concordance of strong vertical lines, geometric shapes (like the repeated chevron motif), and an intricate gold sunburst.*

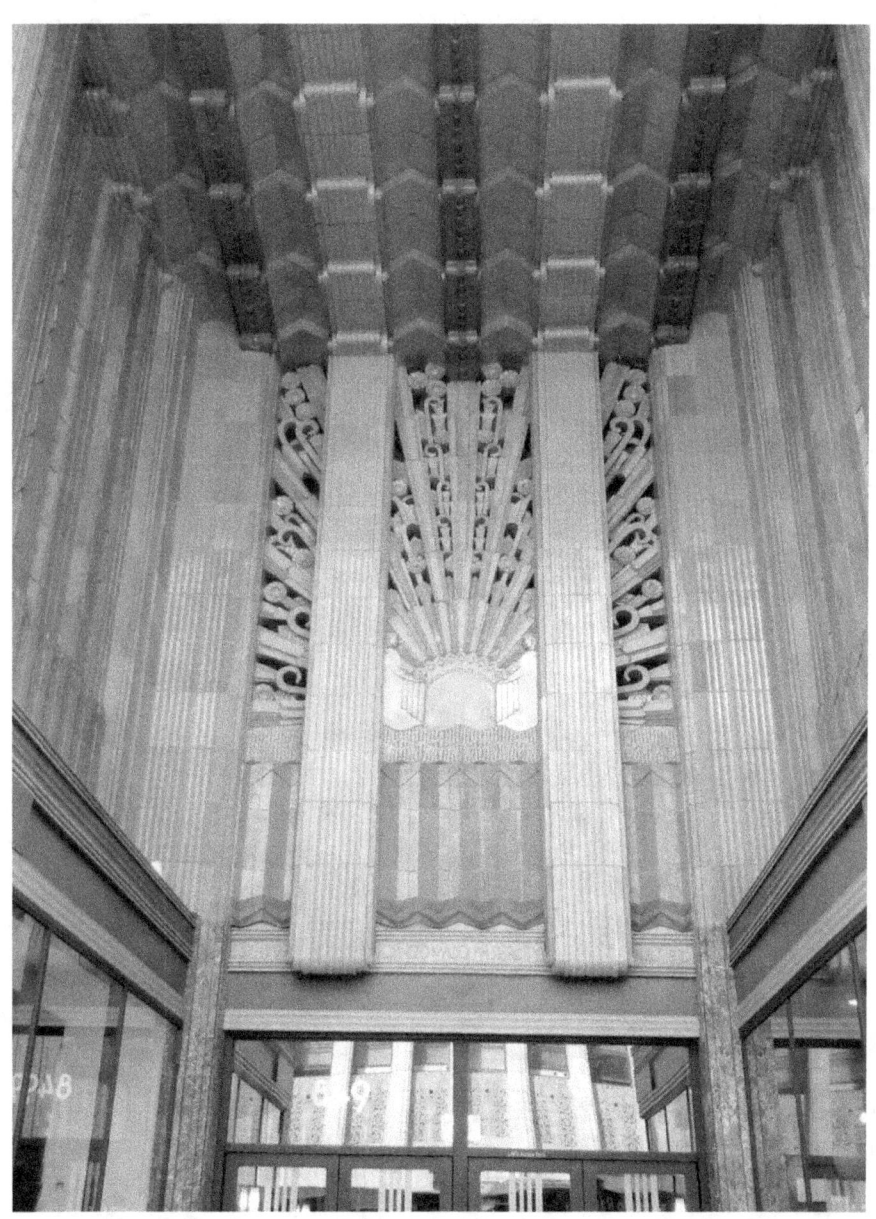

## TRINITY AUDITORIUM BUILDING

855 S. Grand Avenue

*Moving west from Broadway, one finds the Trinity Auditorium Building at the corner of Grand Avenue and 9th Street. The Trinity Auditorium opened in 1914 as a hotel, office space, and an auditorium. The auditorium on the top three floors, often used for religious services, was lit in part by light from windows in the ornate dome. In later years, the building became the Embassy Hotel, and still later it became a dorm; lucky USC students in the 1980's lived on the premises. The present owners plan to develop it into the Empire Hotel, with restaurants and a glass-bottomed swimming pool on the roof.*

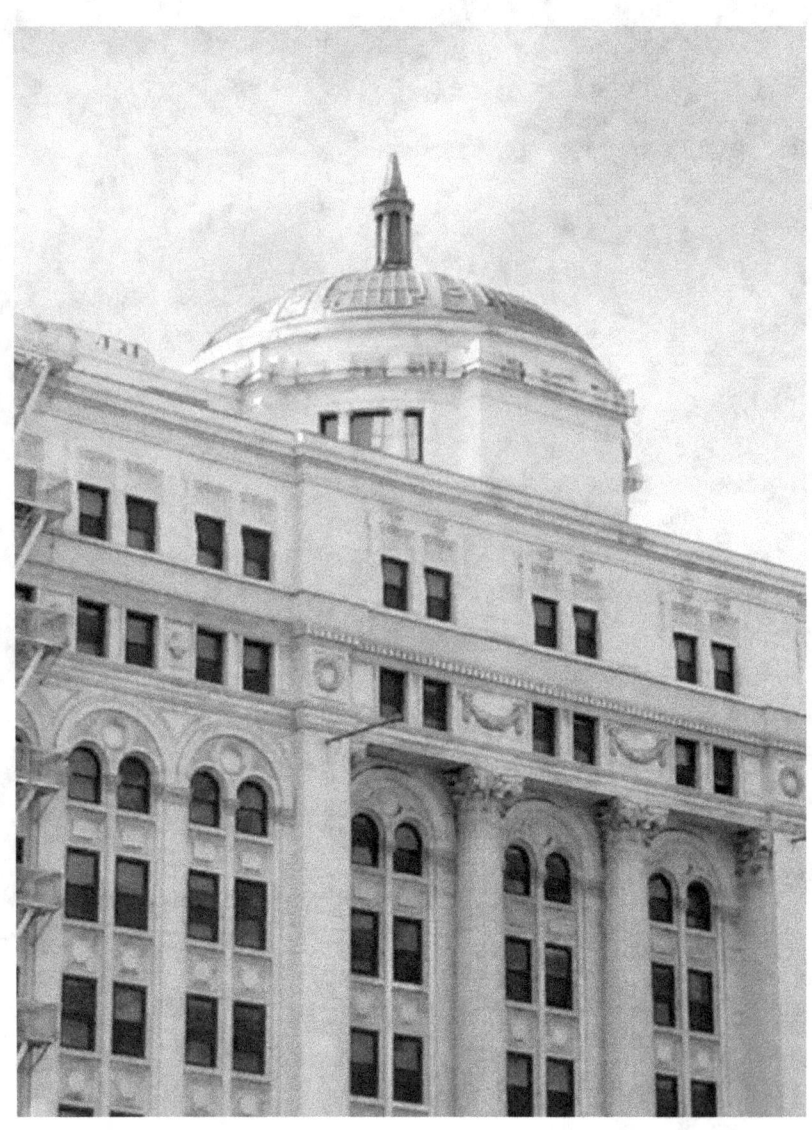

# TRINITY AUDITORIUM BUILDING

855 S. Grand Avenue

*Grand & 9ᵗʰ Steet is one of many nexus points in Los Angeles where the historic eastern core transitions to the more modern western financial district. Note the Trinity Auditorium Building (left) and the historic Stillwell Hotel (right) bracketing the contemporary skyscraper in the center of the photograph. The Stillwell building (838 S. Grand Avenue) opened in 1912.*

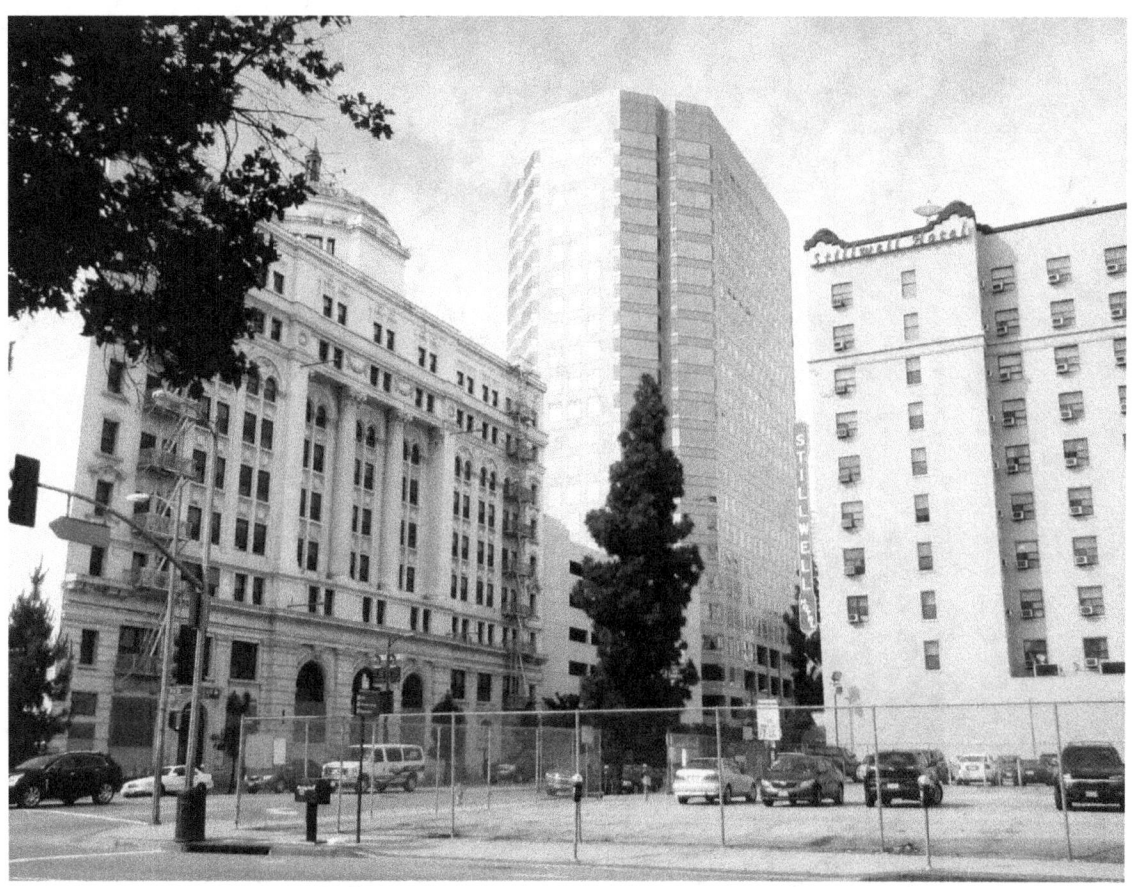

# FASHION INSTITUE OF DESIGN & MERCHANDISING (F.I.D.M.) – L.A. CAMPUS

919 S. Grand Avenue

*Los Angeles is a fashion capital of the United States, second only to New York City. Aspiring fashion designers and merchandisers earn associate and bachelor's degrees at the F.I.D.M.'s Los Angeles campus, which was founded in 1969 and first established on 8ᵗʰ Street, in the heart of the garment district. The present campus on Grand Avenue opened in 1990. Ideally located near L.A.'s garment district and a stone's throw from Hollywood and numerous film and TV studios, the handsome grounds of F.I.D.M. abut Grand Hope Park, complete with palm trees, grassy lawns, and benches.*

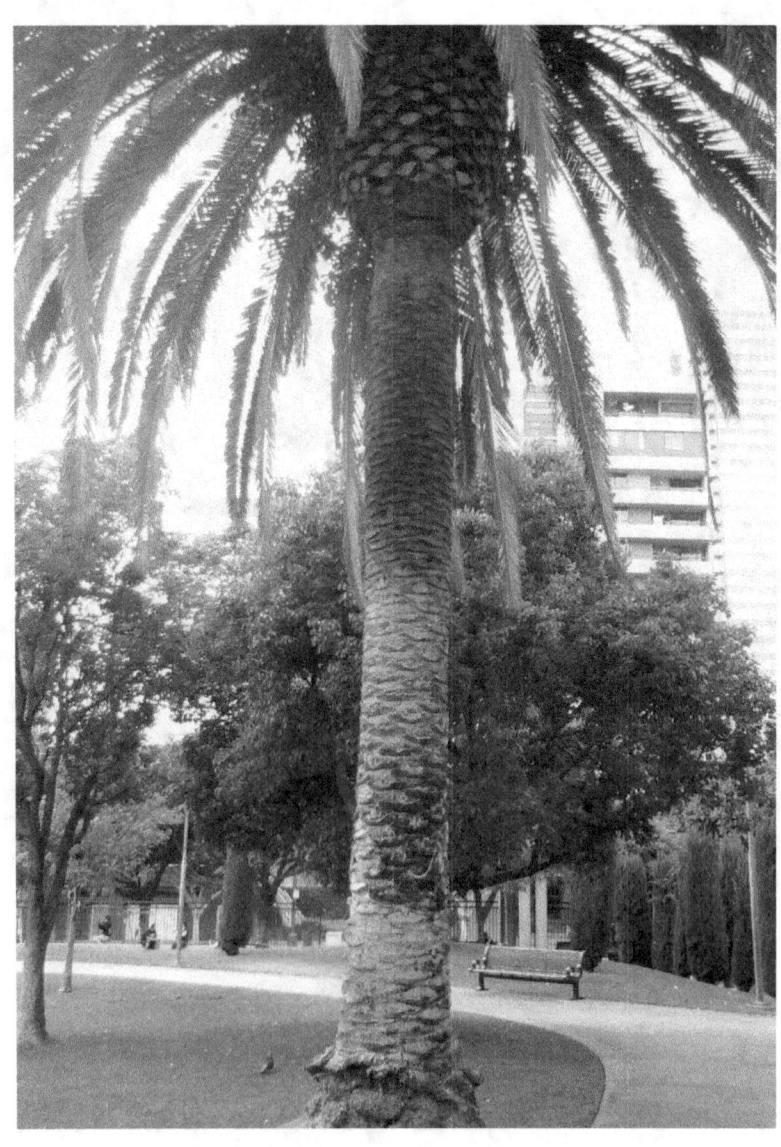

## GRAND HOPE PARK

Between Grand & Hope at 9th Street

*The whimsical clock tower anchoring the northwest corner of the FIDM campus serves as the entrance to Grand Hope Park. The park opened almost twenty years ago, in 1994. A revitalized downtown has grown up around the park – note the modern apartment buildings to the left, center, and right behind the tower, and the financial building in the distance at the top right of the photo.*

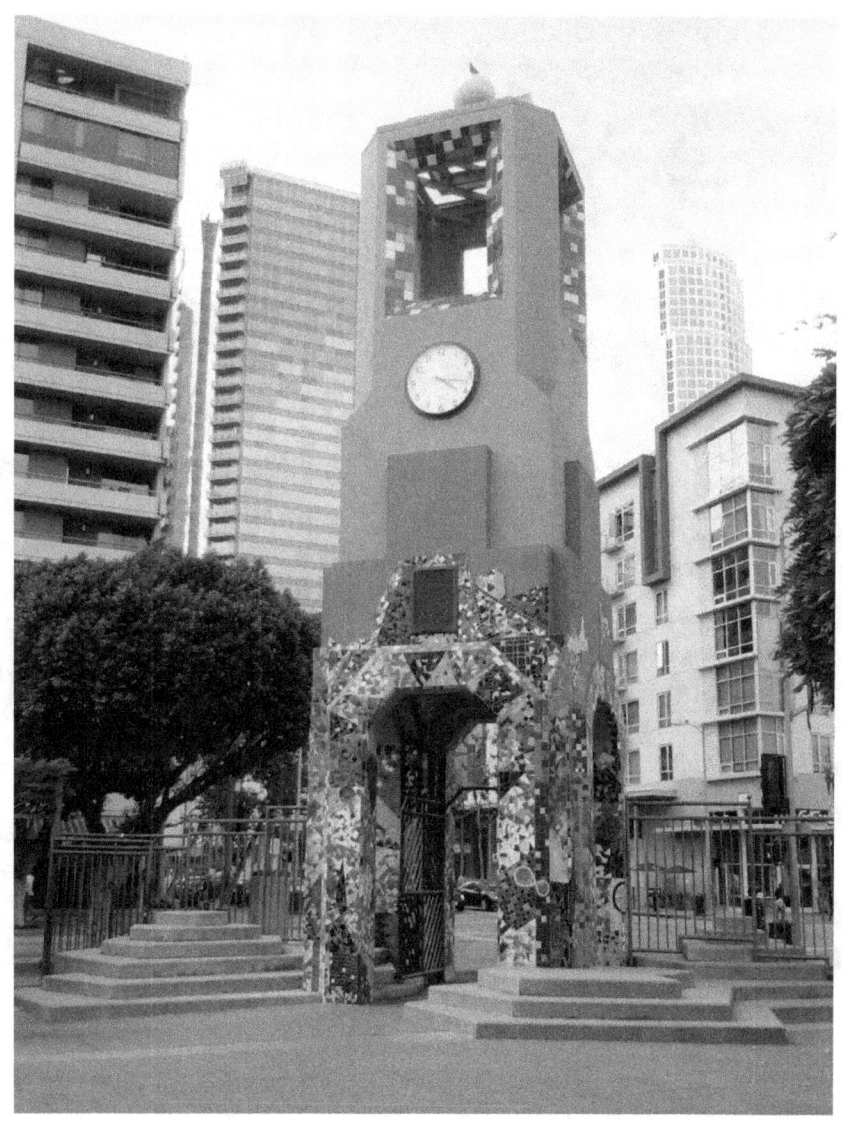

9th Street & Hope Street

*A view looking west on 9th Street, from the corner of 9th & Hope. The southwestern region of downtown Los Angeles is presently the most modern, most prosperous, and – in general – the safest section of the downtown area. Brand new high-rise and low-rise apartment complexes share the tree-shaded streets with modern financial buildings. In the late 1800's and early 1900's, this land was largely residential, a patchwork of fine Victorians, small homes, apartment houses, hotels, and churches.*

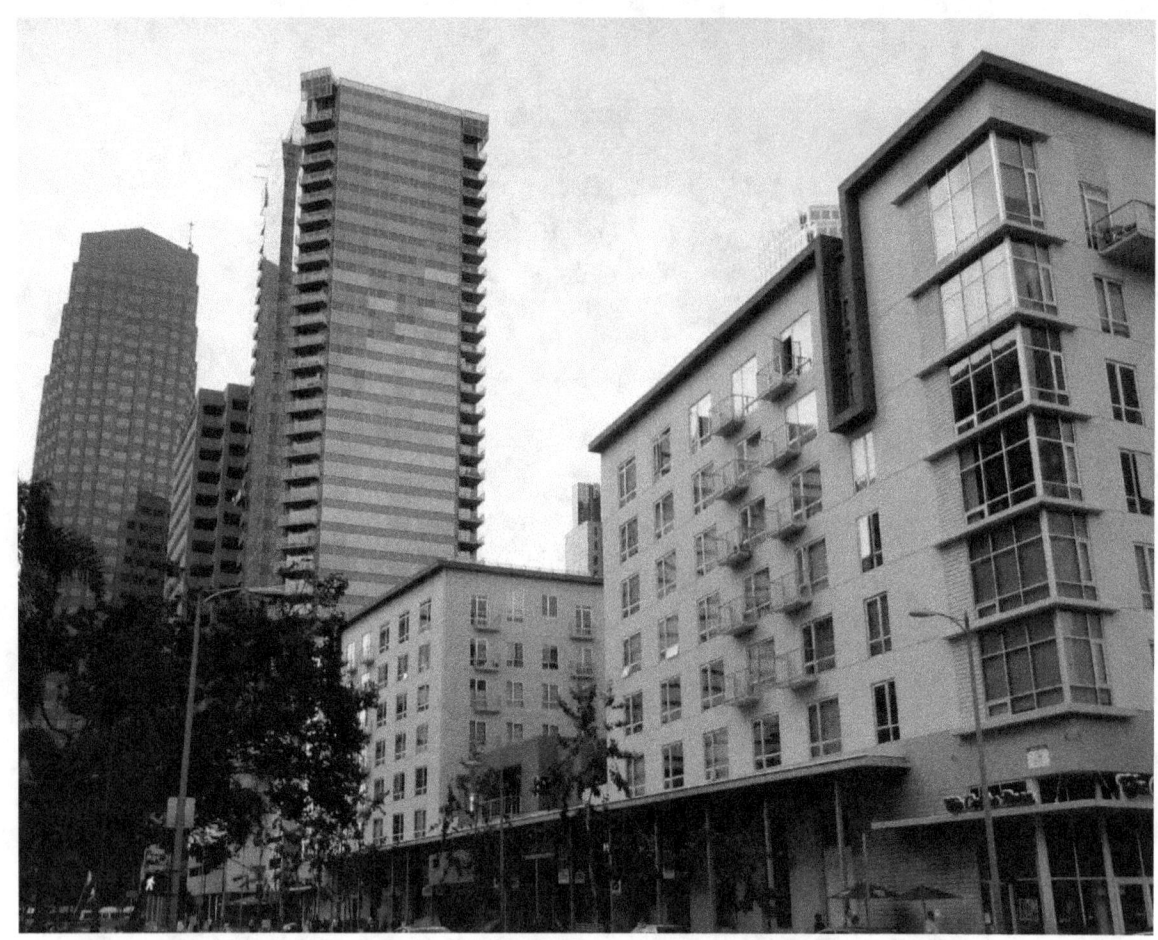

## WATERMARKE TOWER

705 W. 9ᵗʰ Street

*Continuing north to 9ᵗʰ Street and Flower Street, we see the WaterMarke Tower, a new residential skyscraper. Completed in 2010, the WaterMarke rents luxury apartments starting at $3,000 per month and up for a one-bedroom unit. We are not on Broadway anymore!*

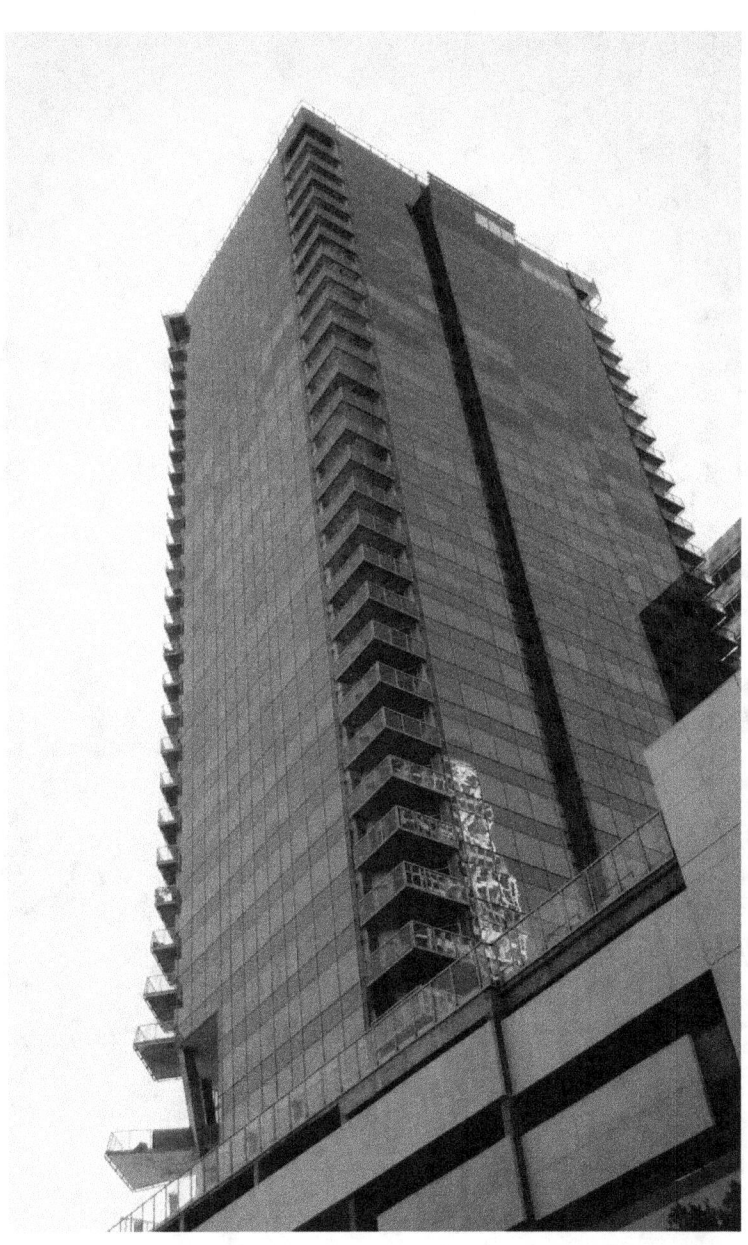

## FIGUEROA STREET & 9th STREET

Figueroa Street & 9th Street

*A view of the financial district, looking north on Figueroa Street at 9th Street.  The round crown of the U.S. Bank Tower is just visible in the distance on the center right portion of this photograph.  A taxi cab parked at the curb (bottom left) is waiting to be engaged by a business person or tourist.*

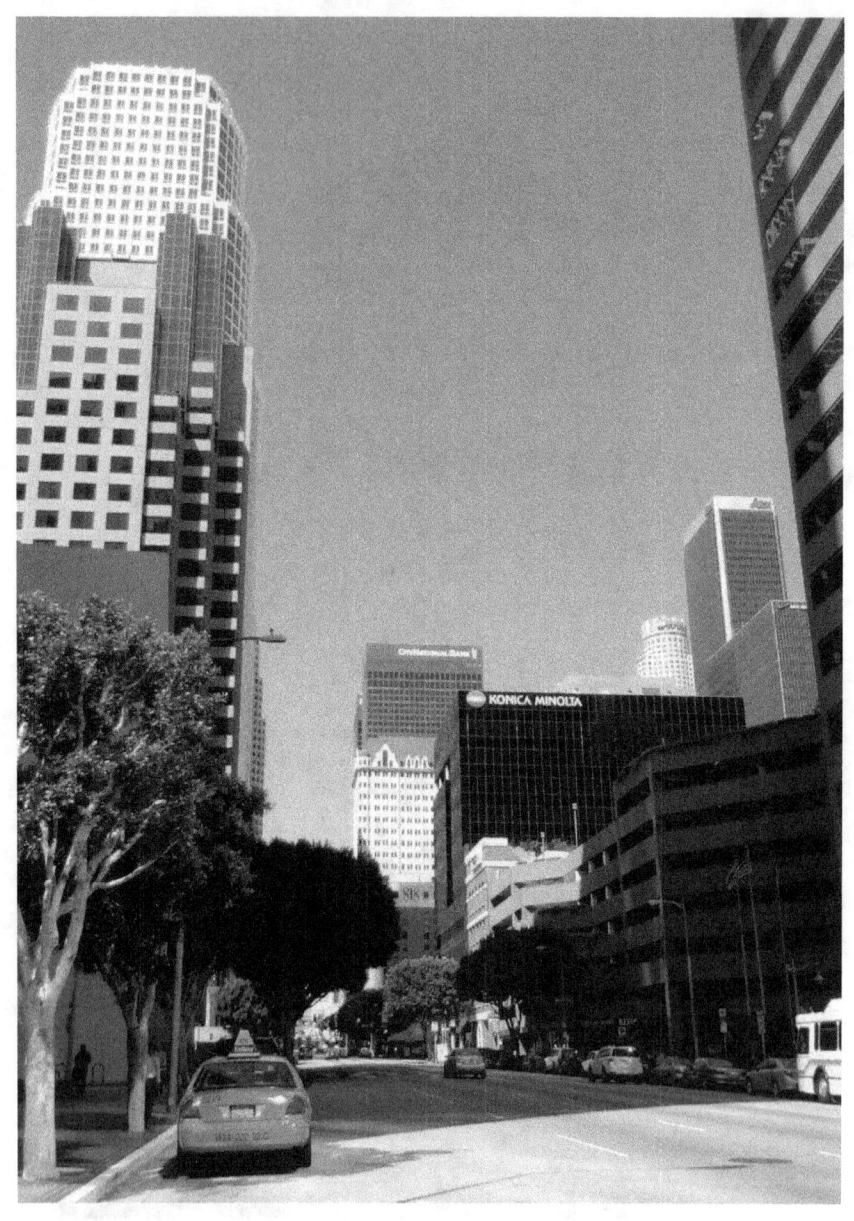

## THE ORIGINAL PANTRY

877 S. Figueroa Street

*It opened in 1924 and hasn't closed its doors since. Open 24 hours a day, the famous Original Pantry serves up simple meals (cash only) to convention-goers and business people in the financial district, and a meal here is an absolute must for visitors to L.A..*

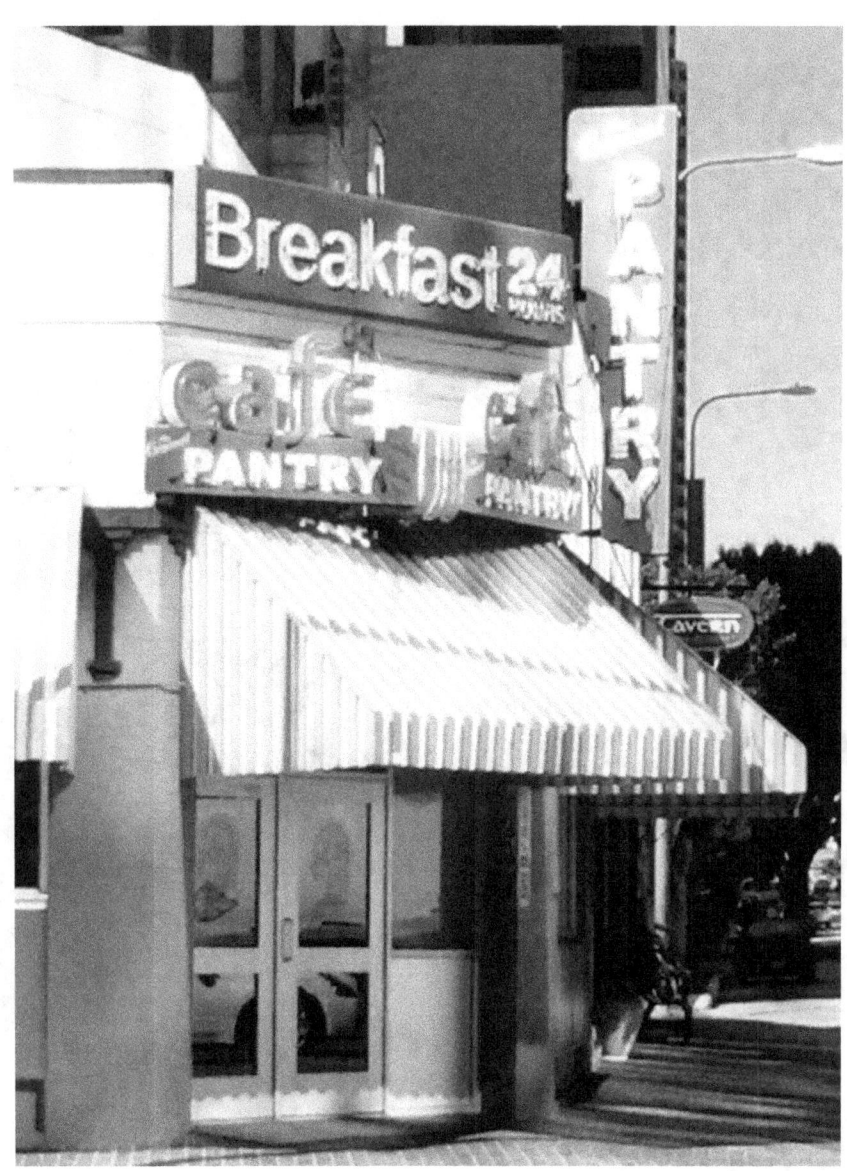

## THE FIGUEROA HOTEL

939 S. Figueroa Street

*This picturesque hotel on the northwest corner of Figueroa Street and Olympic opened in 1925 and started life as a Y.W.C.A. (Young Women's Christian Association). It is known as the Figueroa Hotel, and the Hotel Figueroa, and simply the Figueroa, depending on whom you ask or which sign you read. The architecture and décor has a Moroccan flavor. Sometimes celebs drop by for events or to chill.*

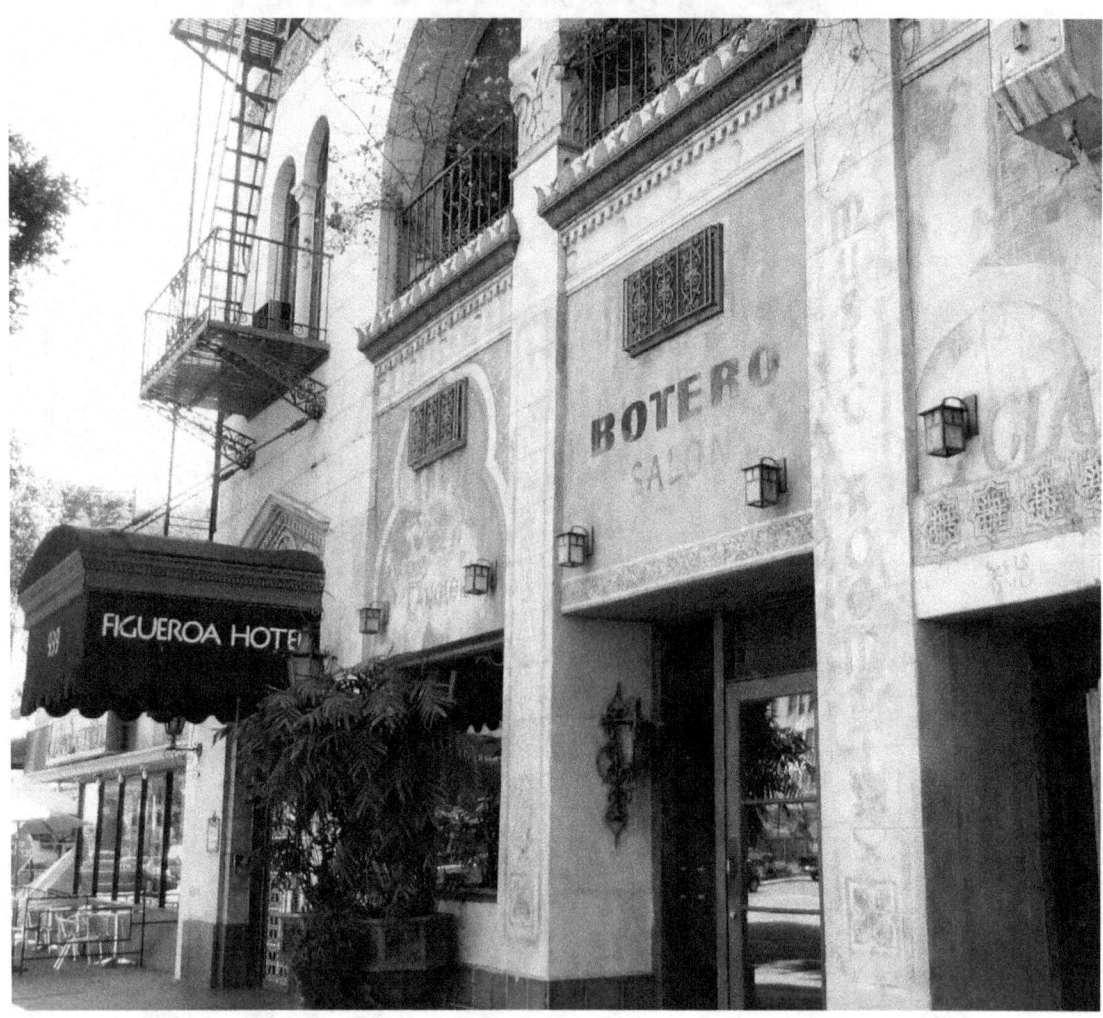

# OLYMPIC BOULEVARD & FIGUEROA STREET

Olympic & Figueroa

*The view: Looking south along Olympic from Figueroa Street. From this perspective, the Figueroa Hotel is on the left of the photographer, out of frame, on the northwest corner of the intersection. The Grammy Museum and L.A. Live complex are out of frame on the right, on the southwest corner. This view shows how modern buildings on the west side of downtown quickly give way to older buildings on the east side, in the distance. Olympic Boulevard, originally 10ᵗʰ Street, was rechristened in 1932 in honor of L.A.'s hosting of the 1932 Olympics.*

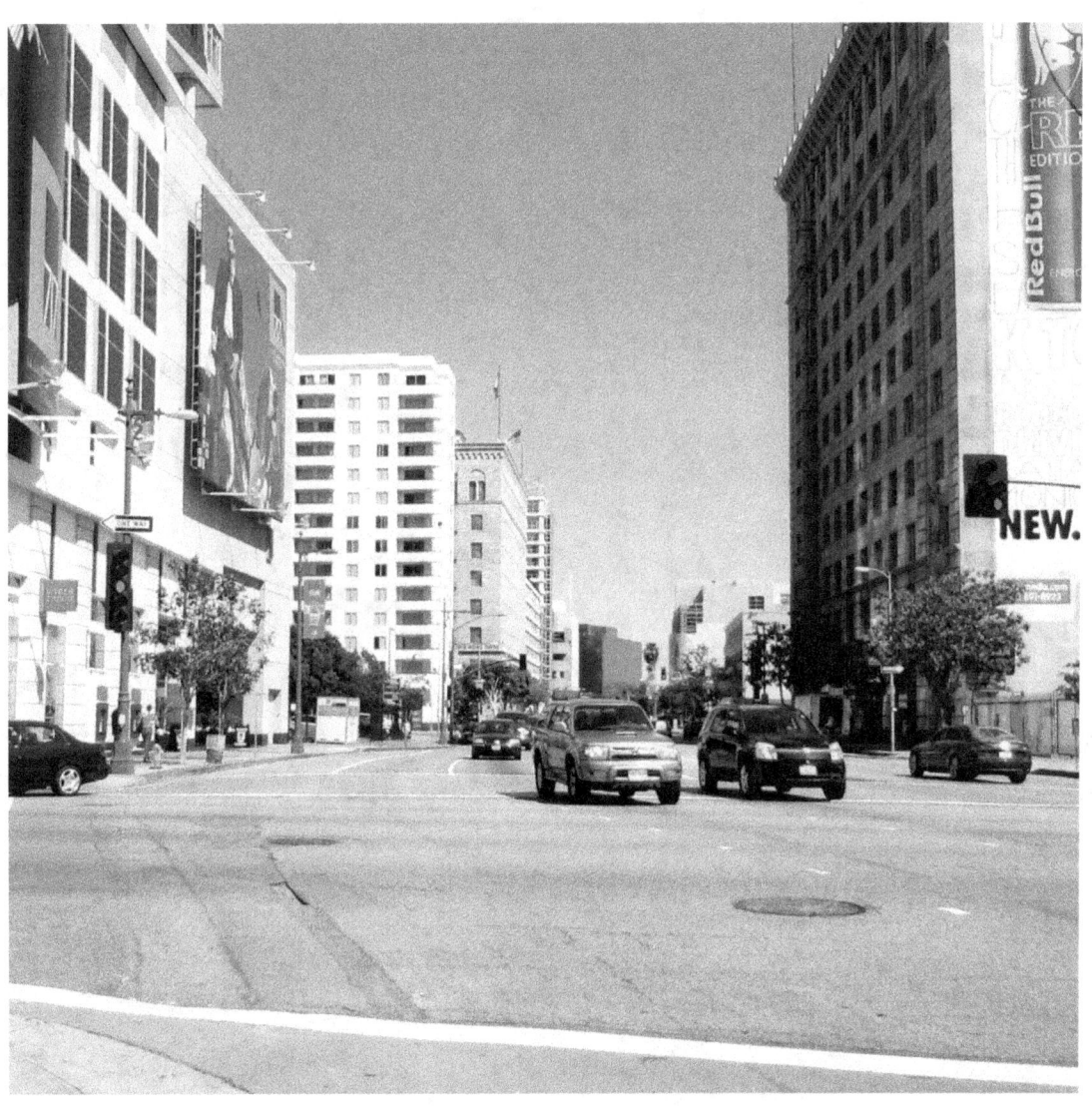

# FIGUEROA STREET & OLYMPIC BOULEVARD

Figueroa & Olympic

*Turning 90 degrees, looking north along Figueroa Street at Olympic.  The Figueroa Hotel is clearly visible on the left side of the photo.  Large buildings along this stretch of Figueroa Street are often plastered with colorful advertisements, in this case for a summer movie (on the walls of the Figueroa Hotel, left) and for luxury apartments (bottom right of photo).*

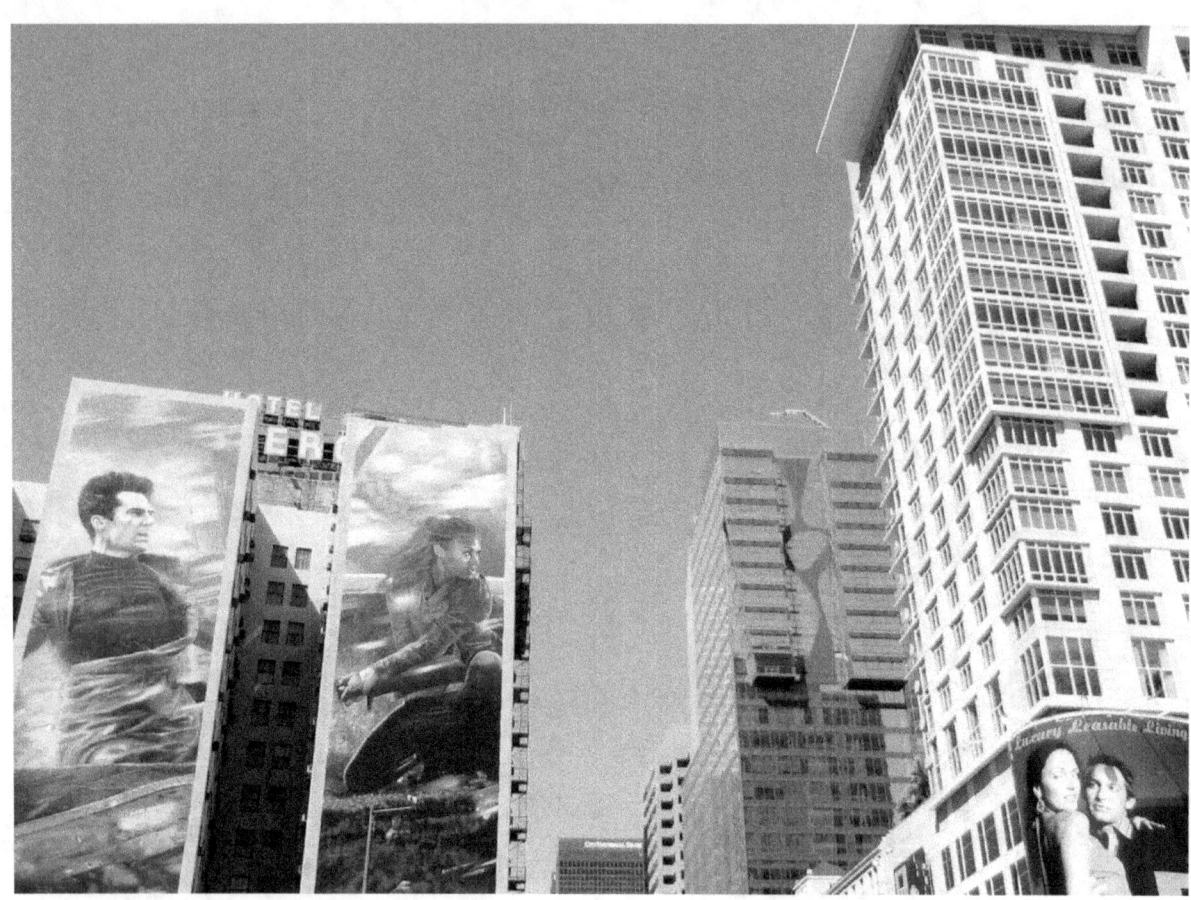

## GRAMMY MUSEUM

800 W. Olympic Boulevard

*In the last decade, a great deal of time, vision, and funding has been expended to revitalize the downtown event corridor. A major part of the initiative included developing the L.A. Live complex; the Grammy Museum opened in 2008, and occupies L.A. Live's northeast corner. Far from a dusty old museum, this is a treasure trove of vibrant, music-related events, performances, and artifacts.*

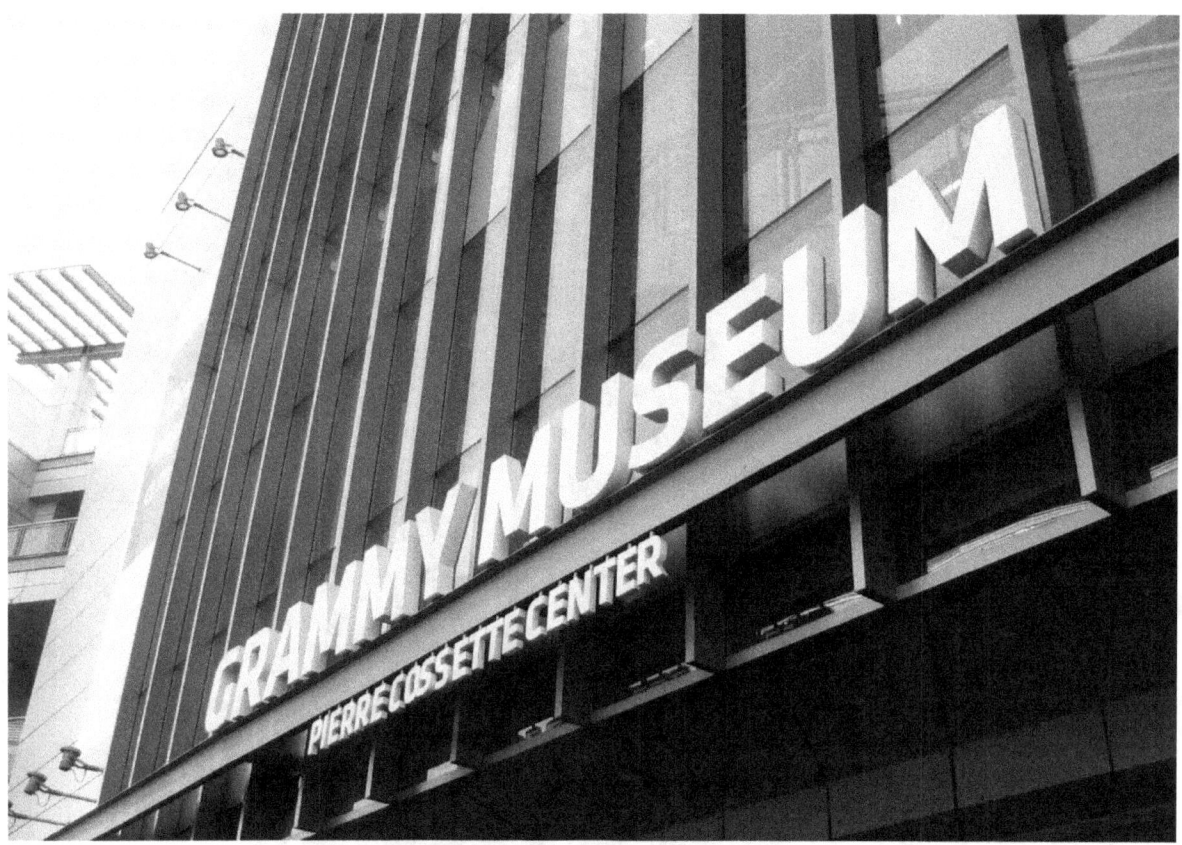

# L.A. LIVE

Figueroa Street / Olympic Boulevard & 11ᵗʰ Street

*A jagged corner of the ESPN building at L.A. Live, the multi-billion dollar entertainment complex that opened near the Staples Center in 2007. L.A. Live features restaurants, movie theaters, hotels, a museum, the Nokia Theatre and Plaza, and various other entertainment venues, including the restaurant and studio sponsored by ESPN.*

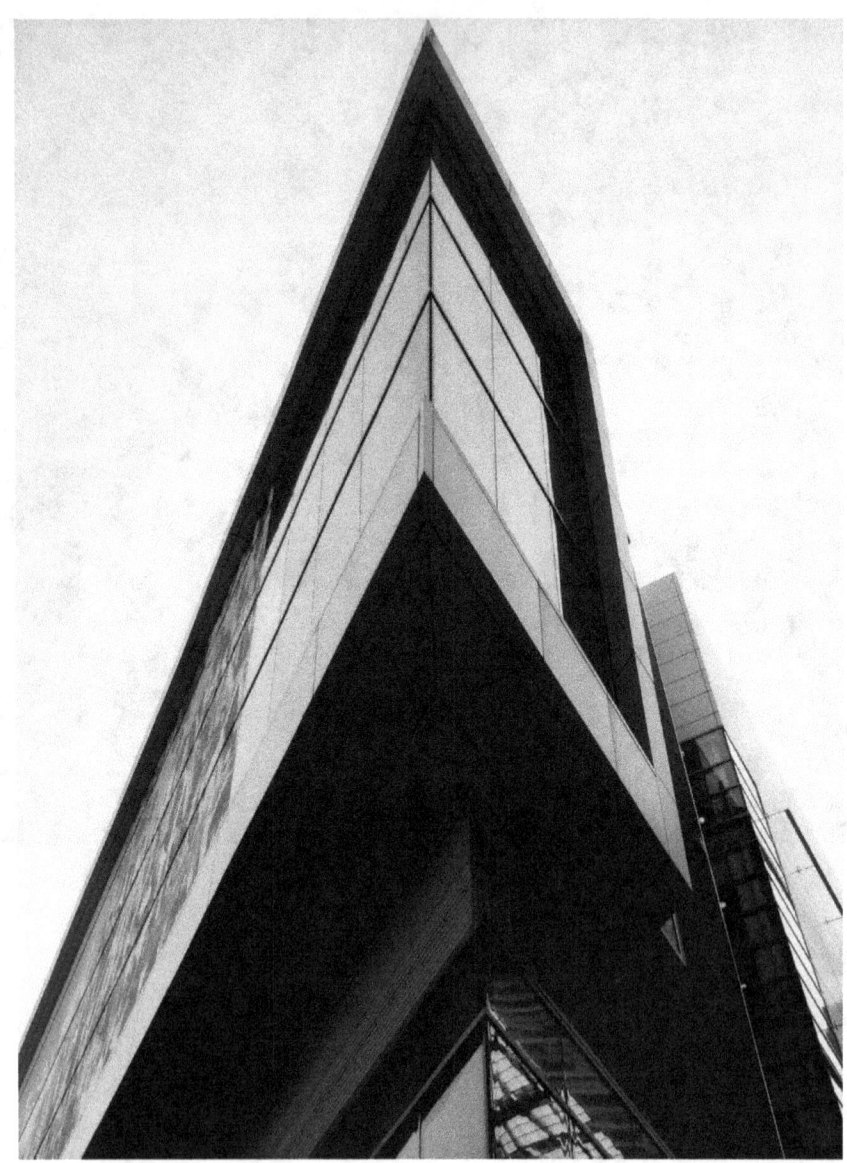

# L.A. LIVE

Figueroa Street / Olympic Boulevard & 11 Street

*Café-style dining at L.A. Live.*

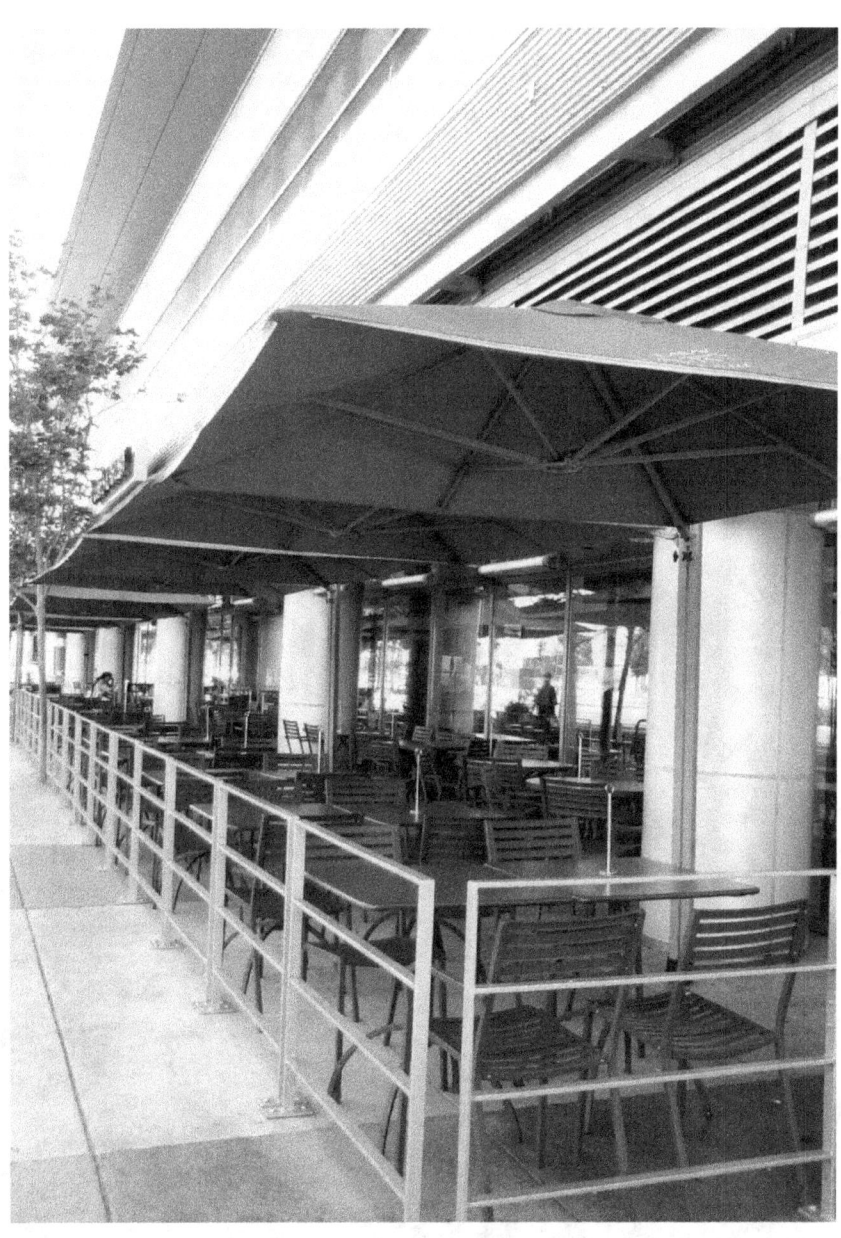

## NOKIA THEATRE

777 Chick Hearn Court

*The Nokia Theatre at L.A. Live opened in 2007, and has hosted a glittering array of performers as well as events such as the MTV Video Music Awards and the Primetime Emmy Awards broadcast.  The adjacent Nokia Plaza hosts outdoor concerts and shows.*

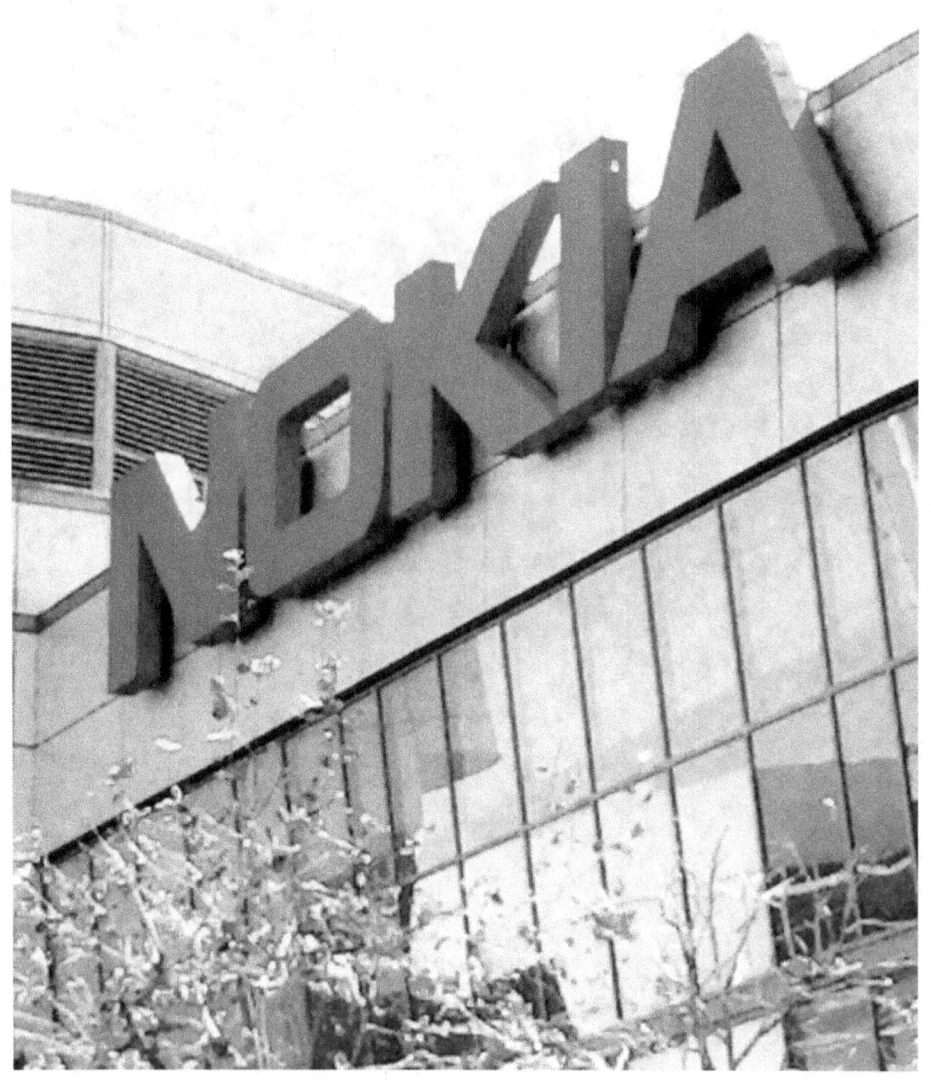

# RITZ-CARLTON & J.W. MARRIOTT

### 900 W. Olympic Boulevard

*The Ritz and Marriott at L.A. Live are the last word in spacious luxury. Their exterior walls serve as canvases on which giant advertisements are projected electronically, á la "Blade Runner". Planes landing at LAX at night can easily identify the illuminated Ritz-Carlton from the air.*

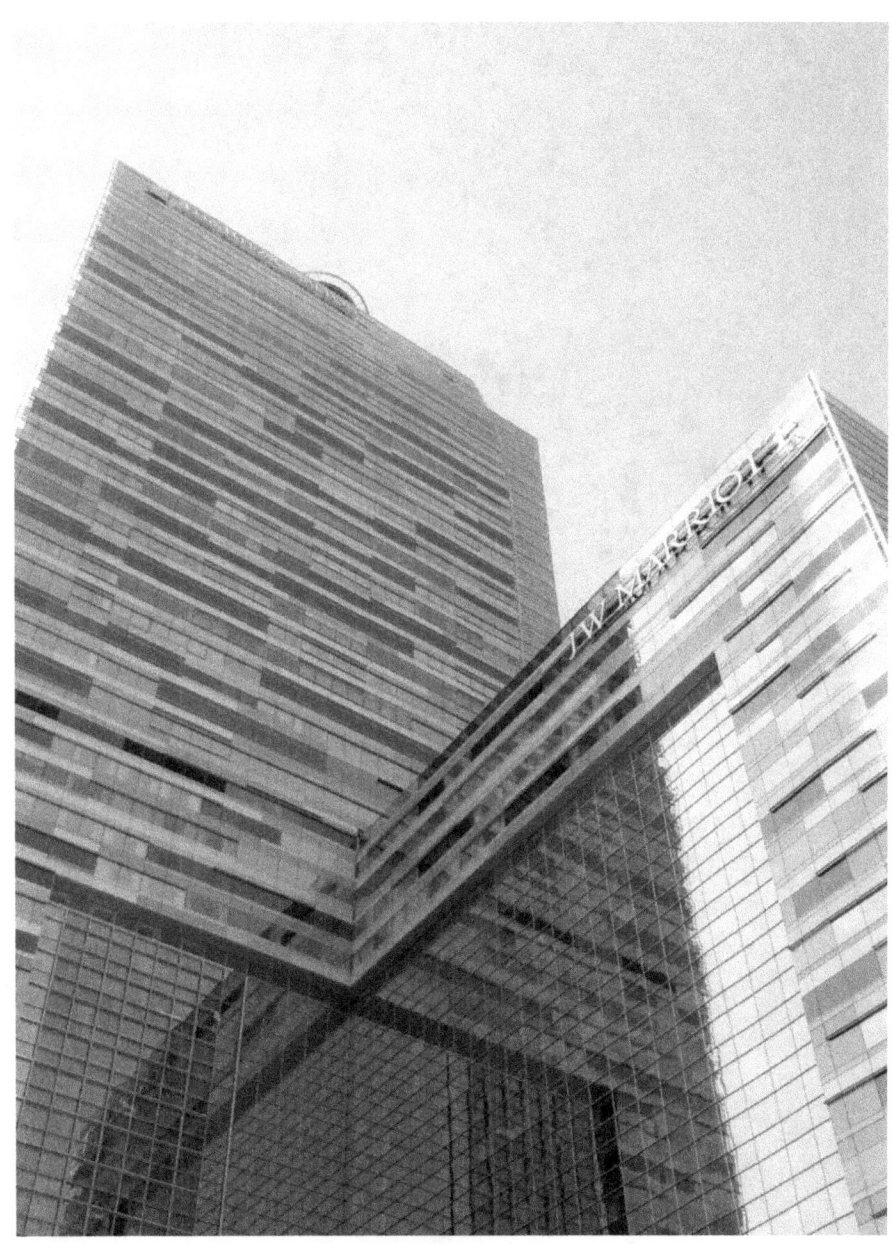

# 11ᵗʰ STREET & FIGUEROA STREET

11ᵗʰ & Figueroa

*A view from Figueroa Street, between L.A. Live and the Staples Center, looking west along 11ᵗʰ Street. The buildings in the distance include residential lofts and apartments as well as offices. 11ᵗʰ Street leads to the garment/fashion district on the southeast side of downtown.*

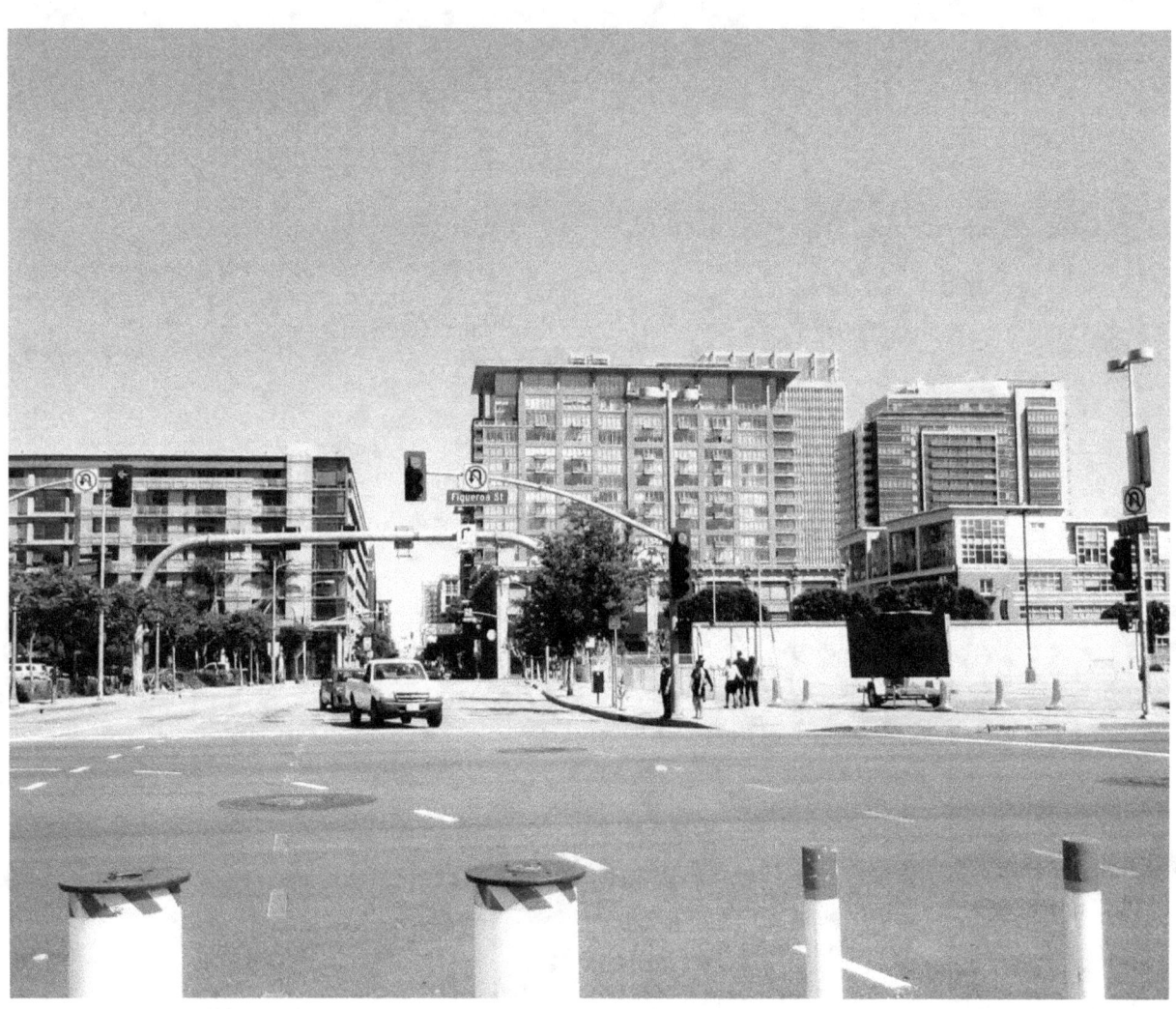

## STAPLES CENTER

1111 S. Figueroa Street

*Although L.A. no longer has a football team, its baseball team, the Dodgers, is world-famous, and the city boasts three winning basketball teams, the Los Angeles Lakers, Clippers, and Sparks. The Staples Center is home to the L.A. Lakers, Clippers, and Sparks, and to the L.A. Kings (L.A.'s ice hockey team). This glorious sports-and-events complex opened in 1999. It hosts concerts and special events as well as sports competitions. In this photograph: the curved northern "prow" of this ship-like building.*

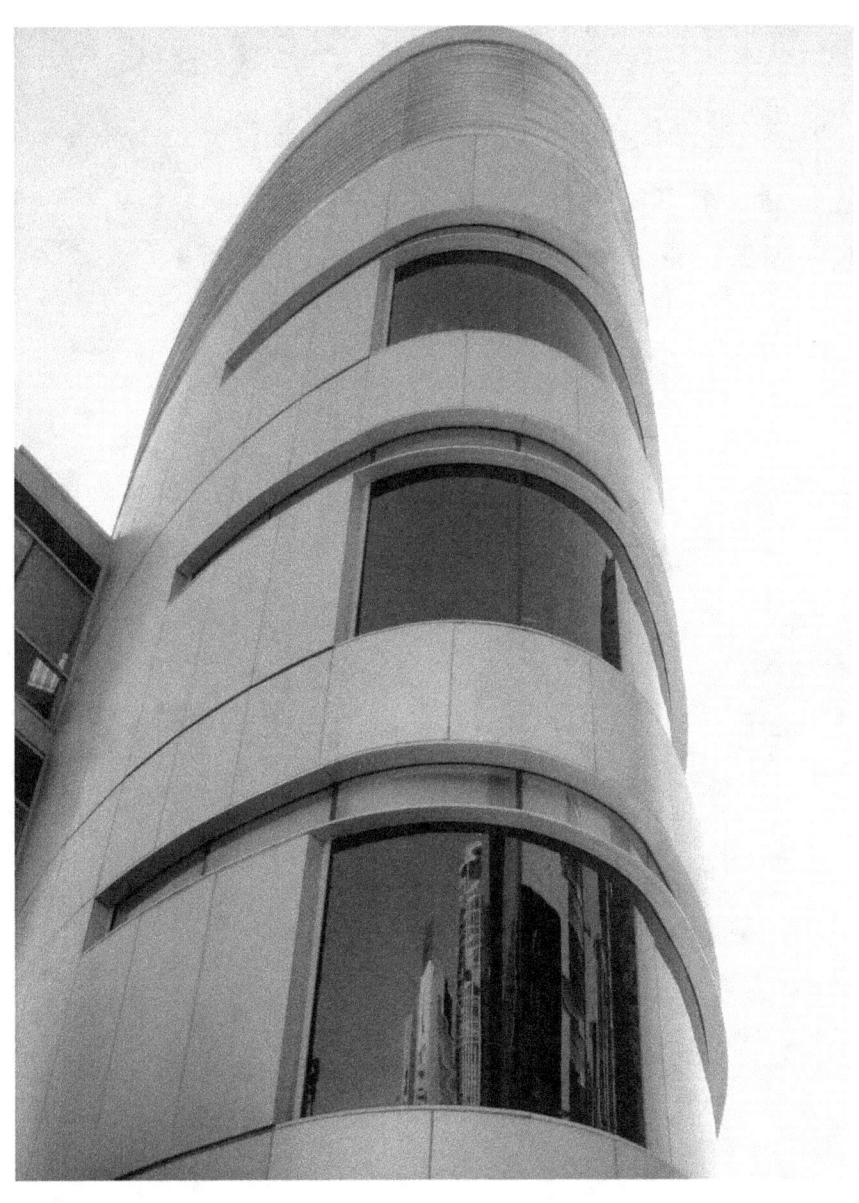

*This exuberant statue of Magic Johnson, Lakers player #32, graces the northern courtyard of the Staples Center ...*

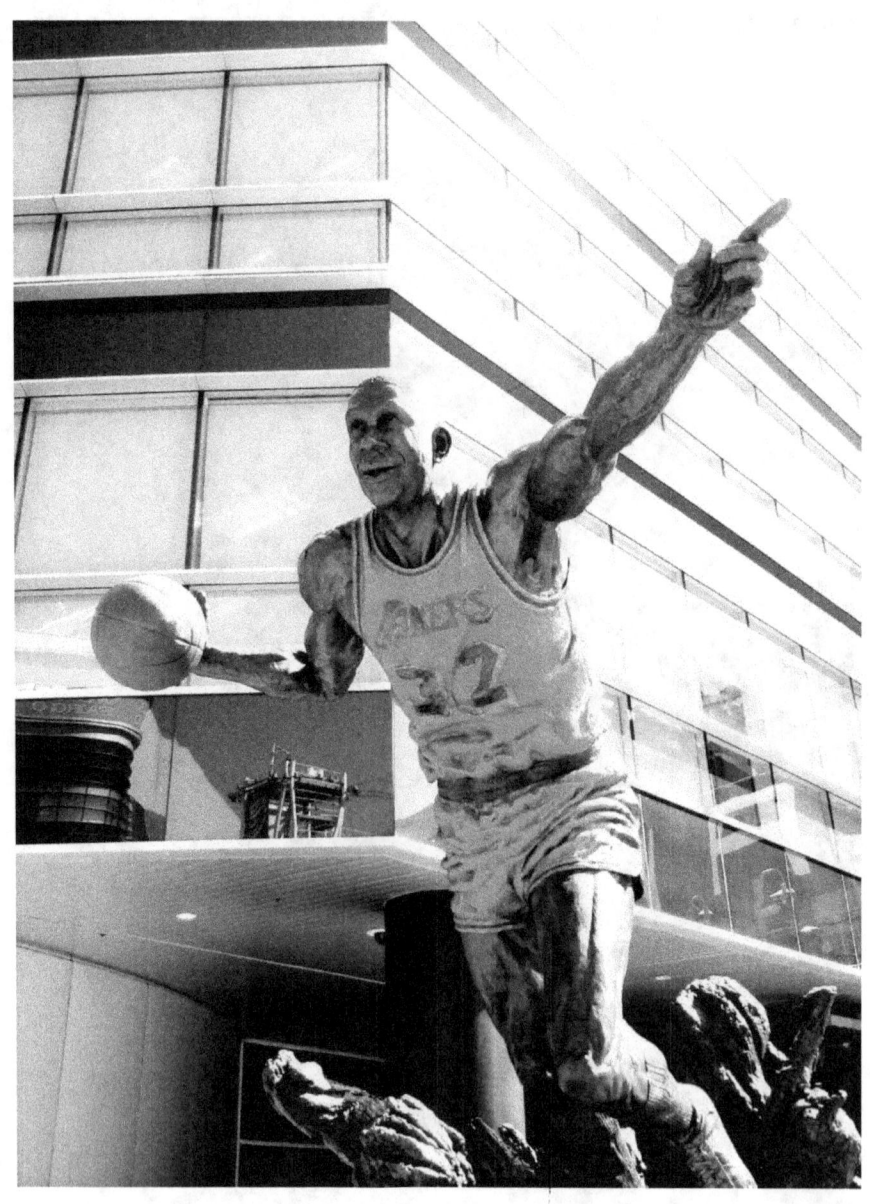

## STAPLES CENTER

1111 S. Figueroa Street

*... As does this gravity-defying statue of Kareem Abdul-Jabbar, Lakers player #33.*

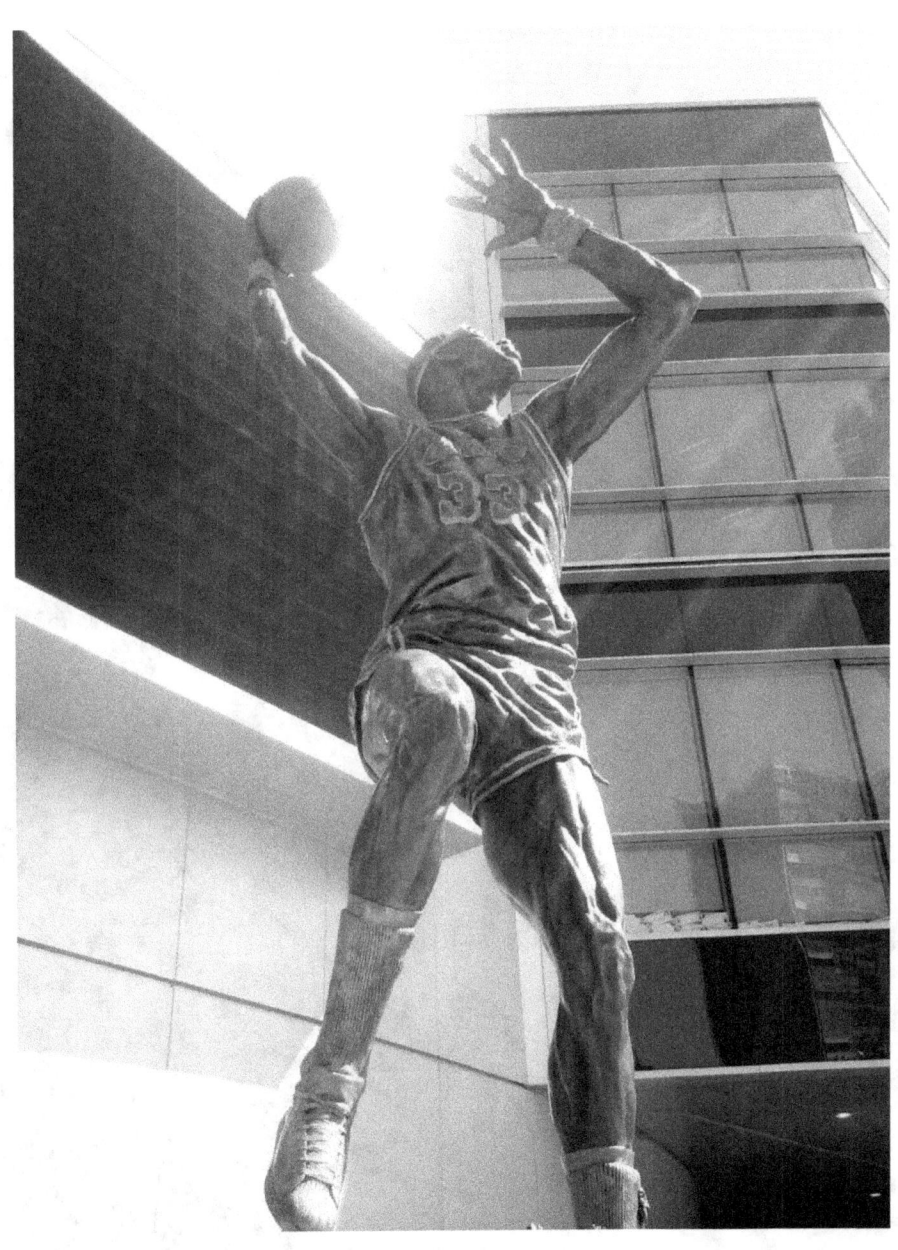

# OLYMPIC BOULEVARD & FRANCISCO

Olympic & Francisco

*The revitalization of Downtown L.A.'s southwest corridor continues, as evidenced by this new hotel under construction just north of the Ritz-Carlton Hotel at L.A. Live.*

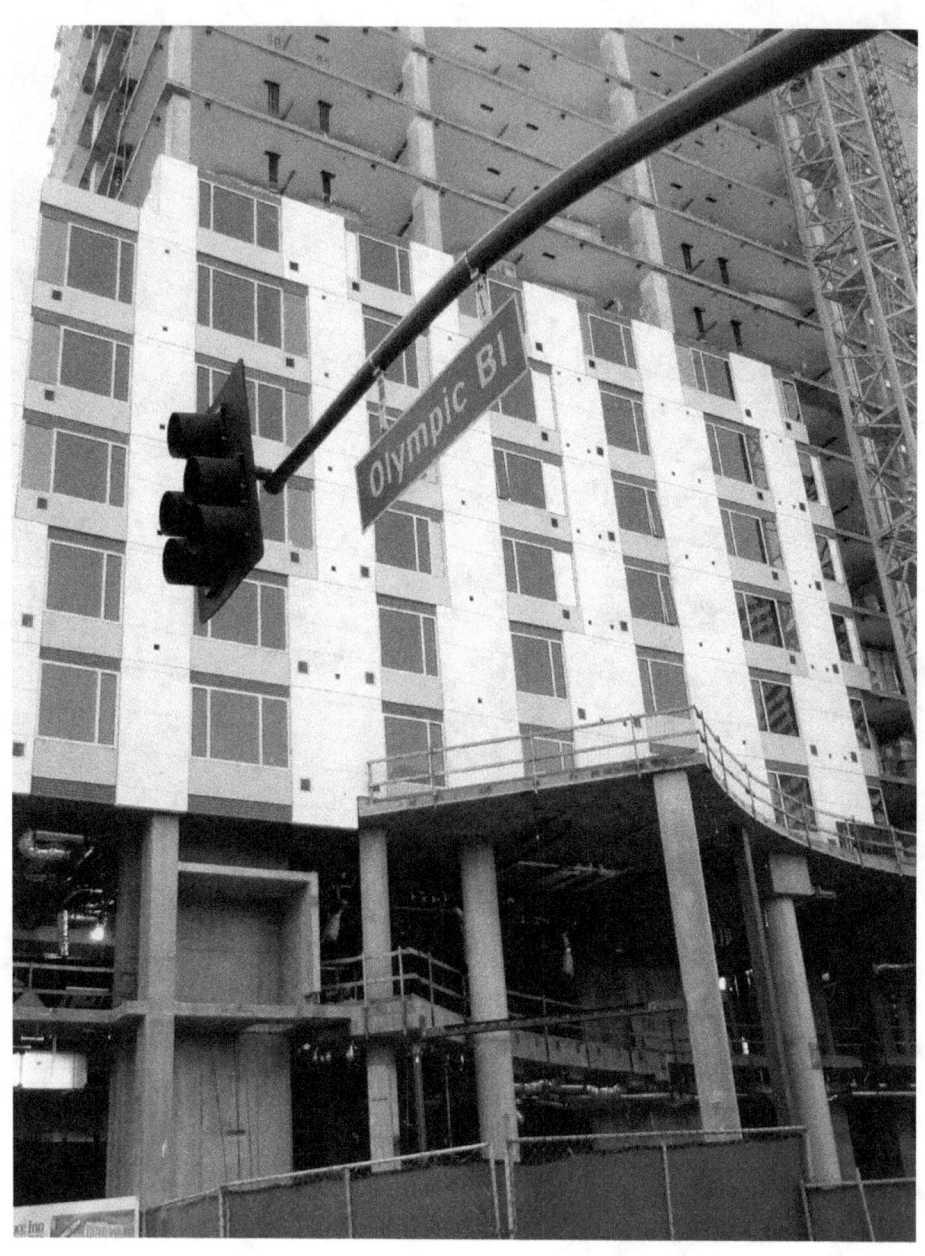

# THANK YOU

*Our photographic journey has taken us from the old postal processing center in northeast L.A., all the way to the Staples Center in southwest L.A. Thank you for taking this photographic stroll, and please stay tuned for more photograph collections covering other areas of Los Angeles.*

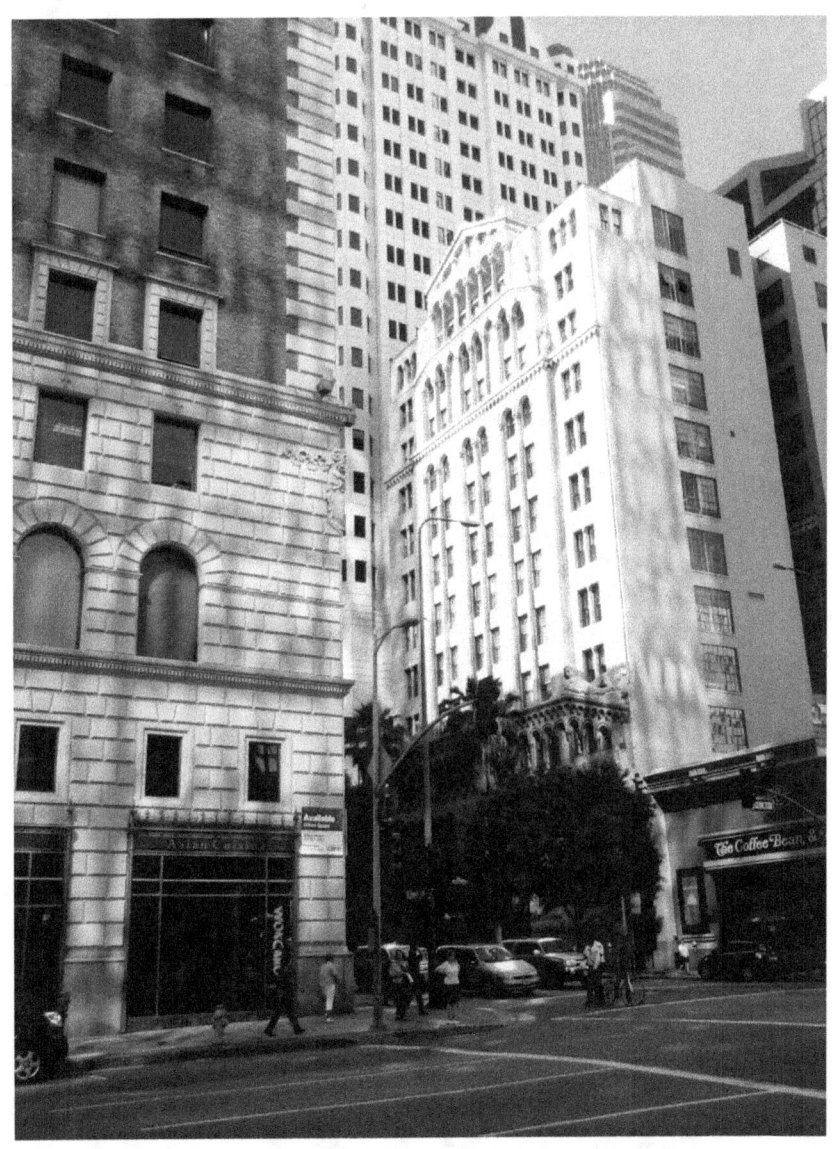

# RESOURCES & RECOMMENDATIONS

*Learn more about Los Angeles.*

## Explore
*Secret City Tours*
www.facebook.com/SecretCityTours
https://twitter.com/SecretCityTours

## Join
*L.A. Conservancy*
523 W. 6th Street, Suite 826, L.A., CA  90014
(213) 623-2489
www.laconservancy.org

## Listen
*L.A. Philharmonic*
151 S. Grand Avenue, L.A., CA  90012
(213) 972-7300
www.laphil.com

## Read
*L.A. Noir:  The City as Character* (Book)
Silver, Alain and James Ursini
Santa Monica Press, 2005

## View
*L.A. City Hall Observation Deck*
L.A. City Hall – 27th Floor
Enter from Los Angeles Street

## Watch
*10 Buildings That Changed America* (DVD)
PBS, 2013

# ABOUT THE AUTHOR

Leslie Le Mon is an author, artist, and manager who has lived in Los Angeles since 1992.

She is an amateur L.A. historian.

Reader feedback is welcome and appreciated.

Please email her at les.lemon.author@gmail.com.

You can visit her website at www.leslielemonauthor.com.

# OTHER BOOKS BY THE AUTHOR/PHOTOGRAPHER

If you enjoy photographs, consider *The Disneyland Book of Photos – Candy Noir*, a digital book of dozens of imaginative, candy-colored and black-and-white images available at Amazon.com.

*Sircus of Impossible Magicks:  Chosen* is an epic fantasy following the adventures of three young heroes time traveling in and around Los Angeles and Pasadena.  Available as a paperback and as a digital book at Amazon.com.

Fans of chilling tales are invited to read *Cold Dark Harbor and Other Tales of Ghosts and Monsters*, available as a paperback and a digital book at Amazon.com.

# COPYRIGHT INFORMATION

www.ingramcontent.com/pod-product-compliance
Lightning Source LLC
Chambersburg PA
CBHW081456170526
45166CB00008B/2453